How to Be a Disney Historian

Tips from the Top Professionals

Jim Korkis

Foreword by Leonard Maltin

Theme Park Press
www.ThemeParkPress.com

Editor: Bob McLain
Layout: Artisanal Text

ISBN 979-8-89609-022-9
Printed in the United States of America

Theme Park Press | **www.ThemeParkPress.com**
Address queries to ben@themeparkpress.com

CONTENTS

Section Three:
RECOMMENDED RESOURCES

Foreword

When I say I am a life-long Disney fan, I mean it. One of my prized possessions as a child was an illustrated book of *Grimm's Fairy Tales*. At the end of one chapter where there was blank space on the page I wrote in crayon: "A Walt Disney Production".

My image of Walt's world was not created by people in costumes parading through the streets. It came from a total immersion in Disneyana: addiction to the daily *Mickey Mouse Club* television show, attachment to a Davy Crockett coonskin cap, subscription to *Uncle Scrooge* comic books, and the firm belief that the arrival of each new Disney film at my local theater was "A Major Event".

Most important, I watched Walt Disney himself on television every week, an affable man who might have been a favorite uncle sharing stories and taking me behind the scenes at his Magic Kingdom. I have a feeling that younger people who did not experience this blitz and only know of Disney as a corporate name, not a living person, might not understand the way so many of us feel about Walt and his work.

Was I brainwashed at the age of 5? I suppose you could say so ... but I've never regretted it. Walt was my Pied Piper.

That's why, on December 15, 1966, when I was home from school nursing a cold and heard the news that he had died, I knew I wanted to do something about it. Earlier that year I had taken on the roles of editor and publisher of a monthly magazine called *Film Fan Monthly* from its founder, who lived in Vancouver, Canada. I was 15 and bursting with energy and ambition. I knew how I wanted to pay tribute to Walt Disney: I would compile an annotated list of all his feature films.

I picked up my copy of the Manhattan telephone directory and made a cold call to Walt Disney Productions (as the company was then known). I asked for the publicity department and was connected to a nice young woman named Arlene Ludwig. I told her what I wanted to do and she immediately replied, "How can I help you?" I said I was going to do my own research but could use some stills, which she promised to provide—and did.

My local library in Teaneck, New Jersey, had the other resources I needed to build an accurate filmography, and that's what I published in February of 1967. The last complete entry was for *Monkeys, Go Home*, which was about to be released. Other titles yet to come, which I listed, were *The Happiest Millionaire*, *Bullwhip Griffin*, *The Gnome-mobile* (which I mistakenly spelled Gnomobile), *Blackbeard's Ghost*, and *The Jungle Book*, which I said was "one to look forward to".

When the issue came out, I sent a handful of copies to Arlene in New York. She called me to say how pleased and excited she was. "We don't have a list like this," she explained, to my great surprise, and asked if she could purchase more copies. I said I could provide as many as she needed and wouldn't think of charging for them.

Several years later, when I made my first trip to Los Angeles, Arlene arranged for me to get a tour of the Disney Studio in Burbank, California, which was arranged by their publicity chief, Tom Jones. It was an unforgettable day: the genial Mr. Jones arranged for me to meet animator Ward Kimball, walk onto a soundstage where Norman Tokar was directing a blue-screen shot for *No Deposit, No Return*, and get a private screening of a 35mm print of *The Reluctant Dragon*, which was impossible to see in those days.

At the end of the afternoon, Jones said how helpful my *Film Fan Monthly* filmography had been to him and his colleagues and asked if I had considered expanding it into a book. I hadn't thought of it until then, but he planted a seed that soon began to grow in my mind.

I pitched the idea to Crown Publishers, which had just issued my first hardcover book, *The Great Movie Shorts*, and they said "yes". I knew what I had to do next: screen every one of Walt Disney's movies. My friend Arlene Ludwig (who, it turns out, was the daughter of Irving Ludwig, the head of Disney's distribution arm Buena Vista) arranged for me to borrow 16mm prints from their local depository in Paramus, New Jersey, not far from where I lived.

Every Friday afternoon I would drive to a modest, unmarked building and take home one or two prints to screen over the weekend in my basement. This distribution center handled all non-theatrical prints for rent and also maintained a special cache of prints that were earmarked for VIP use. The label on one of the shipping boxes indicated that it had just been to Gracie Mansion, the home of New York City's mayor.

A few key titles like *Snow White and the Seven Dwarfs* and *Fantasia* were notably absent, but virtually every other Disney title was available to me in beautiful Technicolor copies. I decided to watch the films in chronological order, which would help me retain a sense of context as I made notes for my book.

I learned, early on, that there was no place where I could find complete credits for these movies, so I took to using my projector lens as a kind of loupe and laboriously copied down every name on-screen. (It was then that I came to believe that music editor Evelyn Kennedy possibly had more Disney credits than anyone else alive.)

In the early days of this process, my basement theater was full of friends as I screened Disney classics every weekend. When I got to the mid-1950s I borrowed a CinemaScope lens from a friend and hung a bedsheet in order to project the widescreen images of films like *The Great Locomotive Chase*. By the time I got to the later True-Life Adventures, my audience shrank and then disappeared altogether. Undaunted, I plugged away through the 1960s studio output.

When, after one year's time, I finished my homework, I contacted Arlene again to take the next step: interviewing Disney staffers. It was here that I hit a major snag. Since we had last spoken the company had arranged to publish a coffee-table book, *The Art of Walt Disney*, with the prestigious art-book house Harry N. Abrams. Unbeknownst to Arlene, my project was considered a rival or spoiler. Thus began a long series of cross-country telephone calls with a man at the studio in Burbank who could have shut me down but instead let me plead my case.

I kept insisting that I didn't need their permission to write about Disney, but I did want their blessing. I finally got it, with one proviso: I couldn't have access to the studio archives or anyone employed by the company. (By this time, Dave Smith had been employed to create an official studio archive. Part of my bargain with the company was that he would vet my biographical chapter on Walt and correct any mistakes he found, which I'm glad to say were few.)

This left me to do my own research for *The Disney Films*. Fortunately, Walt's career was well-documented, and fortuitously, many of his live-action features were directed by freelancers who were no longer employed by Disney and only too happy to respond to my queries.

After *The Disney Films'* publication in 1973, I received corrections from noted Disneyphiles Peter Adamakos, Brian Sibley, and of course, Dave Smith, who sent me pages and pages filled mostly with errors in nomenclature. I was delighted to be able to update the book and make corrections in 1984, 1995, and 2000. It gives me great satisfaction that the book is still used as a reliable resource decades after its inception.

But, as I came to realize, there is no end to the research to be done on Walt Disney's long, multifaceted career.

I have known Jim Korkis since the 1980s. I was a contributor to Gladstone's magazine *Cartoon Quarterly* (1988), edited by Jim and his friend and then-writing partner John Cawley, where I discussed my concern about the re-release of *Snow White and the Seven Dwarfs* in the wrong aspect ratio (cropping the top and bottom of the image) and my response from Michael Eisner. I even contributed a foreword for their first book about animation history from Pioneer Books, *The Encyclopedia of Cartoon Superstars* (1990).

In that foreword I wrote, "I salute their efforts and applaud their work. I just wish this book had been around when I was young."

Nearly a quarter of a century later, those same sentiments apply to this book where Jim has gathered some of the top Disney historians around the world to offer guidance, advice, and "secrets" of the trade to a new generation of Disney researchers. Jim has always been sincere in helping others with their research and has long since proven himself to be a knowledgeable Disney scholar in his own right.

I'm sure this book will introduce me to things I didn't know. That's the exciting part about diving into Disneyana: there's always more to discover.

Leonard Maltin
October 2015

● ●

LEONARD MALTIN [leonardmaltin.com] is one of the most recognized and respected film critics of our time. He appears regularly on Reelz Channel and spent 30 years on the television show *Entertainment Tonight*. He is an internationally respected writer, film critic, historian, and the author of well-received books about the movies. He has assisted on many historical projects, books, and documentaries.

He currently teaches at the University of Southern California School of Cinematic Arts and was the host of the *Walt Disney Treasures* DVD series, a project that he created and supervised. He hosts the *Treasures from the Disney Vault* special showings on TCM, and he sporadically publishes a newsletter for movie buffs entitled *Leonard Maltin's Movie Crazy*.

For links to all of his books, visit themeparkpress.com/historians

(The issue of *Film Fan Monthly* that Leonard mentions in his foreword was issue No. 68 released February 1967. It cost thirty-five cents. From that tiny seed grew a mighty oak of Disney scholarship.)

Introduction

Prove yourself brave, truthful, and unselfish,
and someday, you will be a real boy.
— The Blue Fairy in *Pinocchio* (1940)

...or a pretty good Disney historian.
— Jim Korkis (2015)

Over the years, I have received a mountain of heartfelt and lengthy pleas from people I don't know begging me to help them (or some relative) get a job as a Disney animator or Imagineer. It never seems to occur to any of them that if I had that type of influence, I would have gotten myself such a job long ago.

Several of them even suggest that they would be willing to sweep the floors for free, just to be in the same building as their Disney heroes.

"We would never hire any of them to do that job," laughed a good friend who has worked for WDI for many years. "We would want someone who passionately cared about sweeping the floors and had some great skills in that area to do it and do it well. We wouldn't want someone doing a mediocre job while they were trying to look over our shoulders, ask endless questions, or try to show us things they had drawn. We would never get anything done."

In the last several years, I have been also receiving similar requests from people who want to be a Disney historian.

Many of my good friends and colleagues who write about Disney are the recipients of similar entreaties along with the usual assortment of "What is this torn and used paper plate of Mickey Mouse I found at a garage sale worth financially and is Disney interested in purchasing it from me for their archives?"

Some of these people who want to be Disney historians are truly sincere about wishing to spend their lives recording Disney history, and those of us who have been researching and writing about Disney history are not getting any younger.

In fact, several notable chroniclers have already passed away in recent years, namely Dr. Robin Allan (who received a PhD for his studies on

Disney from Exeter University in the UK) in 2014 and John Culhane (the inspiration for the characters Mr. Snoops in *The Rescuers* and Flying John in *Fantasia 2000*) in 2015, leaving behind boxes and boxes of notes for things that now will never be written by them.

I decided it was time for those of us who have continued to blaze a trail in an occupation that is just a little over a quarter-century old needed to share some "tricks of the trade" to help and encourage others.

Too many self-proclaimed Disney historians merely cut and paste material from the internet with little regard to its accuracy or even its source. Like the flim-flam con artists of old, they have been able to dazzle an unsuspecting but eager audience into believing that they are experts who have some mysterious and can-never-be-revealed source of information.

Unless something is done, these charlatans will overshadow the hard work done by true researchers who have justly earned the right to be called Disney historians and will flood the world with urban myths, false "facts", and other misconceptions that unsuspecting people will accept as true treasures coming from so-called "experts".

This book is to be used as a guide for those seriously interested in exploring Disney history. These are not the Ten Commandments of Disney History but merely a selection of advice and suggestions from veterans to get people started and point them in the right direction. Everything from technical to philosophical information has been shared to provide a firm foundation for the budding historian.

This is not a text book. It is a conversational and anecdotal coaching seminar filled with personal experiences. It is also filled with tools that have been hewn over many years and unfortunate experiences. Pick the tools that are most useful to you.

I grew up in Glendale, California, a city adjacent to Burbank, the home of the Disney Studio.

My first-grade teacher at Thomas Edison Elementary School was Mrs. Margaret Disney, the second wife of Walt Disney's older brother Herbert who spent most of his life working for the U.S. Post Office.

When I learned of this Disney connection, I immediately took a large sheet of easel paper and proceeded to create a full-figure drawing of Jiminy Cricket, my favorite character at the time for a number of reasons, including that his first name was similar to what I was called in elementary school: "Jimmy".

I also liked that Jiminy knew so much about things, as demonstrated by his appearances in short animated segments on the original *Mickey Mouse Club* television show.

One day, after much labor and much erasing, I proudly gave the drawing to Mrs. Disney in the hope that she would rush to the Disney Studio where I would without a doubt be instantly offered a job and I would not have to learn my multiplication tables (which I still do not know to this day). Apparently, portfolio review was backed up for a couple of decades, because I did not start working for the Disney company officially until 1995.

At the age of twelve, I was enthralled by the weekly Disney television program, especially the episodes devoted to animation, since I maintained hopes of being a cartoonist until I became a good enough artist to fully appreciate how bad I really was and that I wouldn't get much better.

I later realized I was more interested in writing about animation than actually doing it, although my brief experience with the art form helped me to better understand the process and the answers I got from the animators I interviewed.

Diligently, I scribbled down the names in the credits at the end of those television shows. At that time, I still didn't know the difference between an animator and a background artist or a special effects person.

I went to the Glendale-Burbank phone book (the cities were then small enough to have just one book to cover them both), looked up the names I had written down, and called those people.

"I saw your name on the Disney TV show. How did you make things move?" I innocently but firmly inquired.

Eighty percent of the people I talked to were incredibly patient and kind and invited me over to watch them draw and listen to stories about working at Disney. About fifteen percent thought that it was some type of gag, being perpetrated by one of their work cronies, having a twelve year old phone and say he liked the way they did cartoons. Five percent were wrong numbers.

Fortunately, the first person who agreed to talk with me was the legendary Jack Hannah who had animated, done story work and directing assignments at the Disney Studio, and was currently teaching classical animation at the California Institute of the Arts.

He also lived in Glendale, but in the richer part about fifteen minutes away. I arranged an appointment for a Saturday afternoon since I still attended school during the week. My mom dropped me off at the address about an hour early, at my request, because I was fearful of being late or Mom getting lost driving to an unknown location.

I was dressed in the same black suit I wore to church with a clean white shirt and thin black tie, looking very much like a teenaged undertaker. I had a bulky tape recorder, several school notebooks, and my shirt pocket was filled with multiple ballpoint pens for fear that they might all somehow run out of ink.

To kill time, because it would be rude to show up so early, I walked slowly around the block in the California heat. That was not enough, so I walked around the block the other way and then finally once more. It was now about ten minutes before my scheduled interview. I walked up the steps on the hilly incline to the front door.

A kindly older woman opened the door. I explained that I was Jimmy Korkis and that I had an appointment with Mr. Jack Hannah.

She turned to the living room and yelled, "You were right, Jack. It IS him."

Jack came to the door wearing a short-sleeved shirt. He laughed, "We've been watching you from the front window for about an hour. We were wondering when you might come in."

He ushered me into his living room. It was a pleasant, homey room, and he sat in an overstuffed chair by the front window. Near it was a coffee table with a lamp. I set up my tape recorder and sat in a straight chair that was on the other side. Mrs. Hannah left to do something in the kitchen.

I think we both expected that the interview might be a half hour. It lasted for over three hours, so I was lucky I had brought several extra blank cassette tapes.

Fortunately, Jack was enthusiastic about talking about the good old days to an appreciative and awestruck teenager. It was as if the doors to Wonderland had been opened wide to me as he rattled off unfamiliar names, interesting stories, and patiently explained some animation concepts.

Jack was 64 years old when I first interviewed him. He embraced what he was then doing as an instructor in the animation department of the California Institute of the Arts rather than nostalgically living in the past. In that first interview, his statement that "nobody seems old in this business" was never truer than when applied to Hannah himself.

It took me over two weeks to transcribe the interview, something I had never done before in my life. Then I typed it out using my dad's old manual typewriter. I mailed it to Jack and in a few days he told me to come up again so we could go over some changes.

It was my first experience of having someone I interviewed remove things that they had said, not because I had misquoted them but because they felt such things didn't need to appear in print.

"It doesn't add to the knowledge of animation to attack guys who can no longer defend themselves," he told me as I pleaded with him to let me include some of the stuff he cut out about Ben Sharpsteen. "Sometimes you get in a mood and days later you start thinking a little clearer. I think you've got enough stuff here."

An edited version (for space) of that first interview appeared in the animation fanzine *Mindrot* #11 (July 1978) published by David Mruz in Minneapolis. Jack even did a quick sketch of Donald painting a painting for me to include in the piece. Other contributors to that issue included Jerry Beck, Mark Kausler, Ron Hall, and Jeff Missine.

With Jack's help, I was even able to put together a filmography of his work at Disney. It was the first time Jack received published recognition outside of Disney.

At the end of that meeting, Jack smiled and said, "You know, you should also be talking to Kimball," and he picked his phone and called Disney animator Ward Kimball to explain that there was this nice kid interested in animation and that Ward should talk with me sometime. That is another much more interesting story.

Little did I realize it at the time, but it was that encounter with Jack Hannah when I became a Disney historian. Quotes from that interview have appeared in several Disney books including John Grant's *The Encyclopedia of Walt Disney's Animated Characters* (HarperCollins 1987).

So, for the next few years, thanks to living in the Los Angeles area, I got to talk with other Disney animators and Imagineers and write about it for my school newspaper and local newspaper, as well as "fanzines" (non-professional magazines self-published by fans) that were focused on the world of Disney. In college, I wrote for professional magazines and newspapers as well.

I spent many, many hours in different libraries, haunted used book stores for books and magazines and pressbooks, attended local events like the ASIFA-Hollywood show and sales, and ran up huge phone bills talking to people in other parts of the United States trying to find any information I could about animation and Disney.

Fortunately, I took notes or recorded the conversations and transcribed them, because most of those wonderful folks who then already seemed ancient to a teenager are no longer around to share their stories.

In the last few years, I have felt an obligation and urgency to tell those stories that never seem to appear elsewhere. Those stories were a great gift and they needed to be shared and not hoarded.

When I think back, I also recall how patient, generous, and helpful all those people were to a much too eager kid. In the last few years, I have felt an obligation to pay back those kindnesses to a new generation as well as share the stories they shared with me.

I was fortunate to be in the right place at the right time, but I also worked hard and made mistakes. I have boxes of index cards, school notebooks, and decaying cassette tapes in my storage unit, and my house looks like a library and a toy store exploded and I decided to live amid the debris.

I have done many different jobs over the decades, from being a professional performer to a newspaper cartoonist to a public school teacher to even cleaning toilets (which can prove to be a wonderful Zen experience), but nothing has given me greater satisfaction than researching, writing, and sharing Disney history.

No one has ever written a book on this topic, and I doubt anyone else ever will. This book may never be a best-seller, but hopefully it may inspire people to be better Disney historians both now and in the future. Even I have learned valuable new things from the contributions of others in this book.

When I was younger, one of the books I most frequently checked out from my local library was entitled *Tips from the Top Cartoonists*. A wide variety of cartoonists including Mort Drucker, Doug Wildey, and VIP Partch were each given two pages to explain what they did and how they did it. They had to communicate complex ideas clearly in a limited space, and I used that same format as the model for this book. *Tips* was a helpful and revealing book for me as an aspiring cartoonist as I hope this book will be for those interested in Disney history.

For those not interested in being a Disney historian, I think the material is still fascinating and imparts good advice that will be valuable to people in whatever endeavor they decide to do or at least to better appreciate what a really good Disney historian does.

Just go ask Alice:

*I give myself very good advice. But I very seldom
follow it. Will I ever learn to do the things I should?*

— Alice from Disney's *Alice in Wonderland* (1951)

Jim Korkis
October 2015

The Basics

Every Disney historian seems to have started the same way.

They got interested in some aspect of Disney, whether it was animation, the theme parks, music, comic books, or whatever. They were unable to locate the information they wanted to know about the topic. So, they had to start searching for the material themselves and share the information they found.

Read. Read everything and anything you can. Not just about Disney. Reading will give you more knowledge and a wider perspective; you will learn how others have phrased ideas and information and can apply it to your own writing. It is true magic seeing a good writer take just 26 letters in the alphabet and a handful of punctuation marks and create something riveting and entertaining. In addition, the more you read, the easier it will be to spot false information.

A good book to avoid is *Walt Disney: Hollywood's Dark Prince* by Marc Eliot. It is an error-ridden, mean-spirited, sensationalistic, and poorly researched biography of Walt Disney. Disney historians dislike it not because the author shares some of Walt's flaws, but because he focuses on them in a tabloid manner to the exclusion of Walt's many accomplishments, and because he uses anonymous interviewees and completely misinterprets documents as well as fabricates myths like Walt was born in Spain. The list of simple errors of proper nomenclature, names, and dates is almost longer than the book itself.

Yet, the book remains in print and is used as a source by many unknowing writers because they feel it must be the truth since it was not approved by Disney and casts shade on Walt. Read books that have received good peer reviews.

Go to the originals. Don't just use descriptions that already exist. Watch the movie or TV show yourself when you can. Don't just take the quote excerpt that appears in another book or an article. Read that original source because the quote may have been taken out of context, been misquoted, or there may be more to it.

Good writing is rewriting and editing. I spent many years as a junior high public school teacher, so I have always had to battle being in love with the sound of my own voice or what I had written. When you first write a piece, you want to include everything. In general, the piece is usually better after you have set it aside for several days and then looked at it again. That heated rush of creation is seductive, but in the cold light of day, it is easier to see things that don't fit, overly florid adjectives that should be eliminated, and even things that you left out like a proper description because you had "seen" that information in your head but not included it in the article.

Write something every day. If you just write when you feel like it, you will get very little done. Writing is work and often frustrating work. Treat it like work. Treat it like an athlete practicing each day, often rotating the routine to strengthen different muscles. Write a blog posting, an Amazon review, a short article, or an outline, or rewrite something you wrote years ago. Varying what you write will keep you fresh and sometimes unblock a writer's block. Schedule a specific time each day to write, even if at the end of the day you decide to toss it away or drastically edit what you have written. The structure of a routine will help you produce more material you can use. Schedule a time each day to do casual research, including re-reading a chapter of a book in your collection or skimming an article in a magazine or even checking out the various unofficial Disney websites.

When you write, ask yourself: "Is it true? Is it necessary? Is it kind?" No, that is not a quote from Buddha, but if you use the internet you will find it constantly attributed to him, just as you will find quotes attributed to Walt (like "If you can dream it, you can do it") that he never said. That "Walt" quote was created by Imagineer Tom Fitzgerald for the Epcot attraction Horizons, but it sure sounds like something Walt would say, doesn't it? That's why it is important to double check and not just parrot something "everyone knows". Remember that the words you write carry emotional weight, so think carefully before putting something in print. Other people are depending upon you to communicate clearly and accurately.

Let it go. There will always be more information to discover. Sometimes when you write a piece, you need to let it go so that it gets in print. Some historians have been working for years on things that may never ever see the light of day. Good enough is sometimes good enough for now. The publication of the material might result in the discovery of additional information.

Don't take yourself seriously. You have the responsibility of providing accurate information, but you are not curing cancer, ending poverty, or colonizing Mars. Be like Walt: take your work seriously, but don't take yourself seriously. No one is going to remember you a hundred years from now. However, if you have written something extremely well, *that* might survive.

What Is a Disney Historian?

A Disney historian is much like Bigfoot. Over the decades, there have been many claims of sightings and some physical evidence, but no one is quite sure exactly what the thing is.

Like Bigfoot, who has been called a variety of names including Sasquatch, Yeti, Abominable Snowman, and Skunk Ape, Disney historians have sometimes been labelled Disney trivia experts, Disney authorities, Disney scholars, and often just Disney fanatics (to indicate an extreme Disney fan).

The purpose of this book is to help define what a Disney historian is and does and to offer guidance and some practical tools to help those people who might be interested in becoming one.

A Disney historian is a career and a passion. It is not a job. A job has regular working hours, reasonable financial compensation for doing the work, and sometimes other perks like health benefits or the use of a company car.

No one has ever made a living as just a Disney historian. In general, they have some other source of income like an actual job or a working spouse or a pension in order to pay the bills and cover the bare necessities. Doing interviews, obtaining research material, contacting people, and related tasks all cost time and money that never even come close to being repaid when the research is finally published.

A Disney historian has to be obsessed with finding and sharing the information, because even a minimum-wage employee at a fast food restaurant makes more money by the end of the year. The career can be frustrating, as well as emotionally rewarding.

Today, there are fewer magazines seeking articles on Disney history and an increased amount of people who want to write about Disney history.

Traditionally, websites do not pay, or pay very little, for your article. Unless you are a J.K. Rowling or a Stephen King, it may be challenging to find a publisher, and most books don't generate much income. At best, you may be offered a small advance, to be deducted from the first royalties you are due after the publisher recovers all of his upfront costs from the cover art, the proofreading, the formatting of the text, and other expenses. If the publisher recovers his costs, then small royalty checks are often sent only annually. (My own publisher, Theme Park Press, is an exception to these rules.)

A publisher may only be committed to marketing your book for the first few weeks it is released and then will move on to the next book in his queue. It will be up to you to do the lion's share of the publicity work which will be even more time consuming.

In general, a Disney historian is someone who has done original research about some aspect of the many worlds of Disney and has published that research so it can be used by others.

The term "Disney historian" did not exist until the mid-1980s. I know this for a fact because I am the one who coined the term and was the first to be identified with it in newspapers, magazines, and on television.

The term "film historian" *did* exist but usually referred to people like Kevin Brownlow or William Everson, who researched and wrote about silent movies. Eventually, as years passed, the area of cinematic research kept expanding, and today it is not uncommon for film historians to write about films from the1980s from a loving, historical perspective.

Leonard Maltin began writing about film history when he was fifteen years old for *Classic Images* magazine and published his own film fanzine, *Film Fan Monthly*, so that he could legitimately meet and interview old-time film celebrities. His work appeared in a variety of newspapers and magazines and later television. Maltin became one of the best known and respected film historians. He also wrote and lectured extensively about his other passions, Disney and classic American animation.

Maltin was the first film historian to write books about Disney (*The Disney Films*, 1973) and classic animation (*Of Mice and Magic*, 1980). In a world with no internet, these were vital and groundbreaking references with their detailed filmographies and historical information. Even the Disney company did not have this information easily accessible at the time.

Maltin was the first person to be identified as an "animation historian". At first, he identified himself as an "animation writer", intending it to mean that he wrote *about* animation, but the general public was confused by that term and repeatedly asked him what films or animated characters he wrote.

It was a natural extension that a film historian who was focused on the history of animation would be an "animation historian". I, and many others who were writing about classic animation, immediately adopted that same term. Maltin never complained.

Whether I wrote a monthly column for *Animation* magazine or for a host of other publications, I was comfortable using the term "animation historian". I was also identified as a "comics historian" because of my expertise in classic comic books and comic strips when I wrote for a variety of comic fanzines and magazines like *Amazing Heroes* and *Comic Book Marketplace*.

In the 1980s, there were a plethora of Disney fanzines and I wrote for just about all of them.

A fan magazine, or "fanzine", is an amateur publication produced by fans of a particular genre. Most people believe that fanzines began with science fiction fans in the 1930s. The term "fanzine" originated in the 1940s to distinguish these types of amateur publications from "prozines" (professional magazines).

Over the years, there were fanzines devoted to *Star Trek*, horror movies, rock'n'roll, sports, comic books, and just about anything that could be imagined, including animation and Disney. To help clarify for younger readers unused to such things, a fanzine was sort of a printed version of a website or a blog but only available intermittently, often just annually.

Before too long, it became confusing to identify myself as an animation or comics historian if I were writing about the history of Disneyland or Walt Disney World or a live-action Disney film. I felt uncomfortable with the usual identifications like Disney expert (since I didn't consider myself an expert) or Disney trivia fan (because I was doing in-depth research and not just "fun facts").

Again, trying to identify myself as a "Disney writer", someone who wrote about Disney, brought up questions as to what films I wrote or what comic books I had scripted. So, following Maltin's example, I coined the term "Disney historian" as a natural extension of "animation historian".

It seemed to perfectly describe what I was actually doing, researching and recording Disney history, and newspapers and television shows loved having a title to describe me when I was interviewed.

The first time that designation appeared under my name on television (although I had been previously identified in print and convention events by that same term) was the April 20, 1989, episode of *Entertainment Tonight*.

I was brought on to discuss the controversy surrounding the publication of a comic book series from Malibu Graphics entitled *UnCensored Mouse*. The series featured reprints of the earliest Mickey Mouse comic strips that had fallen into public domain. I was writing historical introductions for each issue.

It wasn't an amazing stroke of genius to coin the term "Disney historian". If I hadn't devised it, it was only a matter of time before someone else would have; it sounded so natural and right. Just like explorer Christopher Columbus, I get the credit because the general public assumes I was the first one.

Just as others including myself copied Maltin's identification as an animation historian, many others started identifying themselves as Disney historians to the extent that there are now many self-proclaimed Disney historians today who dishonor the intent of that original designation. These so-called experts merely cut-and-paste the often false work of others on the internet and claim it as their own.

Some prominent Disney historians now refer to themselves as simply historians because they do not want to be lumped in with these spurious Disney "authorities".

A true Disney historian does original research, uses multiple sources, gives credit when he is using work done by others, and strives for the highest journalistic standards even if he sometimes precariously balances on the line between strict academia and general pop culture entertainment.

Disney historian has never been an official role at the Disney company, even though I was identified by that title in publications and videos produced by the company when I was a cast member.

The Disney company does not have a job for a Disney historian, though it has a great need for one. While working at Walt Disney World, the manager of Disney University officially decreed in memos, conversations, and presentations that there was no such thing as a Disney historian.

It would upset her terribly when anyone identified me by that title, even different Disney departments like Entertainment, Marketing, and Imagineering that eagerly used my research. She would take them to task, and they would back down because she was so incensed over the issue.

However, since 1970 Disney has operated the Walt Disney Archives at its corporate offices in Burbank, California.

So what is the difference between a Disney archivist and a Disney historian?

A Disney archivist is like a librarian. He gathers material, catalogs material, organizes material, sometimes makes copies of the material that can be used, and preserves the material. An archivist helps people locate the material they need. In the case of the Disney Archives, at one time its most frequent client was the Disney Legal Department, which needed information about dates and names and copyrights to generate lawsuits or to defend the company against lawsuits every single day of the year.

By contrast, a Disney historian is someone who does original research, such as interviewing people, locating material (in the old days, we did some of this by going through newspaper files and trying to read microfilm and microfiche files in libraries or renting films to watch), verifying information, networking with others who have expertise, and organizing that material into a coherent structure.

Most important, a Disney historian takes the raw facts and connects them together into a story so that people can better understand those facts.

For instance, most people know that *Steamboat Willie* (1928) is considered the first theatrically released Mickey Mouse animated cartoon. That is a fact. A Disney historian can tell the story of why that is such a pivotal film, how it connects with other things, share the stories of those involved with the cartoon, discuss the steps in making the cartoon in relation to other animation of the same time period, examine how it built the foundation of a company, and so much else that helps people truly understand and appreciate that it all started with a mouse.

Someone who is a Disney archvist can sometimes also be a Disney historian when they share not only the information but the story behind the information. For instance, the articles that Chief Archivist Dave Smith wrote for the *Starlog* line of magazines and others are still considered classic examples of scholarship.

Today, Disney historians may share their information through websites, podcasts, Twitter, Facebook, and blogs—although a few of us older folks still prefer to do so through magazines and books as it was originally done.

I am still unique in the world of Disney historians because my interests and expertise span many different arenas, from live-action entertainment to animation to comics and other fields. Often a Disney historian will concentrate on a particular area like animation or Walt Disney or Disneyland or comic books or television or a host of other narrowly focused topics.

Even within those topics, some Disney historians tighten their focus even further such as concentrating just on Disneyland during the years Walt was alive or just the original televised *Mickey Mouse Club* show or just the Polynesian Village Resort at Walt Disney World or just a particular artist like Carl Barks or Ward Kimball or even just a particular character or film like Mickey Mouse or *Snow White and the Seven Dwarfs*.

It can be more effective to devote all your attention to just one subject or it can offer a wider perspective to have an interest in multiple areas. As you continue to pursue your research, that choice will usually become apparent.

Remember that Disney history today also encompasses the ABC network, ESPN, the many worlds of George Lucas, the Muppets, Marvel Comics, and other franchises. So future Disney historians may be held accountable for knowing the names of all the creatures and their characteristics in Pandora from the film *Avatar* (2009).

I was extremely excited the first time I knew something that Dave Smith did not. He replied, "Nobody can know everything about Disney." Over the years, I have seen the great truth in that reply and have used it many times myself when fans have tried to stump me. There is so much to know and so much being discovered every day that no one can know everything.

However, the more you know and the more you know about a broad range of subjects, the more your writing will become richer and more interesting.

Dave told me that one of the major reasons he wrote *Disney A-Z: The Official Encyclopedia* (Disney Press, 1996) was so that he could have the most commonly asked information that he needed at his fingertips without having to go through massive file folders.

Cicely Rigdon, who supervised Disneyland Guest Relations among many other accomplishments, told me that Walt Disney himself gave the early Guest Relations hostesses only two expectations that he had for them: know the answers or know where to go get the answers.

Those would be the same guidelines Walt might give to Disney historians today.

Dave shared with me the secret for the famous challenging trivia contests he came up with for the Disney Stores:

> Someone may be an expert on Disney animation or the Disney parks, but if you toss in a question about the Disney Channel or Disney music, they fall apart quickly. So I put in a broad mixture including things I wouldn't be able to answer myself (like Hannah Montana's best friend) if I hadn't written the question.

So you can call yourself a Disney historian or a Bigfoot if you want. There is no organization that will officially grant you that title. There is no test that you have to pass. People will still debate whether you actually are one, so just keep doing the best you can and let your work and history be the final judge.

Keep a good sense of humor. Develop a thick skin against criticism and so-called experts who seek to diminish you or your work. You can get 499 things correct, many of them never before shared, and someone will still focus on the one thing that is misspelled, left out, or insist you should have written "Ubbe" rather than "Ub" when referring to Walt's first superstar animator.

Just like in the old movie Westerns, once you are known as the fastest gun, people will seek you out to challenge that title. You will never win. If you get something right, people will be unimpressed because you are supposed to know those things. If you get something wrong, people will be disappointed since you are supposed to know those things.

Try to ignore the haters. You will never win or change their minds. They may criticize you in public or behind your back on their Twitter feeds or Facebook posts. Trust that those people who do appreciate what you do may come to your defense.

Strive to match the high standards achieved by the Disney historians in this book, and maybe some day you will live happily ever after surrounded by stacks of decomposing paper, worn VHS tapes, other outdated technology, and memories.

Remember that in the final accounting, the title Disney historian is a gift word. You cannot give it to yourself. It is given to you by others who have enjoyed your work. While I dubbed myself with the title, I have worked hard for over three decades to deserve that designation.

The History of Documenting Disney History

In the earliest days, Disney history was provided by the publicity people working at the Disney Studio. They produced a standard multi-page biography of Walt Disney, a handout with a simplified description of how animation was done, short anecdotal stories or fun facts about a movie to be released, and later, similar information about Disneyland.

Although this material was designed for newspaper and magazine journalists or radio show interviewers, it was also sent to curious fans who wrote to the Disney Studio for information.

Joe Reddy spent almost half a century in promotions beginning as a copy boy on the *New York Morning Telegraph* in 1907 where famous Western lawman William Barclay "Bat" Masterson was the editor. Reddy went on to be a publicist for film comedian Harold Lloyd and child star Shirley Temple.

He spent twenty-five years as the Disney Studio's public relations director and Walt's personal consultant and image maker. Reddy was a respected and beloved friend of practically every major newspaper and magazine in the country. As he told one of his assistants, Charles Grizzle, in the 1950s:

> These people should be treated as friends, as valued allies in the great game of show biz; they deserve respect. And they deserve a laugh once in a while, to lighten their burdens. That's why I usually begin most conversations with a joke.

Reddy died in his sleep June 24, 1967, on the Saturday after pumping hands and giving bear hugs to those in attendance at the big premiere for the Disney feature-length movie *The Happiest Millionaire.*

He was a growling cigar-smoking, boisterous throwback to the old school of Hollywood publicists. He worked in Room 240 S (the Shorts building) at the Disney Studio and was not shy in letting people know he loved being Irish, Catholic, and a Democrat. In his office, he would pound away at an old manual Royal typewriter using just his two index fingers.

Journalist Charles Ridgway interacted with Reddy during Ridgway's tenure at the *Mirror-Daily News* in Los Angeles:

> Joe was a former New York sportswriter—you know, the tough guy with a heart-of-gold type. He was the best of the publicists who came around, always ready with a new joke or a wild take about scandalous behavior in Hollywood's good old days.

Magazine and newspaper journalists like James Bacon got their Disney information from Reddy, who also set up interviews with Walt. Of course, all of that material had to be approved by Walt himself when he was alive, including quotes attributed to Walt that were sometimes crafted by Reddy for the story.

Bacon, labeled the Dean of Hollywood Columnists, specialized in writing about the entertainment industry. He began as a writer for the Associated Press, and then spent almost twenty years with the *Los Angeles Herald-Examiner*. Bacon wrote frequently about Disneyland and said:

> I once asked Eddie Meck, Disneyland's longtime publicity director, what made Disneyland the greatest man-made tourist attraction of all time. I fully expected him to give me a long spiel. Instead, he said: "I can give it to you in two words—Walt Disney. We don't even mail a postcard out of here without his okay."

The original manager of publicity at Disneyland was Eddie Meck, who stood roughly five-foot-two inches tall and usually wore a hat, coat, and suspenders. Before working for Disney, Meck promoted A-list motion pictures for Columbia, including Frank Capra's *It Happened One Night* (1934). Meck was hired in early 1955. His philosophy was that the Disneyland park was so wonderful and unique that it could sell itself.

Charlie Ridgway, who eventually took over Meck's job, remembered:

> He was a very interesting little guy. He was very small, barely five feet tall, and he had huge ears. Herb Caen, a columnist for the *San Francisco Chronicle*, used to call him "Mecky Mouse" because he had ears like Mickey Mouse.

> He worked for a couple of studios, including RKO, where he was a "planter". In those days, they had some guys who wrote the stories and other guys who used to "plant" them with a newspaper person. In the course of doing that, he got to know anybody of any consequence in the newspaper business in the Los Angeles area.

> RKO was distributing Disney's films, so that is how Walt met him. From the beginning, the marketing for Disneyland was almost entirely done by publicity. Very little advertising. And it was done by personal contact by getting the news guys to come, bring their families, and getting them to see for themselves.

Ridgeway was hired by Meck in 1963 and began to do the bulk of the publicity writing. He shared his office at Disneyland with Marty Sklar, who was also hired to help write publicity material. Ridgway said:

> My office was in the police station, which was a little attached building [to Main Street City Hall] about maybe fifteen feet square at most and packed to the gills with all the Publicity department's press releases, fact sheets, and photos ready to hand-out or mail-out to writers and editors for newspapers and magazines across the country.
>
> Eddie's office was in the main part of City Hall, right in the middle of the building. He knew how reporters and editors thought and what they wanted. They all knew and liked Eddie. And he taught me all those things.

When Meck passed away in 1973, Ridgway took over completely and that included continuing to do the early publicity for Walt Disney World.

So, for the early decades of the Disney company, the only stories about Walt and his studio appeared in newspapers and magazines, and those stories were often generated or shaped by Joe Reddy and Eddie Meck.

The first book about Disney was written by a Harvard professor.

Professor Robert Durant Feild (1893–1979) of the Harvard Fine Arts Department loved modern art, in particular the cartoons of Disney. He was one of the most popular (and one source also described him as "provocative") instructors on campus, with full attendance at his lectures.

Harvard's then conservative Art department let him go in February 1939 (roughly seven months after the university gave Walt his honorary degree), supposedly because a committee of professors felt Feild had "too much enthusiasm for modern art, particularly Disney's".

When he was terminated for undisclosed reasons unrelated to his teaching ability, there were articles in *Time* magazine, *Boston Evening Globe*, and the *Christian Science Monitor* that covered the situation, and all intimated that it was Feild's love of Disney that was the primary cause.

While in the Los Angeles area on a six-week visit to study art, Feild in August 1938 gave a lecture at the Disney Studio. At that time, Feild had discussed with Walt the possibility about writing a book on Disney animation. Whether Walt felt it would be a good way to support the recently released Feild, or whether it tied in with Walt's dream of an updated book on how to do animation, he agreed in a May 17, 1939, letter to Feild:

> Naturally I was very sorry to hear what happened at Harvard, but after all, who knows, it may be for the best. We definitely feel that you are qualified to write this book, and we want you to know that you have our complete confidence and cooperation, not only in the writing of this material but also in the marketing of it.

Feild spent almost a year at the Disney Studio from June 1939 to May 1940. He was pretty much given unlimited access to all areas of the studio and he took a massive amount of notes. Feild observed every department, talked extensively with animators and technicians, and even had multiple conversations with Walt himself.

The result was the hardcover book *The Art of Walt Disney*, released in October 1941 (Macmillian) that was the very first book ever devoted to the world of Disney. This makes Feild one of the earliest Disney historians.

However, in the tradition of the time, no one working at the studio, except Walt and Roy, are identified by name in the text. All the other artists are discussed anonymously, either by their role "the head layout man will...", "the director says...", or when reproducing story notes, only the initial of the last name was used.

The book includes some rarely seen illustrations and some insight into the preliminary concepts for several animated projects and is an effusive love letter to Disney animation.

Feild explained:

> While not in any way technical, this book describes how things happen in the Disney Studio—how Walt Disney himself acts as inspiration and coordinating spirit for all the several hundred artists and production men and women who work with him.

In 1955, the *Saturday Evening Post* approached Walt about telling the story of his life in a series of installments that would be "told to" staff writer Pete Martin, who had done the same type of thing with such other celebrities as Bing Crosby and Arthur Godfrey.

Walt wasn't interested but realized that it would be a way to help his daughter Diane and her, husband Ron Miller, get enough money to buy a house if the series was formatted such that Diane was telling the story of her dad's life. Diane Disney Miller said:

> Throughout that summer [June-July 1956], Pete, Dad, and I met in a poolside room at my parents' home. Dad told the story of his life, occasionally interrupted by Pete, and Pete got it all on tape. Although my father had given many interviews and was always willing and eager to talk about his life, this exercise presented an opportunity for him to offer the whole narrative—a story he loved to tell. I was at times spellbound. It was a precious experience for me and we did, eventually, buy our first home.

With the November 17, 1956, edition, the *Saturday Evening Post* began an eight-part series titled "My Dad, Walt Disney" by Diane Disney Miller as told to Pete Martin. Diane gave Martin full credit for shaping that raw interview material into such an entertaining series that with some editing it was issued by Henry Holt and Company in 1957 as the first biography of Walt titled *The Story of Walt Disney* by Diane Disney Miller. For five dollars, people could purchase a copy at Disneyland personally autographed by both Walt and Diane.

For the 50th anniversary of Disneyland in 2005, Disney Editions released a limited-edition reprint that includes end notes by Dave Smith of the Disney Archives to correct and enlarge on some of the information, since Martin took Walt's recollections at face value and Walt was not always correct on titles or chronology.

In 1950, Walt Disney asked Chouinard art instructor Don Graham (who had taught classes at the Disney Studio from 1932 to about 1940) to investigate the possibilities of producing a book on animation. Dividing his time between Disney and his teaching at Chouinard Art Institute, Graham's research eventually ended up in a book he didn't write, *The Art of Animation* by Bob Thomas (Simon & Schuster/Golden Press, 1958).

Graham's approach seemed "too technical" for Walt's approval, so Thomas was brought in to make it more accessible and to use the chapters to help promote the forthcoming animated feature *Sleeping Beauty* (1959). A staff of Disney artists headed by Paul Hartley worked for months to assemble the illustrations for the book.

It was the first book to identify and feature a picture of the famous Nine Old Men, as well as giving credit to a number of other Disney artists who had worked in obscurity for decades. This original edition is much treasured by both animators and Disney historians and inspired a very young John Lasseter.

Revised editions from Hyperion in the 1990s are missing much of the fascinating technical information and illustrations of the original edition as well as the detailed information on *Sleeping Beauty*. The technical information and history is simplified and half of the book devoted to promoting the studio's newest films, *Beauty and the Beast* (1992 edition) or *Hercules* (1997 edition).

In 1965, Thomas was approached by Grosset & Dunlap who wanted a biography of Walt Disney geared for children. While Thomas felt he would have to write the book based on file material, he soon discovered that Walt, despite being busy with numerous projects, was excited to participate and allowed Thomas to interview him at length four times during the writing of the book. Thomas recalled:

> He seemed eager to sum up the lessons he had learned as a boy and tell young people how he applied them in his later life.

Walt Disney: Magician of the Movies was released in February 1967 as part of Grosset & Dunlap's "Pioneer Books" series of children's biographies (and will be re-released in 2016 by Theme Park Press). It was the first children's biography of Walt and had been reviewed and approved by the Disney Studio.

With Walt's death in December 1966, there came an "unofficial" and often critical biography titled *The Disney Version: The Life, Times and Commerce of Walt Disney* by entertainment writer Richard Schickel that appeared in 1968 from Simon & Schuster. It was not a balanced book, and since Schickel was denied cooperation from the Disney Studio, he had to interview ex-employees who sometimes had an axe to grind.

It is the first book that grossly misrepresents Walt Disney by making unconfirmed assumptions. If you feel the necessity to add this book to your collection, you should get the third edition (1997) that features a new introduction by Schickel where he reflects that he may have been unfairly critical of Walt.

When Bob Thomas' biography of Walt was released in 1976, Schickel stated:

> I wanted to do an independent, objective book. I don't consider it an assault. In many respects, I gave Disney high marks. In any event, it is always good to have a second biography.

In 1973, Thomas was invited to lunch with a few Disney executives at the Disney Studio. They told him that two other writers (Richard Hubler and Lawrence Watkin) had both tried their hand at writing the official biography, but both of the attempts had proven unsatisfactory.

Ron Miller, who was then vice president of production, represented the Disney family and told Thomas that he would "have complete freedom to write Walt's story as you see it".

Out of respect for the family in the final draft, Thomas left out that Sharon Disney had been adopted and that Lillian was two years older than Walt, although that information now appears in the current edition. In the text, Thomas does not shy away from talking about Walt's flaws, but he does not dwell on them in a tabloid fashion.

Thomas had previously written biographies of entertainment figures like Harry Cohn, David O. Selznick, and Walter Winchell. However, this was the first time that Thomas had full unrestricted access to family members, studio employees, letters, and official documents, as well as others who might have refused to be interviewed if it were not an officially sanctioned project.

For *Walt Disney: An American Original* (Simon & Schuster 1976), Thomas also drew upon his own acquaintance with Walt. Walt had toured Thomas through Disneyland as it was being built. Thomas had interviewed Walt many times over the years for newspaper stories and, in addition, had worked with Walt in authoring two books about Walt's life and the Disney history of animation.

Maintaining a demanding schedule of writing four articles and two columns a week for the Associated Press, Thomas wrote the Walt biography on weekends and vacations. Instead of working with index files as he had done when compiling his previous books, he adopted the same method of storyboarding material that Walt himself used for animated cartoons. Thomas wrote three drafts and that was unusual compared to his previous books.

Because of its sense of balance and accuracy, the book is still in print today and considered one of the best biographies of Walt.

Two decades later, in 1998, Thomas wrote a companion book from Roy O. Disney's perspective: *Building a Company: Roy O. Disney and the Creation of an Entertainment Empire* (Disney Editions, 1998).

While there were magazine and newspaper articles and a couple of books, Disney fandom as we know it today began with the celebration of Mickey Mouse's 40th birthday in 1968. There was a new interest in collecting classic Mickey Mouse merchandise that led to the exploration of early Disney history.

Of course, there were the mainstream magazines, like *Saturday Evening Post*, *Look*, *Life*, and *National Geographic* that might do a feature article on Disney, as well as newspapers that did stories when a new movie was released or for a special anniversary.

By the late 1970s, there were also a variety of collector publications, fanzines, and museum catalogs that might devote a cover article or even an entire issue to Disney.

Of course, most Disney fans eagerly awaited issues of the much loved and much missed *Disney News* for their primary information about the Disney company.

Disney News/Disney Magazine (1965–2005)

Disney News was a subscription-only magazine published four times annually, at a cost of $1 per year, for Magic Kingdom Club Families. It featured news and stories (sometimes recycled from official Disney publications) and, of course, was designed to get families excited about visiting Disneyland.

The magazine continued to grow and was re-dubbed *The Disney Magazine* (Spring 1994) when it also began to be sold on newsstands for $2.95. It was still published quarterly but with expanded articles and pages. Sadly, the magazine ended with the Summer 2005 issue devoted to celebrating Disneyland's 50th anniversary.

Disneyana Collector (1982–1987)

The first issue of this subscription newsletter was released in the summer of 1982, published by Grolier Enterprises, with a mailing address of the Disney Studio in Burbank. Each issue would feature an artist or collector profile (sometimes both in a single issue) as well as a mail column, news blurbs, and brief articles on new Disney collectibles. Twenty issues were published with the last one (Vol. 5, No. 6) in Fall 1987.

However, the desire for more information was overwhelming, as was the need to personally connect with others who shared similar interests. So fans turned to "fanzines", self-published, limited-print fan magazines. Originally, fanzines were produced on ditto or mimeograph. By the mid-1970s, they were more frequently done by Xerox or photo-offset printing. They all had limited print runs and were mailed out, sometimes without an envelope to save on costs.

The majority of Disney fans either collected comic books or toys, and some of the first Disney fanzines were glorified sales/want lists with a sprinkling of trivia, badly photocopied illustrations, and not much substance.

The Mouse Club and the National Fantasy Fan Club (NFFC)

There were two West Coast collector organizations that focused on Disney, the Mouse Club and the National Fantasy Fan Club. NFFC was later renamed the Disneyana Fan Club and is still in existence today. Their entire history, including their conventions and publications, are detailed in *The Vault of Walt: Volume 3* (Theme Park Press, 2014).

They each had their own newsletters, *The Mouse Club* (first published in January 1980 and ending in 1992) and the *Fantasy Line Express* (January 1985 to current), respectively, filled with Disney news, articles, and photos.

Here is a brief overview of some of the other zines that in the early days would be in any true Disney historian's collection and are examples of the earliest Disney scholarship.

Funnyworld (1966–1983)

Funnyworld began as a self-printed mimeographed contribution (October 1966) to an amateur press alliance called *Capa-Alpha*, the very first comic book apa. The first issue was 14 pages and the original focus was on funny animal comic books, usually those inspired by their animation counterparts. It was produced by pioneering animation and Disney scholar Michael Barrier.

Six months later, in *Funnyworld* 5, April 1967, Barrier included his first animation information. Little did Barrier suspect that animation articles and interviews, especially Disney-oriented, would soon almost completely displace all talk of comic books. A year later, in *Funnyworld* 9, 1968, the fanzine had expanded to 46 mimeographed pages and Barrier was selling the extra copies he printed for fifty cents.

The summer of 1970 saw the release of *Funnyworld* 12. It was the first offset issue, sold for one dollar, and received its widest distribution, sometimes appearing for sale in bookstores.

The magazine was published sporadically until *Funnyworld* 16 (Winter 1974–75), which was intended as the final issue. Its infrequent publication made it a money-losing situation and resulted in Barrier stopping the fanzine to concentrate on researching a book about the history of animation.

Funnyworld was revived in 1977 when the magazine was sold to publisher Mark Lilien, while the editorial control remained with Barrier. However, after six issues, Barrier withdrew because of strong disagreements with the way the magazine was being handled. His withdrawal officially sounded the death knell for the magazine with issue No. 23 (Spring 1983).

The Duckburg Times (1977–1992)

Originally written and published by teenager Paul Anderson, beginning December 1977, *The Duckburg Times* ("Dedicated to the work of Walt Disney and Walt Disney Productions") cost one dollar an issue. It was a mixture of very short articles, reprinted material, and traced drawings.

With issue No. 8 (October 1980), Frank and Dana Gabbard took over the publication and editing of the magazine and upgraded both the format and content. Those issues included fascinating interviews with Disney artists and articles by writers like Brent Swanson, Andrew Lendaky, Steve Eberhar, Joe Torcivia, and Jim Korkis. The final issue was the double-sized Nos. 24/25 published in August 1992.

StoryboarD (1987–1995)

In early 1987, a few Disney fans were sitting around talking about all things Disney. One of them was enthusiastic about a magazine he had just discovered on Civil War memorabilia. It was slick, with color photos, lists of dealers, and other features. Using that magazine as a template, *StoryboarD* was created (with the final "D" being large to suggest "Disney"). The first issue appeared at the end of 1987. George Timmons was the original editor and publisher. However, since it was just a part-time enterprise that quickly grew too large for the small group, by issue No. 6 (December 1988) it was taken over by Bobit Publishing.

Unlike other Disney fanzines, *StoryboarD* looked like a real magazine with slick glossy pages, color photos, and impressive graphics. Its focus was on all things Disney and became a popular location for animation galleries and collectible dealers to advertise.

The Fall 1990 issue was renumbered Vol. 1, No. 1, and renamed *StoryboarD: The Art of Laughter* (The Journal of Animation Art). Steve Fiott, who was an animation art collector and gallery owner (and folk musician), took over the publication of the magazine with his Laughter Publications, Inc. While the primary emphasis remained Disney, Fiott expanded the focus to other animation studios, especially Warner Bros and Walter Lantz, and related collector products like limited-edition animation cels. The final issue was Vol. 6, No. 3 (May/June 1995). Fiott died June 6, 1995.

Fiott also started his own series of conventions called Disneyana Showcase. The first one was held at Pan Pacific Hotel in Anaheim on May 20–22, 1994. The event had a mascot, a beaver named Wally (after Beaver Cleaver's older brother in the popular television show), designed by animator Nik Ranieri.

The second Disneyana Showcase was held on October 15-16, 1994, at the Inn at the Park. By 1995, the show expanded into a Disneyana Showcase East held in Virginia on April 30 and a Disneyana Showcase West held at the Inn at the Park in California on May 28.

In addition, Fiott published limited editions (less than 1,000 copies) of books like Van Arsdale France's memoir of working at Disneyland, *Window on Main Street* (an expanded version was in the planning stages at the time of Fiott's death and has now been published by Theme Park Press); Ken Anderson's children's book *Nessie and the Little Blind Boy of Loch Ness*; and Andreas Deja's children's book *Puss'N'Boots*.

E Ticket (1986–2009)

One of the most beloved and most valuable Disney fanzines was *The E Ticket*, first published in Winter 1986 by Leon and Jack Janzen. These two brothers grew up in southern California in the 1950s and 1960s, and wanted to recapture some of their memories of that time period by sharing photos, facts, and stories of not only Disneyland but Knott's Berry Farm, Pacific Ocean Park, and other venues. However, the fanzine gradually became focused solely on Disneyland.

It was Jack's wife, Mary Ann, who came up with the name of the magazine. The first issues were sent out anonymously because they were fearful of what response they might get from the Disney company, and they only charged three twenty-two cent stamps for those first issues. The first issue had a print run of 200 copies.

Glossy, coated paper was first used in issue No. 15 and limited interior color in No. 21. It was until No. 23 that the format became a new color cover and full interior color. While they shared the duties of editor, proofreader, and art director, Leon Janzen did most of the writing while Jack Janzen painted the covers and did interior art.

The E Ticket evolved from a 14-page, photocopied, double-stapled fanzine to a slick 46-page (or more) magazine with full-color that unfortunately ended with issue 46 (Summer 2009). The brothers had planned to "steam through", as Leon said, to issue No. 50. Unfortunately, Leon Janzen died of a massive heart attack on September 9, 2003, just as issue No. 40 was completed. It took his brother another year to publish the next issue because he was so heartbroken.

In Summer 2009, Jack produced the final issue (No. 46) and invited friends to enjoy "one last ride" on the Griffith Park carousel where Walt had supposedly began thinking of a place where a father and his two daughters could spend some time together. On December 31, 2009, Jack Janzen announced he had officially retired the magazine. The good news was that the Walt Disney Family Museum acquired all the assets of the magazine, including back issues and CD ROMs, and sells them at their museum store.

There were two annuals (1988, 1991) featuring a mixture of new and reprinted material published, in addition to a special very-limited edition "Mr. Toad's Enchanted Evening at Disneyland" issue (October 1999) and three CD-ROMs that collected the first 24 issues along with some additional material. The index created for the magazine was produced single-handedly by long-time Disney fan Jerry Edwards.

Persistence of Vision (1992–1998)

Ten issues of this groundbreaking and much-loved magazine were published by Paul Anderson. The magazine was intended to be called *Walt's World* with a logo drawn by Disney artist Ken Anderson, but just two days before taking the first issue to the printer, Paul Anderson received notice from Disney Legal that the title was unacceptable, so he had to quickly invent another one.

Beginning with the second issue, subscribers also got a homemade cassette tape filled with audio treasures from Paul Anderson's collection. After the publication of the 10th issue, Anderson seemed to disappear from public view because of family and health issues. His research on Disney and World War II that he had put into the planned issue No. 11 has expanded into an as-yet-unpublished book on that subject. Along with Todd James Pierce, he now hosts the Disney History Institute website devoted to Disney.

Tomart's Disneyana Update (1994–Current)

Published by Tom Tumbusch (a frequent speaker and dealer at Mouse Club East Disneyana shows in the early days of Disney fandom), this publication is not just a supplement to the four-volume *Tomart's Illustrated Disneyana Catalog and Price Guide* (1985) but a valuable historical resource for Disney fans and researchers. There are over eighty issues published and most of them are still available at a reasonable price at the Tomart website. Tumbusch is also responsible for the Disney Pin Collecting Guides.

In addition, there were several publications devoted just to the work of artist Carl Barks who had an impressive career at the Disney Studio as a story man primarily on the Donald Duck cartoons and then left to work for Western Publishing writing and drawing Donald Duck comic books where he created the character of Uncle Scrooge.

Other fanzines included *Disneydom* (March–October 1969), *Mouse Rap Monthly* (1988–1995), *Magical Moments & Memories Disneyana Enthusiasts Club* (Early 1990s), *Theme Park* (Winter 1992–1993), *The Barks Collector* (1976–1990), *Vacation in Duckburg* (1971), *Barksburg* (1982), *Scrooge Hunter* (1992), as well as many other short-lived attempts at documenting Disney.

In the late 1980s and early 1990s there were a plethora of collector's magazines like Collector's Showcase, animation magazines, and dealer auction catalogs (like the wonderful ones by Howard Lowery with valuable annotated notes) that contained information about Disney animation and memorabilia.

Howard Lowery began buying and selling original animation and comic art in 1970 as an employee of Collectors Book Store in Hollywood, California. He gained experience and knowledge in these and related areas as interest increased among collectors and the general public, and in 1984 he purchased that section of the business.

In September 1989 Lowery moved his business to Burbank, California, where he opened a retail gallery and organized nearly fifty full-scale auctions of animation art, comic art, and movie collectibles. His annotated auction catalogs packed with rare Disney documents and merchandise are desirable collectibles today. His marriage to the charming and knowledgeable Paula Sigman, who was a Disney archivist for fifteen years, introduced him to the artists behind the art. He still operates on-line auctions at HowardLowery.com.

Leonard Maltin wrote two ground-breaking books: *The Disney Films* (Crown, 1973), listing summaries and commentary on the feature films made while Walt was alive, and *Of Mice and Magic* (McGraw-Hill, 1980), a history of various animation studios and a listing of their cartoons, including a chapter devoted just to Disney.

The Disney company authorized a huge coffee table book detailing the history of Disney entitled *The Art of Walt Disney: From Mickey Mouse to the Magic Kingdoms* (Harry Abrams Publishers 1973) by Christopher Finch that remains in print in an updated and revised edition.

In 1968, Finch was an associate curator at the Walker Art Center in Minneapolis. From there he moved to New York and contributed articles to *Arts, Art News, Art in America,* and other periodicals when he was tapped by the Disney company to write the book.

Finch also authored a companion book, *Walt Disney's America* (Abbeville, 1978), with material that could not fit into the first book; *The Art of the Lion King* (1994); and *Disney's Winnie the Pooh* (2002). He has written other books about art and pop culture, including three on Jim Henson.

With the surge of interest in collecting cels, new books focusing on animation and Disney were produced.

Disney animators Frank Thomas and Ollie Johnston retired from the Disney Studio in 1978. However, years earlier they realized that they needed to pass along the knowledge they had gained over the decades to a new generation. It took them five years to write *Disney Animation: The Illusion of Life* (Harry Abrams Publishers 1981). The book not only gave a clear discussion of the technical aspects of drawing for animation but included stories and personality profiles from Disney's Golden Age which were important, first-hand accounts of Disney history.

That book was followed by three others written by Thomas and Johnston: *Too Funny for Words: Disney's Greatest Sight Gags* (1987), *Walt Disney's Bambi: The Story and the Film* (1990), and *The Disney Villain* (1993).

Now there are hundreds of books and magazines devoted to all things Disney.

There was a time when publishing Disney history meant newspapers, books, magazines, journals, catalogs, and pamphlets. Today, anyone with a passion for Disney history can publish online and potentially reach an appreciative global audience. It takes as little as a free computer at a public library and a free account on one of many online publishing platforms.

The transition began well before web browsers and websites. Personal computers and inexpensive modems in the 1980s allowed text-based discussions using proprietary online services. Disney fans found each other online.

Public access to the internet in the early 1990s fueled Disney-focused Usenet newsgroups and list servers. The Mosaic graphical browser, introduced in 1993, set the stage for browsers and websites of ever-increasing complexity.

Every subsequent year brought new innovations for sharing information online—including blogging platforms, community forums, podcasting, video-on-demand, social media services, and mobile apps. Google and other search sites make it easy for those who are interested in Disney history to find it.

The Walt Disney Company publishes Disney history online through its D23 ("The Official Disney Fan Club") website, the Disney Parks Blog, and other official websites when Disney history provides context for marketing current Disney entertainment.

The online presence of the Walt Disney Family Museum in San Francisco includes a blog which makes content from *The "E" Ticket* magazine available.

But most online Disney history is not from the company or the museum. It's on personal blogs that reflect the interests and personalities of the bloggers. It's posted to YouTube or offered as podcasts. It's in wikis, such as Wikipedia and the Disney Wiki. It's published on the big independent Disney websites, on obscure fan websites, on university servers, and on the sites of the biggest mainstream publications, but it's then shared through social media such as Facebook and Twitter.

The roots of the big independent Disney websites often go back to the Usenet newsgroups and fledgling websites of the early public internet in the mid-1990s. Some of these sites were spawned from discussions that a small group of Disney fans held informally when they met at Disneyland.

Al Lutz wrote on June 1, 1997:

> The Disneyland Information Guide (or "The DIG" for short) originally started as a monthly posting of Disneyland hours to the Disney Usenet Newsgroups (because I and many others got sick of answering the same questions about schedules over and over again)—it has expanded over the past two years into a web site at http://members. aol.com/alweho and a seven-part FAQ that is also now posted monthly (if I can get to it) in the rec.parks.theme, rec.arts.disney.parks, rec. arts.disney.announce, and alt.disney.disneyland groups. You can also find it in the news.answers, rec.answers, and alt.answers groups.

A former music recording producer, Lutz started writing about Disneyland on Usenet, then on a series of websites. For fans used to the always positive coverage about Disney and its theme parks in the traditional press, Lutz focused on some of the flaws at the Happiest Place on Earth, from chipped paint to burned-out lights to dangerous maintenance cutbacks, as well as the pixie dust.

In an interview with Robert Niles in October 2007, Lutz said:

> I used to work for RCA Records; spent ten years there. When the problems started hitting in the music business, I got out. Then I got into helping with my family business, the [real estate] appraisal business,

which isn't going so good right now. But I had started going on to Usenet, because that had fascinated me when we'd started talking about it in the music business. I started on alt.disney.disneyland. There was one guy handling the Disneyland FAQ at that point, and he'd kind of given up on it, so I took it over because I got tired of answering the same questions all the time—"What time is Fantasmic! this weekend?"—you know.

Then Werner Weiss from Yesterland [a website devoted to now-closed Disneyland attractions which began in May 1995 and is one of the most popular and respected sites still operating today] contacted me and said, "You really should have a website," and that was the start of the DIG. It just started as an FAQ, but then we developed it into a gossip column. I think having the viewpoint is what's important to me. Because that's one thing they'll kill you for on the Web is not having one.

Deb Wills' AllEars.net began in 1996 as WDWIG (Walt Disney World Information Guide), the Florida counterpart to what Lutz was doing for Disneyland in California.

LaughingPlace.com, launched in 1999, grew out of Doobie Moseley's twin projects: first, a listing of all of the Windows on Main Street at Disneyland, and second, an attempt to create a directory for all the Disney-related websites. Doobie's wife, Rebekah, was instrumental in the creation and evolution of the site as well. John Frost was also involved but left in 2004 to start his own site, the Disney Blog.

At the time there were 196 websites that devoted at least part of themselves to things Disney. Today there are thousands.

DIG evolved into MousePlanet.com. The core columnists who launched MousePlanet in 2000 included Al Lutz, Kevin Yee, Adrienne Vincent-Phoenix, Shelly Smith (now Valladolid), and Jim Hill.

These were all strong-willed and opinionated writers. Within two years, some broke off to create their own websites to communicate Disney information in the way they each felt was best.

Jim Hill Media began in 2002 when Hill launched his own website with the help of Shelly Valladolid after spending a year writing for LaughingPlace.com. He now also writes for the Huffington Post.

MiceChat.com began as MiceAge.com, also in 2002, when Al Lutz broke off from MousePlanet in December of that year. The parting was amicable and the decision was Al's so he could have independent control of his material.

Todd Regan was not originally part of MiceAge but launched MiceChat in 2004 as a separate site to provide discussion forums for MiceAge and general Disneyland topics. Eventually, MiceChat grew to become the primary site, with MiceAge as one of many columns.

Pete Werner's DIS (formerly WDWINFO) website and DISboards forums began as a modest personal fan site. DISboards gets over a quarter-million visitors each week. Werner said:

> I was homeless when I was 21 years old and had other self-destructive problems that caused that to happen. And I promised myself, as long as I kept my life together, I would come back to Walt Disney World every year after my first visit during a business conference I attended in Orlando in May 1991. And that was kind of what I used to reward myself for staying on the right path. And when the internet came along, I'd always been involved in computers, I built a website just for myself, just to learn how to do websites, and I did it around Disney.
>
> And one thing led to another, and all of a sudden people started showing up. And within a year I realized I had something special here. Then I moved to Orlando not too long after that. The site (1998), the boards, the travel agency (Dreams Unlimited Travel 1999) all happened within about three years of each other.

None of these long-established and popular sites is primarily about Disney history, but all include significant historical information, mostly about the parks. And the archives from these sites' early years have increasingly become valuable resources.

Today, there are a plethora of websites, podcasts, and blogs devoted to all aspects of Disney but primarily the Disney parks and the travel planning issues involving them, such as food, ticket prices, and special events.

When asked what advice he would give those who wanted to start yet another Disney website, Lutz responded:

> Two words: be honest. Have a viewpoint and be honest. People might not like what you have to say, but they will respond to it.

The internet has changed many things for Disney historians, from access to information, to a larger audience, to instantaneous feedback from readers.

Disney fans are knowledgeable experts about what is happening, whether it's checking filed building permits or knowledge of new construction or researching copyrighted names of upcoming movies and websites for a glimpse of things to come or even getting leaks from legitimate sources. The internet is becoming a major source in presenting Disney history, especially since corrections can be made quickly.

However, whatever changes in technology happen in the coming years, the role of the Disney historian will remain constant: find the information, verify the information, and share the information.

David R. Smith and the Disney Archives

David Rollin Smith, more commonly referred to as just Dave Smith, was born October 13, 1940, and raised in Pasadena, California. He was the son of librarians and educators. He earned his B.A. in History and a Masters Degree in Library Science from the University of California at Berkeley.

Before Disney, he had library and archival experience while working in the Manuscript Department of the Huntington Library in San Marino, interning at the Library of Congress in Washington, D.C., and being on the staff of the Research Library at UCLA.

The proposal for a Disney Archives was submitted in January 1970, but it was not officially approved by the Disney company until June. Smith became a Disney employee on June 22, 1970, and was the company's first archivist and the only person in his department. His first assignment was to document all the items in Walt Disney's offices.

For decades, Smith has been regarded as the ultimate authority on all things Disney. He authored several books and magazine articles and assisted on many others. He wrote a continuing "Ask Dave" question-and-answer column beginning in 1984 for the Disney Channel and *Disney Magazine*. It still appears today on the D23 website.

In his spare time, Smith collected stamps, historical autographs, and material on author S.S. Van Dine. That is a nice reminder that even a Disney expert should have outside interests.

In 2007, Smith was made a Disney Legend. He retired in October 2010 on his 70th birthday after over four decades with Disney. He continues to work for the Disney company as a consultant with the title Chief Archivist Emeritus.

I have known Dave for decades. In 1980, I received my first letter from him on Disney Archives letterhead paper. It was two short paragraphs. In the first paragraph, he wrote about how much he had enjoyed an article I had written on two Mickey Mouse cartoons featuring animation by Fred Moore. Disney staffers often called those cartoons the "Drunk Mickeys" because of the fluidity of movement and goofiness of Mickey. The second paragraph pointed out two errors I had made. One was proper nomenclature, a particular source of aggravation to him. I had left off the word "The" in a cartoon short title.

I have interviewed Dave many times. The following is an excerpt from one I did with him on March 16, 2005, at the Walt Disney Story Theater in the Main Street Exposition Hall at the Magic Kingdom in Florida. It was done on stage in the afternoon in front of more than three hundred eager cast members. I have eliminated all of my questions to allow Dave to tell his own story in his own words.

Disneyland is very close to my heart because I grew up in southern California. I was a teenager when Disneyland opened and I remember one of my very first trips to Disneyland when I was about sixteen or so. I was walking in through the castle, into Fantasyland, and there was Walt Disney walking in next to me.

Up until then, people didn't really know who Walt Disney was. I mean, they knew the name, but they didn't know him by sight. But, starting in the fall of 1954, he had his television show and people started recognizing him as he was coming into their homes every week on television.

So, I recognized him and I thought—I had started collecting celebrity autographs at that time—I thought, "Oh, here's somebody that I want his autograph." I ran into the first shop that I could find as I went into the castle and it was a magic shop and the only writing implements they had were these two-foot long magic pencils that had different colors in the leads so that when you're writing you get different colors.

Anyway, that was my only choice, so I bought that and I went running out to Walt Disney and he politely declined to sign an autograph for me. He said that when he started signing autographs it created this huge crowd around him and he never got his work done. He told me to write him at the studio and he would send me his autograph. I did, and he did so; at least I have it, and I know it is a real autograph, not one done by a secretary or an artist.

The only other time I saw Walt Disney was when he was the grand marshal of the 1966 Pasadena Rose Parade and I was standing on the sidewalk of Colorado Boulevard watching.

I got a Master's Degree in Library Science from UC Berkeley. I went to the Library of Congress in Washington as an intern for about six months and then left Washington after about a year and a half. I stayed a year at the library after the internship. I figured after working in the Library of Congress I wouldn't be happy in a small library so I searched for a big one in the L.A. area where my home was and UCLA was the one I picked and I spent about five years there.

One thing that I had been interested in, both in library school and in working at the library, was doing bibliographies. I found this very fascinating. I enjoyed that kind of work. And so I had done a bibliography on the *Monitor* and the *Merrimack* during the Civil War and I did one on Jack Benny. They had Jack Benny's papers at the UCLA Library.

But, on December 15th, 1966, what happened? Walt Disney died. And, you know, that was an important happening for people all around the world. I mean, a lot of people remember where they were when they heard that John F. Kennedy died, but a lot of people remember when Walt died, too. I mean, he was a very, very, very famous person and it affected me because I had grown up with the Disney films. I loved going to Disneyland and suddenly this person that I knew so well wasn't going to be around anymore.

So, I thought it'd be fun to do a Walt Disney bibliography. I checked the library sources to see if anything like that had been done before and didn't find anything and so I thought, *Why don't I try?* I contacted the people at the Disney Studio and suggested this and they said they'd be willing to help me. I could tell they weren't too thrilled about this suggestion, but they opened up some of their files for me and let me come in and go through some of the Disney publications and comic books and things like that.

Anyway, I created this bibliography over about a year-and-a-half period. When I finished it, the people at the studio figured that it would be useful to them and so they purchased it from me. I made some money on a bibliography, which is not very common.

A lot of university libraries have what they call their Department of Special Collections and they like to acquire the papers of famous people in their area or in the field they collect to have in the library for their students to do research. The UCLA Library collects a lot in the field of entertainment, of course, being right there by Hollywood.They had contacted the Disney Studio and said, "How about depositing Walt Disney's papers here at the library?"

Dr. Robert Bosker, the librarian, suggested that they come out to the library for a meeting. Two or three Disney representatives came out, and Bosker asked me if I would sit in on this meeting because I had had this contact with Disney before and knew some people at the studio, although I didn't know these people that were coming to the meeting.

And, out of this meeting, it became obvious that this is not a collection that UCLA could handle because you were talking about a huge collection. You were talking about a company that was still very active in business and needing to get into this material all the time and, number three, since this is an active, ongoing company, the company has business secrets that they weren't ready to let out. We didn't want everyone going out to their garage and making an audio-animatronics Abraham Lincoln!

The Disney people figured this really isn't something that could go to the university and the university also said this isn't something they could handle. But I was sitting in the back of the room and my ears perked up and I thought this sounds like a wonderful opportunity, so I went home that evening and typed up a letter to the Disney people that were there and offered my services.

I suggested that I could take a leave of absence from UCLA and do a survey of the whole Disney organization and find out what the quantity and the quality of the material was that the company had saved and then give them some idea of what they could do with it.

They were pleased to get this suggestion. Because here you've got an entertainment company that didn't know anything about archiving, so to have someone like me come along … and I'd had experience at the Library of Congress when I was there as an intern working in all the different areas of the Library—in rare books and manuscripts—so I had dealt with the kind of archival materials that they had at the Disney Studio. They liked the suggestion, and they hired me as a consultant.

I took a two-month leave of absence from UCLA and went to the studio. They gave me the great "grand master key" which opened every door there. This was really exciting for someone that was just brand new on the lot! And they told me, "Go snoop."

I spent weeks going around the studio unlocking doors in basements and closets and all sorts of things that hadn't been opened in years, blowing the dust off the boxes and just snooping to see what was around, what they had saved through the years, and the company also sent me around to see other archives, to see what other companies had done. For two months in the latter part of 1969, I worked full time at the Disney Studio, visiting all departments and sections, sampling both current and retired files.

I also thought the pattern of the presidential libraries was very important, where they had a library collection but also a museum and collection of material related to the president. I visited the Harry S. Truman Library in Missouri, for instance. In response to a letter to one of the presidential libraries mentioning my ideas for the Walt Disney Archives, the director replied that an archives dedicated to Walt Disney could easily surpass a presidential library in interest and educational value and eventually in size.

So, I submitted a proposal January 1, 1970, that the company set up an archives program. It took them about six months, but they decided they liked it so they hired me to come and do it. Essentially, I wrote my own job description. The head of Personnel called me and said, "What do we pay you for this job?"

The Disney people, especially Roy, felt that before they decided where they were going, they better know where they had been. The reason for the Archives was divided into seven categories:

- *Legal*: to aid the general counsel by providing documentation needed for litigation.
- *Publicity*: to furnish material for press releases and advertising purposes, especially important in a company which regularly releases old films
- *Personnel*: to help in the indoctrination of new staff members and in training supervisors for positions of greater responsibility.
- *Public Relations*: to aid in keeping pace with the increasing need for general historical information about Walt Disney and his company.
- *Scholarship*: to make available to serious research scholars information essential for the writing of books, articles, and theses.
- *Management*: to provide data on major decisions made in the past for guidance in making current decisions, and for help in avoiding the same mistakes made in former years.
- *Sales Promotion*: to make available historical materials to be used in promoting current sales, as with an anniversary of Mickey Mouse campaign

Remember at this time Walt Disney Productions was nearing its 50th anniversary in 1973, so there was an increasing awareness of the need for a well-indexed collection of the company's records and products.

With the establishment of the Archives, one of my first tasks was to begin gathering material. The company files fell into three major categories: business records, creative records, and products. The company had a clipping service since the 1920s, so we had literally millions of newspaper and magazines clippings to sort through.

Each class of material has its own peculiarities. Each needed different kinds of main entries and different kinds of subject entries. Specialized catalogs had to be developed.

We couldn't have everything, so we "skimmed the cream from the top of the bottle", you might say.

I surveyed storage facilities. Some old files were found under leaking water pipes. Other files were discovered that had been visited by termites. Termites evidently liked the graphic lines on early drawings, for they would eat only the lines, leaving nicely etched pieces of paper.

The Disney people figured that since I was going to be handling the history of the whole company, I should be at the studio which is the corporate headquarters. About the only place they had empty rooms were in Walt Disney's old office suite which has been locked up since he died. Actually, the secretaries had worked there for about a year after he died, cleaning out the files and things like that, but then they left and they locked the door and the janitor would go in and clean every couple of weeks or so, and that was about it. Nobody was getting in there at all.

And so they gave me for my office one of the anterooms out past the receptionist's room that was, I think, ordinarily just used by Walt for storage. But one of the first things they asked me to do was to go in and inventory Walt Disney's offices because one of the things that I'd noted when I did the survey of other archives and libraries was that, especially with the presidential library, there's one thing you find in almost every single one of those, and that's a reproduction of the Oval Office.

I had thought there might be a day down the line where we might want to reproduce Walt Disney's office. So I was given a temporary secretary and then went in there and sat in Walt's office for about two weeks and inventoried the whole place, counting the paper clips in his desk drawers and everything else. It was kind of an eerie thing, me being a brand-new employee at Disney, having looked up to this man all my life and then suddenly sitting in his desk chair pawing through his desk. It was a little eerie.

People had told me that Walt was not interested in history. He wasn't interested in his history and he wasn't interested in the company's history. Once he made a film, like *Snow White and the Seven Dwarfs* (1937), he would put it aside. He'd go on to the next project. He never looked back. He never went back and saw that movie again.

I was wondering about this statement that he wasn't very interested in his history and then one of the first things I found while I was looking though his desk was the script for *Steamboat Willie* (1928) in the bottom drawer. Now, somebody that's not interested in his history, why would he keep the script for his first Mickey Mouse cartoon in his desk? I think he had in the back of his heart a fond place for the things that started him out in his career.

We did photograph the desk and the rest of the office in color and black-and-white. We were ready if they wanted to reproduce the office, and we measured the room size and the paneling and doors because the architectural plans they had at the studio weren't terribly accurate.

Around 1972, they suddenly decided that we need to use this space. We've been wasting a whole wing at the Disney Studio and it's important space and we need it for our executives now. And so they decided to remove Walt's offices. We had all the documentation, we were fine, and it could be taken out, so we did go in there and pack up all of that material.

That was also about the time they started thinking about the Walt Disney Story, an attraction we had both at Disneyland and here at Walt Disney World, and the idea from the very beginning was to reproduce Walt's offices at Disneyland. We were very careful when we were packing everything up to number the boxes and be sure we knew where everything was so that we could get them out again when we were ready to reproduce Walt's offices.

I remember one story that when we were packing the office, I asked the supervisor of the movers who were helping us if we could have the original telephones. And he said, "No, those belong to the phone company; you can't have those." When he went out of the room, one of the movers went over to the telephone and yanked it out of the wall and handed it to me and said, "What they don't know won't hurt 'em". So, if you go into the One Man's Dream exhibit over here in Florida and you see Walt's office and you see a telephone there, it's the original telephone from his office at the studio.

Back in 1970, I went around the departments. You go up to them and say, "We've started an archives now; why don't you turn over your file set to us that you've been preserving all these years?" What do you think the answer is? "What do you think we are? Why should we give you our file set? How do we know that you're going to take good care of it?" We had to prove ourselves to convince these people that not only would we take better care of their file sets, but we would enlarge them; we'd make sure that if they ever wanted to see anything there, it was always going to be available. Things had gotten lost over the decades.

Things that had happened like, the Danish publisher might have come up to Disney Publishing and said, we want to reproduce the third Mickey Mouse Reader. And so they'd send it off to Copenhagen and it probably never came back again and they just weren't careful about the file sets that they had. So we worked slowly with some of these departments.

Now some of them were very anxious to give us their file sets because they didn't want to take care of them anymore. They wanted the extra space. These were things that they didn't want to concern themselves with at all; get all this old junk into the Archives so we can work on our new projects only. We had both things going on within the company.

The one person I had the hardest time convincing was Madeleine Wheeler, the secretary of Roy O. Disney. Madeleine was sort of the maven of the studio; I mean, she ruled that place. Not Roy, she ruled the place. I remember one summer, the traffic boys that delivered the mail started wearing shorts. She didn't like that. And, within a week, they were not wearing shorts anymore.

I didn't really have a run-in with her, but she did not offer the Archives any of the things that she had until we started working together on various projects. Pretty soon she got to know me, and she got to see what we were doing with the Archives, and then she started opening her drawers and giving us things. She had maintained for Roy all the company's genealogy, the family history. She turned that over to me.

She had ticket #1 from Disneyland that Roy had bought on opening day for $1.00. She turned that over to me. She had Flora Disney's, Walt's mother, family photo album. She turned that over to me. Slowly, these things were getting turned over to me. And of course after Roy died in December of 1971, she turned over a lot of material.

I'm there at my office every morning by 7:30am. What makes the job so interesting is there is no typical day at the Disney Studio. It's a varied job, because this company is involved in many different things all the time.

There are many departments and divisions of this company that need access to historical material. It could be the Cruise Line working on a trivia contest that they're going to have for their passengers, or it could be Disney Publishing thinking about reproducing some of the early Disney books and trying to figure out which ones would be good to reproduce. It could be Walt Disney World working on the telecast of the Christmas Parade and needing information for the emcees to talk about as the parade is going down the street.

Disney Legal is one of our biggest users. As you're no doubt aware, Mickey Mouse is a copyrighted character and we can't allow people to use our copyrighted characters without permission, and sometimes that works to our public relations disadvantage when we have to tell a nursery school they've got to take Mickey Mouse down off their wall, but if we don't protect these characters we're going to lose them, and so we have to be very careful.

Most people that infringe on our copyrights aren't consciously doing it. I mean, Mickey Mouse is everywhere! Can't we use Mickey Mouse? No, Mickey Mouse is a copyrighted character, so a simple cease-and-desist letter from the lawyers usually solves that problem, but there's always the few that are out there to make a quick buck and they think maybe we can make a little money before Disney cracks down on us.

And so those are the ones that the company really has to go after. Very often the lawyers have to come to the Archives and what they're looking for is: the first use of a character—when did Mickey Mouse first appear on a movie screen in Copenhagen, Denmark? We get that kind of question. When did the first Donald Duck comic book get published in Italy? It takes some detective work sometimes to find the answers to these questions.

I don't appreciate getting questions from people trying to trip me up. If they're coming to us with a sincere question that they really want to know the answer, and they've got a reason for needing to know the answer, like it's a project they're working on, then I am fine with that. But it irritates me when people purposely try to show off. There's just no point to that kind of thing and it wastes time, but it still happens more often than I would like.

We have five people in the Archives proper. We also run the Photo Library of the studio which has about two million photographs and there are four people in that department so there's a total of nine people altogether. Our turnover is very little in that department. I'm there thirty-one years now, and my assistant Robert [Tieman] is about eleven years, I think. We've been around a long time. I would not hire a Disney collector—too much temptation in the Archives!

Our collecting policies have changed quite a bit through the years because we didn't really know what the company was going to need in the way of historical material and so we were collecting lots of stuff in the early days. But, as the years went by, we sort of learned the types of things that people were going to be asking about and they weren't asking us to see the old toys and we were collecting a lot of the merchandise that was current in the 60s and 70s.

Today, we don't do that very much anymore. We will take some representative samplings of merchandise, especially when a movie like *The Lion King* comes out. We'll try to get a sampling of *The Lion King* merchandise, but we just don't have the space to store all of this stuff.

If it's an anniversary, 30th anniversary of Walt Disney World, we've tried to get the line on 30th anniversary merchandise; we've tried to get the "100 Years of Magic" merchandise. The things like this that we know the collectors are going to be asking us about in the future. And we do deal with people outside the company by email, by mail, by telephone, these people are calling us and asking historical questions, and if we can answer them quickly and easily, we do!

We do have some objects in the Archives. When I was in Orlando at the time Mr. Toad's Wild Ride was closing at the Magic Kingdom, they asked me if there was anything that I could use for the Archives in the attraction and I picked one of the little devils from the end of the ride. He's kinda cute.

We don't have much in the way of park memorabilia because the parks are, I mean, the main thing in the parks are the attractions and you take a piece of an attraction out, like a piece of the dark rides in Fantasyland, they don't look like much once you get them out. And they're not the type of thing that would fit easily in a small exhibit case which is what we have in the Archives. So big things we have no place for and, if it's a small thing, we want something that really means something when you look at it. Let me give you some examples.

We have the ring that turned the boy into the Shaggy Dog; we've got the snow globe that Mary Poppins had; we've got Dick Tracy's wrist radio; we've got a ray gun from *The Black Hole* (1979); we've got the magic bed knob from *Bedknobs and Broomsticks* (1971).

A few things like that that, if you see them in an exhibit case, you think, "Oh, that's familiar; I know what movie that's from!" But you look at most movies today and is there one hand prop that's really important that people are going to remember? Often there is not.

The first version of the book *Disney A to Z* came out in 1996 and, at that time, Hyperion, which was publishing the Disney books, said this is a great reference book and we should keep updating it every two years. So two years later, in 1998, we did the updated version of *Disney A to Z*, and I expected when 2000 came along, they'd be ready for the next edition. They've been dragging their feet.

What I did though, in 1998, the minute that I shipped off the manuscript for the updated version to the publisher, I started putting onto my computer all of the new material that would then go into the next edition. You know what's happening with the company all the time: we've got new movies coming out, we've got attractions opening at the park, we've got attractions closing at the park, we've got songs winning Oscars, and so forth.

All this information, as it crosses my desk, I just type it into the computer right there! So, I'm up to date as of Friday and it's Disney Editions now that publishes the Disney books; if they say we're ready to do your new edition of *Disney A to Z*, the next morning I will ship off the computer disc and they'll be all ready to go.

For the Disney Store trivia contests, I take *Disney A to Z*, I flip it open to any random page, I see what my eye lands on first, and I think, *What can I think of as a trivia question about this topic?* That's how I approach so many of those questions.

I still write some trivia questions for the *Disney Magazine* every quarter and I'll take maybe half of them from the era covered by my book, but I'll also pick ones from my computer, from those new 73 pages or more, of current films and recent projects that the kids of today are much more knowledgeable about than *Snow White* or *Pinocchio*.

Not only did we do interviews with people who worked at the studio, but we worked with the biographers that started writing biographies of Walt. Some of them never got published, but we have copies of the manuscripts and the interviews they did.

We've got so much in the Archives that there's hardly a day goes by when we're not opening a box to find something else and we find something that's of great interest. I'm always thoroughly delighted when I find something I didn't realize we had.

I was going through a box of old comic books once and tucked in between two issues of very common comic books was a giveaway comic book called *Donald Duck Tells About Kites* (1954). It's very scarce and only about eight pages long. It was a giveaway from an electric company in California. It was valued in the comic book price guide at about $2,500! And I didn't think we had a copy and we couldn't afford to purchase a copy and then here was a mint copy. I think there are still things hidden away in the Archives collection that we don't realize we have, but we do.

You can't go in any archive really and catalog materials just like you would in a library. In a library, you can catalog all your books and you have your card catalog and now your computer and you know what you have in your library. You can't do that with an archival collection. You can catalog a box. You can say here's a box of Winnie the Pooh material, but you can't go through and catalog each piece of paper in that box.

We have about 8500 square feet now. We have about 3000–3500 square feet at the studio in Burbank which is our offices, our reading room, and a large storage area where we have all the materials we have to get to on a regular basis.

But we also have about 5000 square feet in a warehouse building over at the Walt Disney Imagineering facility in Glendale. It's about three miles away from the studio, so it's a very large collection. I think if you surveyed the various business archives in the country I don't think you'd find a larger archival collection than we have at Disney; there's just so many different things that our company's been involved in and more coming in daily.

Now, most libraries don't have card catalogs anymore, but they're still useful for us and we haven't had the time or the staff to go back and convert everything to the computer. So, sure, we're doing everything today on computer, but we still have our card catalog and our reading room and we get a number of people coming in saying, "Wow, you still have a card catalog? How wonderful!"

It takes time to digitize things and people to do it. We'll never be able to digitize the entire collection. We have two million photographs and getting more each day and we've only done about 30,000. First, there are certain photos that are used all the time and those are the ones that they've done first, but we'll never do our two million and it probably wouldn't be worthwhile doing our two million because there may never be a call for some of those pictures.

We are the corporate archives where we're collecting the major elements of the company. However, we have not gone into the detailed separate areas of the company which already had historical collections that they were maintaining. The examples being: the Animation Research Library, which maintains all of the animation art that the company creates (and that's not in our archives), and the Main Files, which contain the legal files of the company—all the contracts and the correspondence relating to contracts. That's not in our collection, either.

Walt Disney Imagineering has maintained their own historical materials, primarily the designs and paintings and that sort of thing done for the creation for all the attractions in the park, but they've also maintained audio, video, and still photography on the elements of the park. So that's the place you would go to find the historical materials related to the parks.

We would have the documentation. We try to keep up with chronology of the openings and closings of all the attractions and shops and restaurants and all that sort of thing. We have files about the buildings of the park and the buying of the land in Florida , but the actual audio and video is primarily at Walt Disney Imagineering.

Whenever they're doing a DVD they come to the Archives very early in the process and ask us what we have relating to that movie. Of course, the first question we usually get is that they want film footage that's never been seen before. Well, we went through video cassettes; they asked us that. We went through laser discs and they asked us that. Now we got to DVDs and they're asking us the same question. That is on top of all the other work we have to get done each day.

I prided myself in being a mentor for young people through my thirty-year-plus career. I get a lot of people that contact the Archives as their first contact with the company. They're interested in Disney history. They have a question they want to ask us and I've gotten to know some of these people and I think if you made up the list there would probably be a lot that I met when they were teenagers and went on to be writers or Disney cast members. I hope they continue to carry on what I have been trying to do over the years and keep in mind the importance of accuracy and being truthful.

So many of the questions you get over and over again you find that maybe 95% of them you can answer without doing any research whatsoever and then the other 5% take a lot of research to try to find the answers. You always have to make the choice whether it is worth the time and effort, whether it is something that can be useful in the future to know.

My advice to those who want to write about Disney history is to be careful. There are a lot of Disney stories and not all of them are necessarily true. One of the things I did was to officially determine in 1973 that Mickey Mouse's birthday was November 18, 1928, the premiere of *Steamboat Willie* at the Colony Theater in New York.

Over the years, people have asked why I didn't select that famous train ride back from New York as the date. It's a great story and even Walt told that story to the press all the time that that's when he came up with Mickey. That needs some more explanation.

There are a lot of dates that could have been used for Mickey's birth; however, all of the publicity releases that the company put out in the 30s and 40s and 50s and 60s said that Mickey Mouse was born when *Steamboat Willie* opened at the Colony Theater, so I figured we should probably just stick with that since the company had been referring to it all along.

Now, the story of Mickey being created on the train is something that is I believe is pretty much publicity hype. It's a cute, quick story, the kind reporters love. This story is not really true. When I started with the studio in 1970, still working there was Ub Iwerks, Walt's first and best animator. Ub was the one, as I'm sure many of you are aware, that actually drew Mickey Mouse for Walt Disney. I met with Ub several times.

Now, here again, like Roy O. Disney, Ub was a very modest man. He was never trying to toot his own horn or take credit. He was never trying to say he did more than he really did, and I asked him how Mickey was created. His answer to me is one I really believe to be the correct story about the birth of Mickey Mouse: Walt came back from New York where he just lost the rights to Oswald and he figured he needed to come up with a new character. He and Ub and a couple of the other loyal employees including Roy sat around in a room and they started throwing around ideas. They opened some magazines and thought, *Well, should we use a horse? Should we use a cow?* I mean, just the different characters that they found there in the magazine.One of them at that meeting, and nobody knows which one, said, "Why don't we use a mouse?"

What character did they have at that time? Oswald the Lucky Rabbit. I don't know if any of you have seen pictures of Oswald the Lucky Rabbit, but if you take those long ears off that rabbit and put round ears on that rabbit, what do you have? You have Mickey Mouse. They didn't really have to work very hard to come up with this new mouse character.

It's always been my belief that it happened out in Hollywood, not on the train, even though Walt said that. He said many things in publicity stories, just as people are wont to do to promote the company or his character or whatever, which may not have been strictly true but makes a good story, and I think that's true with this story about the birth of Mickey Mouse.

Strangely, no one had ever researched when that cartoon premiered, so I had to hunt the date down by locating the program for the theater and checking trade papers for reviews to confirm the date. Previously, the company had celebrated the birthday whenever they had a new film or decided to release a bunch of shorts, so it was in September or October and sometimes as late as December.

I mean, anybody can write anything they want about Disney. Disney has control, though, if they want to use any photographs. But we also want to make sure they're accurate. We don't want them having the wrong birthday for Mickey Mouse. We don't want them misspelling "audio-animatronics". All that sort of thing.

I'm looking at these manuscripts to check the nomenclature, the spelling, the dates. There are certain Disney words that are misspelled all the time. What do you think is the most misspelled Disney word? I haven't heard "dalmatians" yet! Anybody say "dalmatians"? "Dalmatians" is the most commonly misspelled word because Dalmatia's a place, i—a. And a dalmatian is an "i-a-n" and so many people put an "o" in that word.

"Supercalifragilisticexpialidotious" is way up there. Pinocchio, one "n" and two "c's"—that's a very difficult word for people to spell. "Geppetto", two "p's" and two "t's". That's one word that I had some problems with in recent years. Remember last year we did that TV special on Geppetto, the musical version? Well, when the first publicity releases came out on that film, they spelled Geppetto with one "p". I dashed off an email and said, by the way, two "p's", not one.

And, a month or so later another press release came out with one "p" in Geppetto and off goes another email and I was really worried. I turned on the television the night that show was coming on the air and they spelled it right. I was so happy!

Even Disney itself sometimes implies inaccurate things. I don't know if you've seen the film at the finale in the One Man's Dream attraction, but there is a sequence where they're talking about Walt on television and they have the *Wonderful World of Color* opening with all the flashing colors coming on the screen and it says, "And now our host, Walt Disney."

And it flashes immediately to Walt standing in front of the Epcot map and saying, "Here's what we're going to do in Florida." That was never on the *Wonderful World of Color*! That's something I've tried to fight ever since I started the Archives because people are always saying it was, and it was never on national television at all! That was a film made for the people of Florida. It was a film that was shown on some local television stations here in Florida, but it was used more for Disney people that would go down and speak at the local Kiwanis Club or something like that just to show them what some of Walt's ideas were for this project in Florida. It's very misleading for them to have that in the movie. They don't say it's from the *Wonderful World of Color*, but it sure is implied there!

That's why you always have to be careful. There are people walking out of that attraction thinking it was part of the television show. These things bother us, but what can we do about them? We try as much as we can, but people are going to do what they are going to do.

As I mentioned earlier, I pride myself in having been a mentor for young people throughout my career at Disney. I think if you made up a list, there would be twenty or thirty people that I met over the years while working at the archives who were teenagers at the time and who went on to become outstanding writers about Disney history.

I would like to think that will be part of my legacy, as well as that I tried to get people to be accurate about Disney and that I created a place where people can find that information.

Why You Won't Get a Job at the Disney Archives

In 2003, Dave Smith said:

> We rarely have openings in the Archives, since we are a small department (five in the Archives and four in the Photo Library), but when we do have openings, they are listed on the Disney.com website under Disney Careers.
>
> We recently filled an opening for a computer expert in the Archives and a clerk in the Photo Library. Those were the first openings we have had in over five years, and both were listed on the website. For positions in the Archives, we look for expertise in library skills and historical research, and hopefully some Disney knowledge (though we do not hire Disney collectors).

Seven years later, in 2010, Smith gave the same reply that he has given since the 1970s when he was first asked how someone could get a job in the Disney Archives:

> Actually, we have a very small staff; we have five in the Archives and three in the photo library, which we administer. Since it is a small staff, there is rarely any turnover. When hiring, we do like people who have library and history training.

The photo library contains over three million images ranging from Walt's early life to the films of today. There are over 5,000 images of just Walt himself. Many of the negatives and transparences are in cold storage in rolling cabinets next to the brightly lit reference section.

If you check all the "Ask Dave" columns beginning in 1984 up to today, you will discover that an inquiry into being hired at the Disney Archives is one of the most frequently asked questions and that Dave always replied with some variation of the above statements. Even though Dave is retired, the policy remains the same.

D23 ("D" for Disney and "23" for the year 1923 when the Disney Studio first started) is the official fan club for Disney fans. It started in 2009 under the direction of Steven Clark who left in September 2013.

In January 2014, Adam Sanderson was promoted to senior vice president of corporate communications of The Walt Disney Company. His duties include the supervision of D23 and the Disney Archives.

Becky Cline remained as director of the Archives, a role she took over from Dave Smith who retired in 2010, but there is a strong dotted-line connection between the two departments today, so there are roughly a dozen people working now at the Archives in some capacity.

The Disney Archives is not a museum nor open to the public. It is a company research facility started by Smith at the direction of Roy O. Disney in June 1970 to collect and preserve Disney documentation to be used for business needs. Disney reuses its past more than most other major companies and often requires historical information for projects, including lawsuits.

Smith had seven years experience working in libraries (including the Library of Congress) before creating the Disney Archives. One decision he made early on was to only have a small sample of merchandise because detailed photos were sufficient to document those products. He told me:

> The decision on what to save in the Archives is based on years of experience of what our users are going to be asking for. Thus, the most important materials we save are informational materials—publications, press releases, correspondence files, etc. Especially with the expansion into other franchises like ABC, the Muppets, and more, we are flooded with new material every day that needs to be examined and properly cataloged.
>
> Although lately we have been doing some traveling exhibits, that is not our major goal. In the earlier days, we collected more of the merchandise, but in the first thirty years it was rarely requested and was just taking up expensive storage space. So, we de-accessioned some of the items which no longer fit within our collecting policy and made them available to Disney Auctions. We have a limited budget, limited manpower, and limited space, so we had to decide what is most important to have from a business standpoint.

Since its primary function is for the use of the various Disney company departments, the Archives is not open to the public. In the earlier years, Smith did generously open the resources to qualified students and writers outside the company, but with the growth of Disney along with an increased work load and the fear that the material accessed might be used to damage the brand, the Disney Archives has closed its doors to outsiders.

Over the last decade or more, there have been a handful of exceptions, sometimes prompted by the requests of the late Diane Disney Miller or the late Roy E. Disney. At the Disney company, even though there are rules, there are always a handful of exceptions. For instance, the Disney Archives has been opened to some limited tours to the general public, usually in connection with a D23 event.

If you ever got a job at the Disney Archives, you would not spend your day researching or writing.

The Society for American Archivists describes the archivist's primary task as "[establishing and maintaining] control, both physical and intellectual, over records of enduring value".

In addition to handling and cataloging of historical material, archivists are responsible for updating new materials to archival standards (e.g., removing anything that could damage it, such as paperclips, staples, and tape) and then describing, cataloging, and placing those materials in archival storage. Some archivists may have to digitize the materials in the archive, create displays or pamphlets, or assist researchers in using the collection.

Entry-level archivist positions usually require an undergraduate degree in an area like history and a graduate degree like a Masters of Library Science (MLS). Similar degrees may include a Masters of Library and Information Science (MLIS) or Masters of Information Studies.

In the field of archiving, there are many more highly qualified job applicants than there are positions. Due to the small size of most archives, usually there is little to no chance for advancement even if you do get hired.

One job that you would be guaranteed to handle involves the hundreds of boxes that were never fully cataloged (in order to save money, Smith often filled available space in some boxes with material not related to the outside markings) along with all the new material coming in each and every day.

The Animation Research Library emerged from the Animation Department's morgue in the late 1980s. It houses art from all of Disney's animated features and numerous short subjects. It caters to artists in Disney's Feature Animation division and is not open to the public, even for tours.

The collection of over sixty-five million pieces features conceptual design work, model sheets, animation, backgrounds, layouts, exposure sheets, maquettes (three-dimensional models), reference photographs, audio and video tapes, and many story and other reference books. There are over 450 boxes just with material from the Disney's *Lady and the Tramp* (1955).

The Walt Disney Company also has several individual departmental libraries including ones for Imagineering, Entertainment, and Marketing.

Obviously, some people *do* get hired to work in the Disney Archives, and sometimes there is an intern or TA (Temporarily Assigned) position that lasts less than a year. (If it is more than a year, then by law they are required to hire you. It is easier and cheaper to find a new intern even if you have proved yourself valuable.)

Here are some tips that will make it more likely you might be considered if an opening appears. You will need an attractive and professional resume submitted in the fashion that is required. Even if you follow all of these suggestions, it does not guarantee that you will get the job.

- Live in the Los Angeles area and have reliable transportation to work. Disney dislikes paying relocating costs. If you live in the vicinity, then you are "geographically more attractive" and less expensive.

- Already work at Disney. If you are an employee of Disney, then you are already in the system so it makes it easier to process any paperwork to move you to a different department. If you are a Disney employee, it means that you already understand how the company operates and its policies (e.g., where and when to pick up your paycheck, restrictions on information, sexual harassment, etc.) which is considered an advantage. In addition, this gives you an opportunity to network. People generally get hired because of who they know and not what they know. Establish that you are pleasant and easy to get along with and do not challenge authority. In other words, don't act like Walt.

- Have previous experience. The Disney company loves people who have had professional experience elsewhere because it cuts the costs of training and assures that not only can you do the job, but if you crash and burn, they can point at your resume that other businesses were foolish enough to hire you to do the same work.

- Have training or a degree in Library Science. Although this is not a firm requirement, it is an advantage, especially since you will be competing with other applicants who do have the degree. Also, you will have better knowledge of the procedures of properly handling material. Make sure you are adept at the latest computer programs and related technology.

- Do not be a huge Disney fan or collector. While having a general knowledge of Disney is helpful, Smith found in the past that hiring someone who was an avid Disney fan caused multiple problems. Sometimes they were too distracted by all the treasures to do their job. Sometimes they felt they had to "protect" certain items. Sometimes they felt those items were best protected in their own private collection. Sometimes they were argumentative because they didn't understand the difference between the company's business needs and pixie dust. That's just the tip of the iceberg. The Disney company often refers to these people as "Disney Geeks" in the most uncomplimentary manner.

- Make yourself valuable. What skill or background do you have that other applicants do not? What will make you stand out from the crowd in a good way?

- Have good luck. Getting a job at the Archives is much like winning the lottery. People do win the lottery, but the odds of you winning are astronomical. Be pleasant. Be professional. Be reliable. Be careful.

If you find that anything I have done is impressive and you realize that I had library and history training, worked at Walt Disney World (and was the recipient of countless recognitions including perfect attendance for a decade), was friends with Dave Smith and helped out many departments, knew Disney history, then you should also know that I submitted my application for the Disney Archives in 1995 and have never heard back.

I have been told it is "on file". I assume it is a circular file. On the other hand, if they had hired me I would not have written any of the books I have about Disney, especially the one on the making of *Song of the South*. Writing any of those books would have had to be approved and then later reviewed and edited by Disney.

My friend and former writing partner, John Cawley, worked at the Disney Archives and the only time he was allowed to do research was on his lunch hours. He found some amazing things, but that was not his primary job.

Although the vault doors to the Disney Archives may be closed to you, there may be many other options open to you including museums or universities with significant Disney collections as well as the personal collections of some of the historians mentioned in this book. To take advantage of those opportunities, you will still need to learn the skills spotlighted in this chapter.

History Is Happening Today

Your life is already history.

The life that you have led has already exposed you to things that others may never have the opportunity to experience.

I grew up in the southern California area, so I was able to go to Disneyland about twice a year. I got to ride attractions like the Flying Saucers that no longer exist. I got to see Wally Boag perform on stage in the Golden Horseshoe Revue. I got to watch the *Disneyland* television show each week when Walt was still the host. Many of those shows were never rerun or released to home video.

I got to go to newsstands, grocery stores, and drug stores to hunt for Disney comic books off a spinner rack. I got to see the premiere for *Mary Poppins* (1994) broadcast live on my local television station. I got to meet when I was a teenager some very interesting people connected with Disney.

Believe it or not, you have had some experiences that others will never have. You may have sat in a theater on the opening weekend of the release of the Disney animated feature *Frozen* (2013). It is a record-breaking film and you were there when it premiered, remember your personal reaction, and saw how others responded. You may have even seen two of the voice actresses on a talk show sharing their stories about working on the film or participated in some event or contest connected with the film.

You may have gone to a Disney theme park and seen a show or ridden an attraction that is no longer there. No one will ever again be able to tour the One Man's Dream attraction as it was or experience what it was like to have a gigantic Sorcerer's Hat block the Chinese Theater at Disney Hollywood Studios or visit the Big Thunder Ranch area at Disneyland or ride on the original Luigi's Flying Tires at Cars Land that lasted less than three years. You may have watched something on the Disney Channel that never got re-shown or a local television news report about Disney.

It is important not to delay any further in putting together your working archive by gathering material that is easily available today as well as discovering treasures from the past. It is important not to feel that everything of significance has already been accomplished or that you have lost so many opportunities to interview people or experience things. Every historian in this book had the same fears when they began.

Disney history is happening right this very minute and you can be an important part of documenting it and sharing that information with others.

It is not too late for you. Start a file with all the press releases. One day soon you will never be able to locate them as newer things get publicized or changed. Start a folder collection of newspaper and magazine clippings because those disappear quickly and are sometimes difficult to find again.

Keep the paper maps and other handouts at the parks. They are free and often discarded. Paper maps will soon be disappearing entirely to be replaced by an app. Wouldn't you have loved to have in your collection some of those free paper items distributed in the early years of Disneyland like brochures, postcards, and flyers? Those items contain valuable information including how something was described at the time.

Things that you are taking for granted today will be history in the next decade. Disney is constantly changing. Information is constantly getting lost, especially when new things like park attractions, restaurants, and ticketing, or even television shows, debut.

Now that Disney Springs has opened at Walt Disney World, no one talks about Pleasure Island or the Disney Village Marketplace that preceded it. In fact, if history is any guide, within the first few years some of the stores and restaurants at Disney Springs will close and be replaced by something else.

I would recommend saving every Disney-related interview you can find. This will prove to be a wonderful source for quotations in your future articles; everyone loves hearing from people who were actually there when something was happening.

Did you know that songwriter Alan Mencken spent two pages talking about the stories behind the music he wrote for Disney films in *Entertainment Weekly* magazine (January 23, 2015)? That's a pretty popular magazine. Many popular magazines have this type of information and many obscure ones as well. For instance, the June 2015 issue of *Reminisce* magazine had a full-page article where Larry Williams remembers being a child riding on Walt Disney's lap on the steam train around Disneyland on July 17, 1955.

Those magazines were published during your lifetime and disappeared within weeks. There are many more magazines, including some that were highly popular during their time period, that are no longer published that include Disney treasures waiting to be discovered. Don't take it for granted that these things will always be around or easy to find.

In addition, newspapers also have articles. Obviously, newspapers that were published in the Los Angeles area like the *Los Angeles Times, Los Angeles*

Herald-Examiner, Los Angeles Daily News, Glendale News-Press, and *Burbank Leader* featured a great many terrific articles about Disney.

Once place to start to search billions of newspaper articles is NewspaperArchive.com. Some newspapers have their own archives. Todd James Pierce offers several great sites to locate newspaper articles in his essay in Section Two.

Remember that websites disappear without notice as well.

I still mourn for Lampwick's Guide to Disney done by Augie Ray and hosted at Prodigy. I wish I had made copies of some of the material before it vanished forever. Some long-lost website material can be recovered via the Internet Archive Wayback Machine at Archive.org . There are only periodic "snapshots" of web content; images are often missing, and many smaller websites are missing entirely. But it can be useful when looking for things that were published online in the past but are no longer available if you know what you are looking for first.

In the beginning, save everything until you decide what you really need to keep.

Get organized. The only thing worse than not having the resource you need is having it and not knowing where to find it. Don't just throw the magazine in a pile. Don't forget to put a post-it note on the cover or the page of the article so you can quickly identify it. More than once, I have had to go on eBay and buy another copy of something because I can't find the copy I know I have … somewhere.

Invest in magazine file cases that are reasonably inexpensive to store your magazines so they can be protected and easily accessible. The time to start organizing your collection is now, not later. What good is a complete collection of *Disney News* if they are scattered all over the place and not in one location and not in chronological order?

Think about bagging and boarding your magazines, especially older issues, to protect them from water damage or further decay. Keep them out of heat, direct light, and humidity if possible.

Yes, you need to invest a lot more time, energy, and money in order to take care of the collection you are accumulating. These are the tools of your trade. Just as you would not want a hammer to rust or a drill bit to get dull, you need to take care of them.

Disney history is happening NOW and you are a part of it. Some day, someone might be asking about your memories, so consider starting a daily journal not just to record information but to record your reactions and thoughts. Ward Kimball's diary of the time of the Disney strike in 1941 has proven a valuable resource for many writers.

Unfortunately, in some instances, you have already fallen behind before you have even started, so don't delay any more.

The Importance of Information

In his lecture for the Reading Agency delivered on Monday, October 14, 2015, at the Barbican in London, author Neil Gaiman stated that all of us have the obligation to support libraries, to read aloud to children, to use the living language to communicate, to write the truth (and that good fiction is a lie that tells the truth), and to never write anything we wouldn't enjoy reading ourselves.

The Reading Agency's annual lecture series was initiated in 2012 as a platform for leading writers and thinkers to share original, challenging ideas about reading and libraries. Gaiman is a skilled wordsmith of short fiction, novels, comic books, graphic novels, audio theatre, and films. His notable works include the comic book series *The Sandman* and novels *Stardust, American Gods, Coraline,* and *The Graveyard Book.* He has won numerous awards. Here is a very short excerpt from that much longer lecture:

> Information has value, and the right information has enormous value. For all of human history, we have lived in a time of information scarcity, and having the needed information was always important, and always worth something: when to plant crops, where to find things, maps and histories and stories—they were always good for a meal and company.

> In the last few years, we've moved from an information-scarce economy to one driven by an information glut. According to Eric Schmidt of Google, every two days now the human race creates as much information as we did from the dawn of civilization until 2003. That's about five exobytes of data a day, for those of you keeping score. The challenge becomes, not finding that scarce plant growing in the desert, but finding a specific plant growing in a jungle. We are going to need help navigating that information to find the thing we actually need.

> I do not believe that all books will or should migrate onto screens: as Douglas Adams once pointed out to me, more than 20 years before the Kindle turned up, a physical book is like a shark. Sharks are old: there were sharks in the ocean before the dinosaurs. And the reason there are still sharks around is that sharks are better at being

sharks than anything else is. Physical books are tough, hard to destroy, bath-resistant, solar-operated, feel good in your hand: they are good at being books, and there will always be a place for them.

Books are the way that we communicate with the dead. The way that we learn lessons from those who are no longer with us. There are tales that are older than most countries, tales that have long outlasted the cultures and the buildings in which they were first told.

Information in itself is indeed important. However, how that information is communicated is often much more important.

When it came to history, my eye-opening experience came as a student at Glendale Junior College. In order to fill a requirement and to find a class that was held in a time frame near my other coursess, I took a class on Civil War history taught by a Civil War historian. I had no idea what a Civil War historian was or did. Someone said that he was called upon to consult on various projects including some mural that had been done at Forest Lawn Memorial Park.

I was casually aware of Civil War history and thought I knew the basics. I couldn't have been more wrong. The instructor's understanding of this time period was so rich that even at an early morning hour, he held the class in thrall as he showed us that history was not about names and dates but about people. The battle itself was less important than the choices behind going to battle and the challenges faced by individuals to make it all happen. He peppered history with little side stories like condiments that made it all come alive.

I applied those same lessons to sharing Disney history. The stories of the people and struggles behind the magic made it even more magical. Disney history truly is the story of people, some too often forgotten or completely unknown.

Having the correct facts is important, but being able to apply that information and connect information is even more so because then it provides a much broader understanding

Sharing and When Not to Share

Disney history is like a gigantic jigsaw puzzle and some pieces have been missing for decades.

As a Disney historian, you need to share the pieces that you have because it will encourage others to share their pieces and eventually there are pieces that connect together and provide a better perspective of the entire picture.

However, you also need to remember that your time, your knowledge, and your resources all have value. You will run into people who expect you to give all of those things to them for free simply because you already "know it" or "have it".

It will not occur to them that it may have taken decades to find certain material or that it might have cost you money you really weren't able to spare at the time or had to borrow. It will not occur to them that it takes you time to find some information, time that could be better devoted to more research or writing or something that will earn you some money.

No one ever offers to compensate you financially for your efforts. Sometimes the only compensation you can ask for is to publicize your books or your website.

You have no unwritten obligation to answer others' casual questions or help them with their school assignment or give them copies of material that you have.

These many requests are like being attacked by a horde of vampires who will never be satiated even after you have given them what they want. They will suck you dry emotionally and steal time from other tasks more deserving and will keep coming back after they have gotten their first taste.

So, while you should not hoard information because that helps no one, you need to be selective in how you share it and who you share it with. Also, remember that once your information is out there, anyone can use it and use it without crediting you as the source.

Ask yourself whether this is a valid project deserving of your time and resources. Ask yourself whether this person has shared with you in the past or is likely to share with you in the future. Ask yourself if you can afford the time to do it. Ask yourself whether it will make you feel better for having done it or whether you are already rolling your eyes and grumbling.

Here is the story of why I no longer assist students asking for help on National History Day (NHD).

The purpose of NHD is to give students an opportunity to learn historical content, develop research and communication skills, and to present what they have found in a variety of ways from presentations and papers to websites and videos. As a former junior high public school teacher and a lover of history, I support that premise heartily.

Some students greatly abuse this opportunity just to get the assignment done. It is not unusual for me to receive dozens of requests for help, and I quickly realized that most of those requests expected me to do all the work.

When I agreed, they asked questions like "When was Walt Disney born?" or "Did he have any family?" or "When did Disneyland open?" indicating that none of them had done even the most basic research. These are actual questions and I received them multiple times.

A high school girl contacted me by e-mail last year asking for my help on her NHD project. I explained to her that I had been disappointed in the past so I had established some restrictions. First, she had to send me her bibliography so I could determine she had done some research before she talked to me and also so I could see what she had been using for reference since some resources have a particular bias.

Three weeks later, she sent me her bibliography. It was apparent she had copied it from someplace, since some of the books she listed as her sources were remarkably obscure or were so academically written that even I haven't completely read them yet.

Giving her the benefit of the doubt, I told her she could ask me a maximum of ten questions. I set that restriction to control the time involved and also to force her to make some hard choices. She had to decide which ten questions would be the most valuable to ask in relationship to her thesis.

She sent the questions which, as expected, were not very thoughtful and included the typical unanswerable question: "What was Walt Disney's greatest achievement?" In what? Animation? Outdoor entertainment? Cultural influence? Hospitality industry influence? Television? Marketing? My answer was that Walt's greatest achievement was always the next thing he was going to do.

I answered all the questions. Two months later, I heard from her again. Supposedly, her teacher had insisted that I be interviewed over the phone. I knew from past experience this was not a requirement; an e-mail interview was sufficient.

Being a nice guy, I set up a time over the weekend (since she was at school during the week) which made me postpone making some other plans with my brother. I made it clear that I was in the Eastern Time Zone. She sent a quick e-mail saying that would be fine.

Over a week later, I e-mailed her the day before since I hadn't heard back from her to re-confirm that things hadn't changed. I never heard back. The time came and I was waiting at the telephone. It never rang. I checked the phone for a dial tone, checked the clock, and continued to wait.

Forty-five minutes passed. The phone rang. It was the student. I pointed out that she was forty-five minutes late. She didn't apologize but explained she had been working on the questions and lost track of time.

Her first question was, "What did Walt Disney think of Disneyland?" I told her I had already answered that question in the e-mail and I felt it was an ill-conceived question, explained why, and offered some alternatives. Her next question after a pause was, "Where was Walt Disney born?"

I told her the interview was over and she should just use the answers I had sent her in the e-mail.

This experience reinforced my decision, one that has been made by many, many other Disney historians, that even with setting restrictions, it was more likely that it would be a waste of time rather than helping a young person to better appreciate history.

Some Disney historians simply ignore requests. Others reply that they have no time but direct them to the Walt Disney Family Museum or the Disney Archives instead. I am sure both organizations already have more than their share of similar requests to handle.

The story is not over. Two and a half weeks later, I received another e-mail from her. It was not an apology. She asked if I could re-send the e-mail answers I had sent her nearly three months earlier. She explained that they were in her spam file and her computer had automatically deleted them.

I thought of just ignoring her request. I thought of asking her to write a short paragraph about what she had learned about the experience before I re-sent the answers. Finally, I searched through my sent mail folder, found the answers, edited them to a single sentence each, and sent them to her.

I never received a confirmation that she received them or a "thank you". In fact, in all the NHD students I have helped, I have only been shown one of their final projects and received perhaps three quick "thank yous" for my efforts over the years.

Basically, she had told me by her actions that I was obligated to do this because I was supposedly an authority on Disney but that my time and input had no value other than checking off something that had to be done.

These students grow up to be young adults and I receive dozens of questions a week. Some of the actual questions I received while I was writing this particular section included "Did Walt Disney wear dentures? His teeth always look so white and perfect.", "How big was Walt Disney's penis?

Did he have a small penis and was just overcompensating?", "When did Disneyland open?" and, of course, "Was Walt Disney born in Spain?"

None of these were for an article, book, podcast, or any specific project. They were just idle curiosity because, after all, they assumed that all I do is write for a living and that means I have plenty of free time.

When I ask for help, even from fellow Disney historians, I try to ask politely and professionally and always indicate that it is a favor and I understand if they are unable to assist. I try to explain clearly what I need, when I need it, and most important, why I need it. In most cases, it is for an article and the deadline is short.

When I was writing an article for a foreign Disney publication about the Indians in Disney's animated feature film *Peter Pan* (1953), I contacted John Canemaker for help about the animation in a particular scene in the film. He was unable to help. He was just about to leave on a trip and his files were in storage. I still thanked him for responding and I understood fully why he was unable to help, especially with a short deadline. I didn't feel that he owed me any assistance at all, and I appreciated him explaining why he couldn't help and that he did it so politely.

I was able to find the information from another person. That's one reason why it is important to cultivate multiple sources for information.

Canemaker, who is exceeding nice and well bred, taught me that it is fine to say "no" but to do it quickly and politely and not leave the door even slightly ajar for any follow-up.

Composer Richard Sherman, a Disney Legend, once told me that the most expensive thing about being a Disney Legend is all the people who send things for him to autograph but never send any packing or postage for him to return the items. Every week, he goes to the post office and pulls out of his own pocket money to send things back to these thoughtless fans. They are not malicious and selfish. They are merely thoughtless, and besides, Richard must have nothing but time on his hands to do this and must have a fortune from all those songs.

Once you are identified as a Disney historian, you will be flooded by requests from thoughtless people who feel you have nothing better to do than to respond to them, scan pages of material, or copy things and send it to them because you have that stuff and they want it. How can you possibly be so rude as to not accommodate them for free? After all, they have real jobs or go to school while you do nothing all day or at least nothing as important as what they do.

I got an offer from someone who said that he would split the profits on a collaborative book project fifty-fifty. He would come up with the idea and read the final draft and make changes. All I would have to do was write the book.

While writing this book, I received a request from the administrative assistant to a top government executive who was writing a book on famous Florida people. She wanted me to write a chapter about Walt Disney and Florida, but my name would not appear on the material since the politician would do some rewriting so it sounded more like him.

I assume he is also having other people write other chapters anonymously. I would not receive any financial compensation, but my name would appear in the acknowledgements. I would not receive a copy of the book. I said "No, thank you" quickly and politely and she was shocked that I would pass up this chance.

I was offered that same opportunity from an author who writes cookbooks to share my knowledge of Walt's eating habits and recipes. When I pointed out that she was getting paid to write the book so shouldn't I receive something for supplying this material that took me time and money to acquire, she responded quite coldly, "You should just be happy to have your name in the acknowledgements since it will be seen by many people. I am sure the Disney Archives has whatever material you have."

I am sure they do if they knew where to look and had the time to do so. When the book came out, there was none of the information and recipes that I had. She went on to write another book.

My general rule of thumb is that if I know it off the top of my head or can find it quickly by pulling a book off of my shelf, I will try to help if I feel the person is sincere or the project is valid.

While there are thoughtless people out there, there are also thoughtful people out there. There are people who are deserving of your help. Make sure you know the difference before you get caught in a pool of quicksand. Sometimes you will make mistakes in making that choice, but learn from those experiences.

This book is a physical example of many busy people taking too much of their precious time to help others and share what they know. They feel that you having this information may be valuable and important. They are asking for nothing more in return than for you to do better work or appreciate good research when you read it.

Thou Shalt Not Steal: Plagiarism and You

Plagiarism is the "wrongful appropriation" and "stealing and publication" of another author's "language, thoughts, ideas or expressions" and the "representation of them as one's own original work", according to most dictionary definitions of the term.

I gathered those quotes from ten different dictionaries that used the same phrases to define plagiarism, so it might be claimed that it is common knowledge. Unfortunately, in the world of Disney websites, it is not.

We live in a cut-and-paste society and too many people who identify themselves as Disney historians merely take material existing on the internet and try to pass it off as their own research. These people consider that if something appears on the internet, then it is public domain property because, after all, facts cannot be copyrighted.

However, according to the 1996 Digital Millenium Copyright Act, how those facts are expressed constitutes unique intellectual property, especially if the same exact phrasing is used.

According to Plagiarism.org:

> A paraphrase is a restatement in your own words of someone else's ideas. Changing a few words of the original sentences does NOT make your writing a legitimate paraphrase. You must change both the words and the sentence structure of the original, without changing the content. Also, you should keep in mind that paraphrased passages still require citation because the ideas came from another source, even though you are putting them in your own words.

I have been the victim of plagiarism multiple times. One of the most egregious examples took place in the last year where a podcaster who takes great pride in proclaiming himself a Disney expert took an article I wrote in 2009 and read it word-for-word as part of his podcast without citing me as the source or even the website where the article originally appeared.

When confronted, he claimed that he had done research from multiple sources and had forgotten to write down those sources because it was done so long ago and put in a file. His partner on the podcast who had read from the same script had no response.

When shown a copy of the original article and that his podcast included ONLY my article presented in the exact same order as I had written it and using personal sources (e.g., quotes from letters sent to me from a Disney Legend) that only I had access to use, his reply was, "Have your lawyers call me. There was no harm intended and so no harm was done."

He even tried to rally others to his cause that I was unfairly defaming his reputation for an innocent mistake. It turned out he had "borrowed" material without citation in the past from some of the same people he had turned to for vindication.

He eventually removed the offending podcast. It turns out he had been "borrowing" a little bit of material from me for years, but this was the first time he went for a full outright theft. I guess the fact that I had not complained earlier gave him a feeling of safety that I was not paying attention to his podcasts.

One of my Disney historian colleagues quoted extensively in this book sent him the following suggestions when the podcaster wrote to him to plead his innocence:

> As writers yourselves, you're aware that facts cannot be copyrighted, but actual wording belongs to the author. Also, as reviewers, you're aware that attribution helps the credibility of the writer (or podcaster) who is using material from another source. And it only seems fair that the original author should be given credit.
>
> In any case, starting with someone else's article and then editing it to make it "different" is not a good approach. It's neither research nor writing. Starting with reading multiple sources (ideally including period sources, such as historical newspaper archives), building an outline, drawing your own connections and conclusions, writing in your own voice, and including quotations with proper attribution will give you much better results.

Ironically, the Disney historian who wrote that response had also been a victim of this same podcaster several times before and had tried to quietly rectify the situation in the past. I made sure that my friends in the Disney history community knew what had happened so they could be wary about their material being appropriated in the future.

In the end, the podcasters only admitted to making an honest mistake and removed the podcast. Their listeners still think they are knowledgeable experts who somehow have magical access to rarely known material.

There is one website that has a Disney article I wrote for the internet reprinted word-for-word except that my name was removed and the webmaster replaced it with his own. Personal references to my growing up in Glendale, California, and mentions of my brothers and an experience we had at Disneyland still remain.

I tried multiple times contacting the webmaster and received one response that I was obviously "crazy" and didn't "know what you are talking about", even though I had sent the link to the original article. All other e-mails and phone calls were ignored. Since his site is so small and receives so little traffic, I decided to just take a deep sigh and let it go.

Do not use other people's work without crediting them. There are a variety of ways of doing this from including it in the text itself to using footnotes or end notes. In the end, it is better to over-credit. Instead of diminishing your expertise, it actually increases your credibility. In the past, reporters and book authors did not always credit. Today, you will see that it is considered proper etiquette to always do so.

People will steal whatever you write. Those facts that took you decades and perhaps a sizeable monetary investment to uncover will be eagerly grabbed as if they were free beads thrown from a Madri Gras float.

Pick your battles if you feel you have been a victim of plagiarism. Try to be polite in the beginning. Escalate if you feel you need to do so. Publicize it to others. If I had been aware that the podcaster was known to "borrow" exclusive material, I might have paid more attention to him earlier.

However, realize that the best you can hope for is that they remove the posting. They may never even apologize. They definitely will not change their habits because they figure the likelihood of them being caught again is slight. They also take comfort that in pursuing legal action against them will result in you spending time and money and emotional angst.

Even the Disney Company itself has sometimes just "let it go" and ignored some things in order not to bring further attention to the trespass and get involved in an expensive battle. Sometimes they have been proven right and the object of controversy disappears from people's consciousness. However, they do not let everything go, because then they would be put in a position of perhaps losing a copyright if they did not defend their work aggressively.

While there might not be justice in the short run, there is justice in the long run. Those two podcasters still do not realize how many doors have been closed to them and how many opportunities they have lost. They feel that their mistake has been forgotten. It hasn't.

That small website that stole an entire article hasn't had a new posting in over a year. A good reputation is the hardest thing to build and one of the easiest things to lose.

In colleges and universities, plagiarism is considered a form of cheating and is subject to severe reprimands including suspension. Reckless or unintentional plagiarism (you vaguely remember reading or hearing something or just forgot to write down the source) is still considered a disciplinary offense in many schools.

All knowledge is built from previous knowledge. Something that you read will inspire you to connect-the-dots. This is a building block, and if it helps you to develop a new perspective or a conclusion, it should be credited as the foundation. By citing the source, you are helping to support your own idea and showing that you did research.

In my early writing, I used too few citations not just because it was the style of the time and seemed intrusive but because of the fear that too many citations might suggest I was relying too heavily on the work of others.

I was wrong and have tried my best to change. Using multiple citations merely shows that you did intensive research and looked at a variety of different perspectives before coming to your own conclusion. Adding the voices of other experts only strengthens your article. Citations also allow readers to discover other sources they might enjoy.

Think of citation as evidence. A parking ticket is called a "citation" because it is evidence that you parked illegally. An award is sometimes called a "citation" because it is evidence that you are deserving of some type of recognition. A citation in your work is evidence that you did your homework.

Be careful to use quotation marks to distinguish the exact words from the writer.

Kenneth Burke, in *The Philosophy of Literary Form* (Berkeley: University of California Press, 1941), provides the analogy of academic scholarship as an infinite, ongoing conversation, which you join, contribute to, and take from, and to which others, likewise, do the same.

Treat the work of others the way you would like your work treated.

Plagiarism is theft and is becoming more and more common on the unofficial Disney websites and blogs. It is a violation of professional ethics. It is a violation of the law if you fail to acknowledge direct quotes or the paraphrasing of another person's work or insufficient acknowledgment of such work.

Common knowledge needs no internal citation. Common knowledge is what is considered a well-established fact (usually verifiable in a minimum of five different sources), proverbs ("Look before you leap", "A stitch in time saves nine"), historical dates and events.

An example of common knowledge would be Walt Disney was born on December 5, 1901, or Disneyland is often referred to as "The Happiest Place on Earth". What Disney animator Ward Kimball ate before he went on stage to perform and what he said to Frank Thomas to make him laugh at the Golden Horseshoe in July 1955 is not common knowledge.

When in doubt, always cite your source. Walt and Roy Disney would have wanted it that way since they were both highly ethical men in all of their business dealings. That is common knowledge as well.

Disney Brand vs Disney Business

You can love the Disney Brand but still have some concerns on decisions made by the Disney Business.

The Disney Brand is that pixie-dusted feeling where people who are true of heart and work hard live happily ever after, often thanks to the help of their comical friends. The Disney Brand is all those memorable characters, classic films, unforgettable music, and breath-taking moments in a Disney theme park. The Disney Brand is very much tied to the vision and philosophy of Walt Disney himself.

The Disney Brand is family, magic, happiness, cleanliness, and quality.

The Disney Business is like any other business. It is responsible to its shareholders to show continuing profits by doing things like letting go long-time loyal and productive employees, outsourcing work to the cheapest vendors, and doing things that may seem questionable but are not illegal and produce greater revenues on the final balance sheet.

The Disney Business counts on Disney fans having short memories and whose attention can be diverted to a new shiny object. It wants to control its image and everything that is written about it, especially minimizing anything bad—whether a death from negligence or a never-repaired audio-animatronics character, and everything in between. The memory of Walt Disney is often considered an impediment to operating the business for the greatest profit.

Too often, people confuse these two very different aspects and think of Disney as just one thing.

A Disney fan's love of Disney is different than a historian's love of Disney. A Disney fan unconditionally loves all things Disney.

If something unpleasant pops up, like a severe increase in parking prices for the theme parks or a poorly thought-out movie that bombs big time at the box office, the Disney fan forgives those flaws as minor aberrations. He stoutly maintains that the Disney company knows what it is doing and has some grand master plan that it is not revealing to mere mortals.

A Disney historian may love Disney as if it were the girl of his dreams but is always still aware of the mole on her face that has a squiggly hair sticking out or her annoying laugh that sounds as if it is coming from her nose or her sometimes inappropriate behavior in public. Actually, a Disney historian may love Disney more than a Disney fan, because he does not ignore the imperfections while still loving the whole.

A Disney historian realizes that Disney is often successful in spite of itself rather than because of itself, sometimes just gets lucky (as with the recent film *Frozen*), and that the company hasn't been reflective of Walt's personal vision for decades.

However, being justly critical of some of the choices the Disney company makes, like cutting back on maintenance while raising prices yet again, often results in being classified as a "hater". Some people feel that you either love everything that Disney does or else you are a hateful, critical person trying to ruin it for everyone else.

A Disney historian loves Disney so deeply that he passionately wants to study it, write about it, explain it, and very often endure its worst moments for an opportunity to discover some greater insight. After all, one of the most important purposes of history is to understand historical events so completely that similar mistakes aren't repeated in the future.

Walt himself made some poor choices, but at the end of the day, he had many more hits than misses. He learned from those poor choices as well.

The Disney company doesn't always learn from its poor choices. When Epcot Center opened, to help distinguish it as a different product, no Disney characters were used. Newly installed CEO Michael Eisner quickly saw the error of that decision and introduced the characters to the park, resulting in almost immediate increased attendance, sales, and guest satisfaction.

When the Disney Institute opened and later Disney's Aulani Resort in Hawaii, the company made the exact same mistake and had to shoehorn in the characters and Disney references within a year to improve those two underperforming business ventures.

On the other hand, the Disney Cruise Line eagerly showcased the Disney characters and heritage from the very beginning and became one of the most successful departments of the company, with continued expansion and profits to this day. This example demonstrates that the current Disney Business has no consistency.

It is not one happy magic kingdom but a series of separate fiefdoms with individual leaders reporting to the same king and sometimes undermining other fiefdoms to make themselves look more valuable.

I have written for official Disney publications and as a freelance writer continue to do so. Disney has multiple publications aimed at specific audiences, from annual pass holders to Disney Vacation Club members to other specific demographics, and all of them feature articles about new and upcoming projects.

When writing for Disney, your work is not just examined by the Disney Archives for accuracy and proper nomenclature but also Disney Legal and Disney Brand to make sure there are no extravagant promises ("happiest place on earth" usually has to be in quotation marks or identified clearly as just a marketing phrase, because without that indication somewhere else on earth may actually be happier so an aggrieved party could challenge or sue for false advertising) and no conflict with current projects (for instance, do not mention that Walt Disney World's Mr. Toad's Wild Ride was once located where the Winnie the Pooh attraction is today, because Disney is selling Winnie the Pooh now and not Mr. Toad).

For one Disney magazine, I had to write an article about the Princess FairyTale Hall in Fantasyland at the Magic Kingdom in Florida that opened in 2013. The point of the article was to get more guests to visit earlier in the day than they planned for the advertised meet-and-greet experience with Disney princesses.

Since this was an approved Disney magazine, I was given the opportunity to interview Imagineer Jason Grandt, who was deeply involved in the development of Princess Fairy Tale Hall, for fifteen minutes over the phone. However, since he was an Imagineer, he was assigned a handler, Diego Parras, to listen in and stop him if he went off the approved publicity "script", started revealing information about other projects, or if I became too aggressive in my questioning.

Grandt described the new meet-and-greet location as an "annex" to Cinderella Castle. Both he and Parras were wonderful and helpful, although sometimes surprised at my questions.

My first question was, "Why do you think that Disney guests are so fascinated by the opportunity to meet the princesses from Disney animated films?" They didn't have an answer, since it wasn't typical of the questions usually asked, like, "Which princesses will be there?" The answer to that question was that no one connected with Disney was quite sure until the area actually opened.

I wrote the article (Disney has strict and limited word counts for articles, so they run only 450 to 1,000 words for the most part) and it was initially rejected because of this phrase: "The Princess FairyTale Hall in an annex to Cinderella Castle which is based on the classic Disney animated feature film."

Pretty harmless, right? At first, I thought the problem might be the word "annex", but I saw that it had been used in the official publicity release as well.

It turns out that someone who reviewed the text was troubled by me identifying *Cinderella* (1950) as a "classic", because the word seemed to indicate something old, and that is not what Disney is selling. We do not want young people to think of Disney's Cinderella as "old", I was firmly counseled.

That is the reason that Mickey Mouse no longer celebrates his birthday because, according to the Disney Business, if kids thought Mickey was over eighty years old, they wouldn't like him. So sometimes the special day is promoted as celebrating "over eighty years WITH Mickey". It is never explained how you can celebrate eighty years with someone if he isn't at least eighty years old.

If you are confused and ready to provide examples where Disney has used the word "classic" to describe one of its animated films, then I can as well. I used it myself to identify another Disney animated feature a month earlier in a different Disney-approved magazine and used it several weeks later in yet another article for that same Disney-approved magazine, with no problems.

Disney has rules, but they are inconsistent. It often depends upon the department or the person in that department who is assigned to do the review. Once I knew the stumbling block, I removed the word and asked why they didn't just remove it themselves. "We don't do things like that" was the e-mail reply I received. That way they can honestly say they never tampered with a writer's submission. The writer made the change on his own.

In November 2010, Disney announced that the former location of Pleasure Island near the Downtown Disney shopping area was to be converted into a brand-new electric wonderland of shopping and restaurants called Hyperion Wharf. I was given the assignment to write a short article for a Disney-approved magazine about this new venture. I made the mistake of including one short paragraph about the former Pleasure Island to emphasize how the changes would be better than what was formerly there.

It was a mistake, because even though there were Disney guests with many fond memories of the early Pleasure Island and its nightclubs and New Year's celebrations every night, it was a tainted brand and the Disney company wanted people to forget it even existed.

As long as Disney never mentioned Pleasure Island or ignored questions about it, then it would somehow fade away. Disney has seen that this has proven true in the past. Not discussing something results in it being extinguished.

This time I was lectured by the editor, dutifully removed the paragraph, cashed my check, and went on to my next assignment. Ironically, Disney never pursued the plans for Hyperion Wharf and removed postings of the concept art promoting the project.

In March 2013, Disney announced the land would be converted into Disney Springs with the Pleasure Island area to be known as The Landing.

"Drawing inspiration from Florida's waterfront towns and natural beauty, Disney Springs will include four outdoor neighborhoods interconnected by a flowing spring and vibrant lakefront," proclaimed the publicity release which, of course, did not refer to either Pleasure Island or Hyperion Wharf.

On September 29, 2015, the name change became official with roadway signage featuring the new name appearing across the WDW property.

If I am assigned to write about this new location, I will wisely forget I even heard of Pleasure Island and Hyperion Wharf. I also need to forget the area was once called Downtown Disney, Disney Village Marketplace, and Lake Buena Vista Shopping Village, at various times during its existence, and featured some marvelous things. That is the Disney Business.

One of the rules of the Disney Business is that whatever is newest is the best thing Disney has ever done, and all those older things can't ever compare.

The magical memories of eating at Cap'n Jack's Restaurant and looking out the windows to see the lights on the *Empress Lilly* riverboat as its paddle wheel slowly turned in place at twilight or the enjoyment for nearly fifteen years of attending the outdoor living nativity scene presented each Christmas season called "The Glory and the Pageantry of Christmas", among many other experiences, is the responsibility of the Disney historian to research and record. Those all took place at the Disney Village Marketplace.

The Disney Business would only like you to only remember the flashiness of the new Disney Springs where Cap'n Jack's has been torn down and the paddle wheel at Fulton's Crab House has not turned in years.

Now is the best time of your Disney life, they claim. You cannot have people thinking that something better was removed by Disney often for financial reasons.

I was a Disney media representative for the "100 Years of Magic" special promotion in 2001. I had to write articles two different ways. Supposedly, the year-long promotion was to celebrate what would have been Walt Disney's one-hundredth birthday.

However, the Disney company worried that younger people would have no idea who Walt was. So I would write one version stating (and these are actual examples): "Walt Disney was an innovator developing the multiplane camera that allowed animation to achieve a three-dimensional approach." I also had to write an alternative version: "The Walt Disney Company has always been known for innovation including the development of the multiplane camera in the 1930s that allowed animation to achieve a three-dimensional approach."

The official publicity release stated:

> The excitement of "100 Years of Magic" extends to all Disney parks with spectacular parades, new attractions and shows for guests. The "100 Years of Magic" event incorporates milestones across Disney parks worldwide. For everyone of every age who's ever been touched

by the magic of Disney, the "100 Years of Magic Celebration" is the chance to share a never-ending dream come true with those you love.

Notice Walt's name is not used in this opening paragraph. By positioning the celebration in such a way, the Disney company was able to claim that Epcot's Tapestry of Dreams Parade and Animal Kingdom's Chester & Hester 's Dino-Rama with its Tricera Top Spin were tributes to Walt Disney simply because they debuted that year.

Disneyland did not celebrate its 50th birthday in 2005. You may think it did and you may have rushed to purchase Disneyland merchandise with the logo on it. However, if you look at all the press releases, what was actually being celebrated was the 50th anniversary of the creation of theme parks, so you could go to any Disney theme park worldwide to celebrate that event. It was officially labeled the "Happiest Homecoming on Earth", not Disneyland's 50th.

No, guests did not "get it". They all swarmed to Disneyland. At the time, the Disney company established there would only be global celebrations in the future and no more "local" celebrations which is why recent anniversaries for other parks like Epcot last approximately fifteen minutes, although merchandise acknowledging the date is still produced for sale but in limited quantities so it sells out before noon on those days.

Michael Barrier covers Disney "revising" its history into an approved narrative more fully in his essay in this book in Section Two.

As a Disney historian you need to be true to history, both the good and the bad. If you are writing for Disney, you need to realize they want you to forget some things ever happened, including Walt himself on occasion. Sometimes official Disney publications even want you to forget the truth.

An editor of an upscale official Disney publication for guests making over $100,000 a year "knew" that purple martins ate mosquitoes on Walt Disney World property and assigned me to write an article about how Disney did this to environmentally control pests on property.

During the annual Epcot Flower and Garden Festival in the spring of each year, purple martins, the largest of the North American swallows, return to comfy white PVC gourd homes behind the merchandise shop Mouse Gear to start new families as well as to gourds backstage at Animal Kingdom. The program started around 1998.

As part of my research, I talked with James Mejeur, a zoological manager at Animal Kingdom, who has been in charge of maintaining the Walt Disney World colonies of purple martins for over ten years.

He told me:

It is a popular myth that we encourage the purple martins to return to Epcot because they control the mosquito population. Actually, the purple martins fly higher than mosquitoes. If the purple martins were dependent on eating mosquitoes, they would have to eat tens of thousands a day and even then they would probably still be hungry.

Of course, that would decimate the mosquito population completely fairly quickly, so if the martins needed to eat mosquitoes, they would then starve. Actually, if martins ever fly lower than usual, they much prefer gobbling up junebugs because they have a nice crunch. We have other methods to control the mosquitoes at Walt Disney World, but the martins are not part of that process.

So I wrote my story and turned it in. The editor was incensed. Everyone knew that the purple martins ate the mosquitoes on Walt Disney World property. He slashed away two-thirds of the article, including the quote from Mejur, before running it and never gave me another assignment. I had written the truth, not the story he wanted told and knew was true despite all evidence to the contrary.

I am sure there are people who still believe the purple martins eat all the mosquitoes on WDW property and may even reference this Disney executive as someone who told them that real story, so it must be true. Be careful of trusting what cast members tell you.

When I was laid off from Walt Disney World, along with thousands of others, I maintained a good relationship with the company and continued to write articles, research and narrate videos, and even do special presentations on Disney history. It was because I understood that you can love the Disney Brand but have concerns about how the Disney Business operates.

Like any company, the Disney Business wants to control its story and, if it can, control how you write the story. Your responsibility is to accurately tell the story that happened. That doesn't mean you have to be mean.

Sometimes you may be in a position to be a critic about something Disney related. Keep in mind whether you are reviewing the work as an example of the Disney Brand or as a product of the Disney Business.

It is not enough to merely label things as "good" or "bad" in a review. You need to describe the facts even to those who know them and hopefully offer additional insights to help them arrive at a conclusion. You need to explain why something is good or why something might have some unfortunate consequences or missed opportunities.

A good critic can help educate an audience if he is consistently fair. When reviewing something, the three questions to answer are: What was the person trying to do? How well did they do it? Was it worth doing in the first place?

Your job is not to describe at great length what you would have done differently. You need to review based on what is actually there. There may be good reasons for things missing, including a restricted page count or being aimed at a wider general demographic than simply Disney fans familiar with such things.

I wrote a book called *The Book of Mouse* (Theme Park Press, 2013) about Mickey Mouse and explained there were no photos because Disney charges substantially for each image plus the company will review and possibly change the text before granting a license for its photos. Regardless, some people still reviewed the book poorly, complaining about the lack of photos and that it wasn't in hardcover.

The book costs twenty dollars. If I had added the photos, the book might have cost seventy-five dollars and much of the information would have been removed because Disney doesn't want some stories told, even if they are true.

I would love to have available a hardcover, full-color, illustrated book that was 1,000 pages, but both the budget and other restrictions like approval from Disney and marketability of the final product prevented that from happening.

I was happy with the final result and that such material was gathered together in one place for future reference. There were many other things I would have liked to have added. There were several things I included where I wish I had had more information. I am satisfied that within the boundaries that were set I did the best I could do. The fact that so many people have spoken highly of the book seems to reinforce that assumption.

Reviewers often want to show off their intelligence and superior taste by being overly critical to demonstrate that they have higher standards than the general audience. They write harshly to show everyone that they have not snorted the Disney pixie dust.

When you review something related to Disney, keep in mind the limitations, especially on writers, and whether what has been done within those restrictions would appeal to an audience interested in that topic. Basically, people should know from your review what to expect from the thing, regardless of your personal opinion of it.

You can love the Disney Brand as it continues to bring happiness to countless people around the world, but you can still be wary of the Disney Business that is only interested in a version of history that will help it to earn greater profits.

As a Disney historian, you do not have to be a commentator or a critic. Your primary job is to share the accurate information and perhaps help lead people to a conclusion. If you are working for the Disney company, then they may require you to tell the story the way they want it told for business purposes.

The Art of the Conversation

Jeff Kurtti, Brian Sibley, Todd James Pierce, and others share excellent insights into doing interviews with people about Disney history in their essays in Section Two. In this short chapter are a few additional thoughts to consider.

An interview is not merely recording a prepared presentation. An interview is not an interrogation or an ambush. An interview is not a forum for you to show off how clever, knowledgeable, and funny you are.

Documentarian Ken Burns removes himself from being part of the interview. "It's part of the tradition I came from, taught by social documentary still photographers who were more photographers than they were filmmakers," he has stated. That means your purpose is to guide the subject into remembering and record those memories and not be a commentator or a participant at that moment.

An interview is a conversation that usually begins with some small talk to warm up the subject and get them comfortable with speaking and assure them you are sincerely interested in their story the way they want to tell it.

You should show that you are grateful that they have given you the gift of their time, especially since some of the older subjects may not have much time left and the more modern subjects may have other much more important projects that demand their attention. Respect them and their time. Come prepared and do not delay them with fiddling with your equipment or anything else.

They should be physically comfortable which is why so many interviews happen at the person's home, where they feel safe.

Also, they don't have to fight traffic going to someplace else, find a place to park, stumble around trying to discover the location of the conference room (and restroom), and other concerns. If it is at their home or at some presentation they are attending, you show up and then you leave, and they don't have to worry about anything else other than talking.

Make sure there is cool water available. It is important to lubricate when talking and the longer the person talks, the more their voice will become raspy and scratchy because if you are doing it right, they are talking much more than you are and have lost track of time because they are enjoying it.

Because of the actions of others who have interviewed them in the past, these subjects may be reluctant in the beginning to talk because they fear what they say may be used to hurt them, people they worked with, or the Disney company.

Make sure you have plenty of time for the interview, because the more time then the greater chance of building trust and allowing them to feel that you are excited to be talking with them. It sometimes leads to them saying something they never intended to say when the interview started.

It is important to establish immediately the ground rules. What are you intending to cover and approximately how long do you think it may take? If the topic is Epcot, is it about Walt's concept, the building of the facility in Florida, what it is today, a specific attraction that no longer exists, their overall experience working there, or what? Sometimes it is good to send them some or all of the questions before the interview so they can get into the proper mindset.

Can the subject review the final interview and be allowed to remove anything they want for whatever reason they have? That procedure has worked well for me for decades. I keep a separate file of the material that they wanted removed along with their objections. If they know they can edit it later, they are more comfortable speaking freely.

Or is the subject just part of a larger narrative contributed to by others in an attempt to get at the truth on some topic and so you can't let them modify their response later? You want them to be a quick sound bite to illustrate or support something and added to sound bites from others. Is the interviewer merely looking for an answer that reinforces what they already know?

You need to prepare for the conversation by doing your research. Learn everything you can about the subject. Always have more questions than you can possibly ask. There are few things worse than coming to the end of the interview and letting it dribble to an end rather than have a strong finish.

"How would you like to be remembered? What project would you like to remember being associated with? Is there anything you would have changed about your career? What project would you have liked to work on, and why? What is something you have never been asked that you would like to talk about now?"

When they worked at Disney may spark some possible inquiries, so become familiar with what was happening at Disney during their tenure. If they worked at Disney in 1971, they might have some impressions of visiting Walt Disney World when it first opened. They might have interacted with some of the people responsible for creating and operating Walt

Disney World, even if their own job was working in some area like finance or parking or maintenance. They might have run into people working on animation, live-action shooting, or the weekly television show.

It is important to have some prepared questions so that you have a roadmap of where you want to go. However, the conversation may turn to other things, and you should allow the person to talk about what they are interested in talking about, because it will prime them to talk about other things as well.

It is okay to go off-road for bit to see the largest ball of twine in Iowa or some roadside museum of lunchboxes. Since you have a roadmap, you will always be able to direct the trip back to the main road. Sometimes those off-road excursions will reveal things more interesting than the things on your planned itinerary.

If I asked you what you had for lunch three Sundays ago, it might take you awhile to figure out the answer and yet you are asking these people to remember things that happened years or decades ago. That is why it is sometimes best to frame the questions in a chronological fashion, because it will help people to remember and those memories will continue to build and build as they continue to answer questions.

Start at the beginning and then progress. Don't jump all over the place in terms of time periods.

Also, any visuals like photographs or illustrations as well as names and events will help them to remember. If I told you your lunch took place at one of your favorite restaurants with one of your best friends and your car was having trouble that day, it might help you remember clearly what you were eating on that Sunday as well as other memories of that day and what you were thinking.

Don't be so dependent that you have to read questions off of a note card or a notebook. Any prepared questions are your notes to help you, something to aid you in remembering what you want to talk about with the subject. It can be easy to get distracted. You can glance at your notes, but don't read off of them. Maintain eye contact when asking and listening to the response.

Listen aggressively and carefully to the answer. Their answer may suggest another line of questioning.

Give them your full attention when they are talking. They are what is important and this may be your only chance to ask these questions. Smile. Be pleased with what they are saying so they get positive reinforcement to continue. Don't hesitate to ask them to explain further something you don't understand. Don't immediately jump into asking another question or interrupt what they are saying. Sometimes amazing and unexpected things can result.

It is sometimes called responding "organically", meaning that what they say may lead to other questions about what they just said that never occurred to you. Think of the conversation as a journey down a river and allow it to flow naturally, but know the destination you have to reach.

Try to make the recording device unobtrusive. Often, people who joke and speak freely will freeze up when a recording device is turned on because now what they say seems "official" to them, and they want to phrase the response carefully because they feel they will be held accountable. Again, if you establish that this is a conversation and you pay little or no attention to the device, eventually your subject will forget about it as well.

When asking questions, "open" ones are more effective than "closed" ones. A closed question is one that evokes a "yes" or "no" answer or some fact. For instance, on what day and time did the Magic Kingdom open at Walt Disney World? The only response is October 1, 1971 at 10:00am.

An open question might be, Why do you think that Disney opened up the Magic Kingdom in October? There are multiple possible answers, including cooler weather, low tourist traffic to work out the "bugs" before the holidays, beginning of the fiscal year, and many more. You are asking for an opinion, and there is no pressure to get the "right" answer. A closed question should only be used to confirm something. For instance: "Let me make sure I understand this. So, you are saying that it was Roy O. Disney who insisted on the October opening despite requests to delay it?"

Ken Burns said in the Spring 2015 issue of *MovieMaker* magazine:

> If I say, "Do you like chocolate ice cream?" and you say "Yes"', it doesn't help me. I need a question that gets a response of "I love chocolate ice cream and I remember a time when..." How can you frame a question that doesn't get a "no" or a "yes"? You need a question that opens doors.

When you are interviewing someone, the purpose is not just to get information but to capture the spirit of the person who is talking. Are they amused at certain things? Are they concerned about others? Do they have a distinctive rhythm of speaking? Do they pepper their speech with casual profanity (something you may find common in older Disney employees) and are you going to include that? Do they have a certain agenda to establish their own legacy or to settle old grudges? Can you convey the tone of what they are saying?

For instance, a famous Walt Disney World story is that the night before the grand opening, they had to lay so much sod at the Contemporary Resort that Disney executive Dick Nunis had to bring in whatever volunteers he could find, from college students to Magic Kingdom cast members, most of whom had no experience laying sod.

Everyone tells the story that in the darkness, they could hear Nunis shouting "Green side up! Green side up!" to the inexperienced crew. But did he say it with a smile in his voice as encouragement to make people laugh or with a level of frustration that it was not being done correctly or with the tone of a harsh command from a strict leader under pressure or any of a half dozen other ways? Just the cold hard words do not give any insight into his personality. It is up to you to help readers understand not only what is being said but how. Was something said as a joke or sarcastically?

Often times, you may have to edit a lengthy interview or only take a handful of samples for an article. In these cases, it is important that you stay true to the intent of what the person said and not manipulate selected quotes for your own purpose.

With older people or people who live quite a distance from you, it is more common to do an e-mail interview than a phone interview. On a phone interview, it is sometimes difficult for them to understand the question or for you the answer. Some subjects don't hear as well as they used to and often have a spouse or a friend listening in to repeat the question.

An e-mail question gives the subject a chance to reflect and research their answer before responding. It can also result in a shorter response than you would like and may require some follow-up questions.

In an e-mail interview, your question may be much longer than usual to establish exactly what you are asking. When you publish an interview in its entirety, it is often best to edit your original question to just a sentence or two so that the reader can understand the answer. You do not have to supply all the detail that you might have originally used to get the subject to remember.

While you should prepare, you can never prepare for everything. The person may not be feeling well or just in a foul mood. I like and respect Disney Legend Bill "Sully" Sullivan and even helped him write a book of some of his memories. However, I learned that some days, he just didn't want to talk or seemed irritated and gave a two- or three-word answer. Other days, the stories just flowed. Fortunately, I had the opportunity to interview him multiple times so it balanced out. Unfortunately, with others, I often get one shot so need to try my best to prime the pump by being patient, positive, and persistent.

A good interview is often a mixture of luck or magic as well as talent. You will always feel you left something on the table that should have been asked. To this day, I regret not asking things I should have asked some of the people I interviewed who are no longer here. When I interviewed them I sometimes didn't know enough to ask them certain questions. There is a fragile dynamic, and yet good interviews have been done by the people represented in this book.

Remember that Disney has employed millions of people over the years. There may be some person in your own community, no matter where you live, who once worked for Disney or had a relative who did. Don't just concentrate on the big familiar names that have been interviewed countless times unless you have some unique questions that might fill in some gaps of previous interviews.

A good source to see what good interviews are like is the *Walt's People* series of books published by Theme Park Press and edited by Didier Ghez. You will see that series mentioned many times in this book by many different people because it is so valuable to have these first-person discussions available to get a greater understanding of Disney. Once you study what good interviews look like, you will be more likely to mimic that same process when you do an interview.

I always remember what my mother told me: "God gave you two ears and one mouth, so He must have meant you to listen twice as much as talk."

Handling the Media

Included in this book are many useful tips on how to interview someone. However, once you are identified as a Disney historian and have work that is published, you may be contacted to be interviewed by a newspaper, magazine, podcast, or radio show.

While it is always pleasant to have your ego stroked by being asked, you need to keep in mind several important things so that it will be a satisfying experience for both you and the interviewer.

You are not being asked because you are famous and fascinating. You are being asked so that the interviewer can have a good quote or sound bite from somebody even vaguely connected with Disney or to fill a blank hole in their programming or print publication.

The Disney company does not want its employees to be interviewed, especially on current topics, unless they are being supervised and sticking to a prepared statement.

For instance, Disney media reps are constantly reminded to never talk about finances or attendance, since that is not part of the story that Disney is telling. They should never damage the magic by suggesting that there is a person inside a costume or that Disney outsources much of its work, including the building of audio-animatronics, to outside companies.

That's a reason why people are coming to you in the hopes that you will talk off the official script.

You need to assert firmly (and sometimes frequently) during the interview that you are not speaking on behalf of the Disney company. You have a right to your own personal opinion, but you can not claim knowledge of proprietary information.

Even if you do have such knowledge, you should be aware that things change constantly and frequently at Disney. Something set in stone can disappear in minutes, while things never considered can be implemented almost immediately, including a new show for the parks or the release date of a new film.

In addition, stick to your area of expertise. Often, someone wants a quote that puts Disney in a bad light from some sort of supposed authority like you to support a particular approach they already have decided on for the story.

In most cases, that approach is something like Disney has become too money-grubbing and that Walt Disney would never have done something like whatever was being done. Be careful about being trapped into talking about things you don't really know because it can damage your credibility and your reputation. If you "mis-speak", that response will remain forever with few if any people ever locating your later correction if one is ever given.

If your area of study is Disney animation in the 1940s, then you are not qualified to comment on whether it is outrageous that Disney has raised the cost of parking at all of its parks or whether Walt Disney hated women or that Disney is discriminating against a cast member. Yet, you will be asked those questions and others like them unless you stop it by saying you are not qualified to speak about that topic other than just as an average person.

Even Disney cast members want to please people by giving the guests answers all the time, whether they know the real story or not, and the result has been many incorrect answers and the creation of urban myths.

Just because someone asks you a question does not obligate you to answer it. Remember to take time before you answer a question. Even Miss America contestants will repeat the question to buy themselves more time to produce an answer or to clarify what question is being asked.

You don't have to resort to "no comment"; simply explain you can't answer because you do not know enough about that topic or "I would need more time to properly research that before giving a good answer". Don't pretend to know answers that you don't know. Don't guess.

If you have a strong opinion and feel you need to share it, then make sure you include in your answer that it is just your own opinion. That opinion will still be labeled as coming from a Disney historian, indicating that it has more weight than a quote from a regular Disney fan.

The Disney company offers credentials and perks to those writers who are "Disney positive". It makes no sense to assist those writers who are constantly criticizing the company. If you get labeled as "Disney negative", you will find many opportunities denied to you, from attending events to receiving information. If you stick to historical matters that can be documented and are honest and accurate, you will be better off and not put on the naughty list.

The initial thrill of seeing your name in print or having your friends and family hear you over the internet, on television, or the radio may be so overwhelming that common sense disappears. So, you should consider the following:

Before the Interview

- Why did you contact me?

- What is the name of the person doing the interview? (Sometimes, for a radio interview, you may be approached by the show producer rather than the interviewer. Make sure you write the name down and their title and know how to pronounce it correctly. Get all necessary contact information including a phone number and an e-mail address and the name of the publication or station. Make sure they have your correct contact information.)

- Who else is being interviewed?

- What are you looking for? What subjects are going to be covered? (Some interviewers are looking for a quote to support a premise they already have, like Disney is trying to cover up something or Disney is negligent or discriminatory. Other interviewers are on a fishing expedition looking to see what information is out there before settling on an approach to a story.)

- What is your deadline? (If this is being set up for a future date, you should use that time to research the interviewer and his previous work. Generally, newspapers need the information right that very minute they are calling you. Sometimes you can buy yourself an additional hour to check material. It is appropriate to have them call you back in an hour or so after you have a chance to gather your thoughts or look things up. They need you more than you need them.)

- How much time will you need to talk with me? (Remember that even if you are interviewed for a half hour or more, they may select just ten seconds to use and it will be the ten seconds where you did not give enough context or just tossed off a casual, thoughtless remark.)

- If it is a recorded interview like a radio show or a podcast, is it being broadcast live or will it be edited and played later? Will there be "show notes" that accompany the link on the website? How will I be identified?

- Will I be answering questions from the audience?

- Confirm the date and time (indicate what time zone) of the interview the day before the interview.

- Sometimes, you can request that they send the questions by e-mail. In those cases, double check your written answers. Spell check and auto correct are not your friends. Wait before sending the answers so you can re-read them or have a friend read them to make sure there are no glitches.

The Interview

- Keep your answers concise. Reporters do not have time for long, complicated responses. They are looking for a quotable quote or good short sound bite. A sound bite is usually considered twenty seconds or less.

- Do not use jargon, acronyms, statistics, or technical language. Newspaper and magazine journalists will usually take more time than an audio interview. Simple direct answers are best and require less editing. The more you say, the more temptation to stray into things you wish you hadn't said. Don't keep talking after you have made your point.

- Wait until the complete question is asked before answering. Don't interrupt or cut off the interviewer. You can repeat the question to buy yourself more time and to make sure you heard the question correctly.

- Never assume the person interviewing you has any knowledge about the topic or you. Sometimes a reporter is just assigned the topic because of availability or proximity. Most are juggling several different stories at the same time. What might be clear to you could seem like a foreign concept to them.

- Often, mistakes in the final piece are from misunderstandings rather than sloppy or antagonistic reporting. You can ask for them to repeat back what you just said to make sure they are recording it accurately.

- Nothing is ever "off the record". If you say it, and especially if it is "juicy", it will be used or referenced. Even if you are told you are now off the air, or the taping has stopped, or the reporter has closed his notebook, anything you say can still be used.

- Don't feel intimidated by the interviewer. You are the expert which is why you are being interviewed. Don't be afraid to gently correct the interviewer if they misunderstand something or have a wrong piece of information. There is no advantage to losing your temper or arguing with the interviewer.

- Don't assume the interviewer is your friend. They may not be antagonistic, but their goal is to get a good story and they may try to prod you into areas where you feel uncomfortable or try to put words in your mouth by how they phrase their question. Your obligation is to tell the truth and share what you are comfortable sharing. You may be asked to incorporate their question into your answer so it is easier to edit.

- Relax. You are not giving a lecture. Talk to the person like a neighbor. You don't have to rush and blurt out information. The best way to be relaxed is being prepared and paying attention to what is being said.

Live in the moment. Anticipate questions (especially difficult ones) and have the answers ready.

- Be prepared. You can use notes. Failing to prepare is preparing to fail.

- If you make a mistake, correct it as quickly as possible. Anything you say can usually be checked within minutes. People remember the flub, never the correction.

- Don't answer hypothetical questions. Questions that begin with "what if" or "let's suppose" never turn out well. This is another way some reporters try to trap you into saying something nasty about Disney that you may not mean. If something is hypothetical, then there are infinite possible answers depending on an infinite number of other things. Nobody knows what Walt Disney would do today other than in the most general sense, and even then the Walt Disney of 2015 might have a different set of priorities or perspectives.

- If you are asked several questions at once, pick one to answer and then let the interviewer re-ask the others. If you were not asked a question you wanted to answer, you can piggy-back on the answer to a question you were asked: "That also reminds me that another point is…" This is also referred to as bridging—building a bridge from one thing to another. "That is important, but what is even more important is…"

- Smile while you are talking on an audio interview. It will communicate to an audience even if they can't see you because there will be a noticeable change in the tone of your voice. Be excited. Be friendly. This is your opportunity to share some interesting information and to perhaps generate additional work.

- If you are doing the interview over a phone, make sure you are in a comfortable, quiet environment with no distractions.

- Don't reference their competitors. "I saw a great article in the *Los Angeles Times* that said…" or "That is the same question I was asked by GeekingDisneyFans.com…"

- Some people who sense the interview might get contentious or fear being misquoted will record the interview themselves so that the reporter knows there is an independent copy of the raw tape. If you record the interview, notify the reporter at the beginning of the session.

- You may ask to review the interview before it appears in print, but they are under no obligation to do so and usually this is considered bad etiquette because it seems like you are trying to control the story. It also adds to the amount of limited time they have to put together the piece. Once you have agreed to be interviewed, you have generally relinquished any rights to edit it.

- You can request that they let you know when the interview appears and send you a copy or a link to it.

After the Interview

- Contact the interviewer. Comment briefly and positively on the piece. Thank them. If there is a significant error, point it out but do not expect a retraction. For minor errors, they will not make any changes or corrections.

- There are many websites and books that will help you handle being interviewed. Remember that a media interview is very much like a job interview. Both require preparation, good personality, and clarity.

What's in It for Me?

- Most people are flattered that someone wants to talk to them or that their name or voice will appear in some sort of public forum. You will not be paid for your interview.

- However, your time and knowledge is of value. I usually request that they plug and include a link to one or more of my books or a website where I often supply material. For a podcast or a radio broadcast, that plug should not only be given on the air but also printed in the show notes. This will allow those who were interested in what you said to easily locate other material by you.

- It is not a problem for a writer to state " Disney historian Jim Korkis, author of *The Vault of Walt*, said..." If it is, they shouldn't be talking to you since the fuller identification gives you more credibility as well as directing the reader to something you have done.

- When being interviewed for a documentary or a book, you should be asked to be listed in the acknowledgements whether your material was used or not. After all, they did take your time and knowledge even if you ended up on the cutting room floor. In addition, you should ask for a free copy of the DVD or book for your collection.

- If they try to tell you that another department handles that matter, then tell them you have to negotiate with that other department for the interview. Always get that promise in writing. As they say in Hollywood, an oral agreement is not worth the paper it isn't written on.

- An interview is an opportunity to introduce yourself and your work to a new audience, even if the focus of the interview is just part of a larger story.

Good Advice

Everybody loves to give advice to others, but very few want to take it unless it reinforces what they already want to do. Yet, we all see the wisdom in good advice, even when we are not always ready to accept it or follow it.

There was no book or video to help any of the people who appear on the following pages. They had to invent how to do it. Everything they learned was from trial-and-error and the School of Hard Knocks. They sometimes learned by reading and watching others who were struggling as they were and little realizing that those same people were reading and watching them.

The Disney historians in this section are highly regarded chroniclers of Disney history who have spent decades contributing to the rich tapestry of Disney. They are all respected, prolific, knowledgeable, and accurate, and each one felt they were unqualified to give any advice to aspiring Disney historians.

When I contacted Michael Barrier, his initial response was:

> I don't have any advice to give. They should study and learn what any journalist or historian should and practice the highest standards of those professions.

That is true. The same skills and tools that any journalist or historian should have are the same that a Disney historian should learn. However, there are some things that are unique to the world of Disney and that is the reason for this book.

I asked each of the people here to write between 1,000 and 3,000 words about whatever they thought they might have liked to know when they first started. Some concentrated on one topic. Some offered multiple tips. Many shared how they got started and the challenges they faced on their projects as an example for others that there are many different ways.

Despite the diversity of these people, how differently they express themselves, and the differences in their specific areas of interest, there is also a common ground among them. They all love Disney and have a desire to accurately record and share Disney history.

None of them saw the contributions of anyone else or my basic text so they could not be influenced and had to be true to their own vision. If there is any repetition of a topic, it is to offer a different perspective or a reinforcement of a concept, like how to effectively handle an interview. They may disagree with what I or others have written.

They are only responsible for their own contribution which is copyrighted in their names and remains their personal property. I learned many things that I had not thought of before as well as being reminded of things I have forgotten, and it will inform the writing I do from now on.

Some of them had many challenges from family concerns to health issues to looming deadlines for other projects, but they all set them aside briefly because they wanted you to have this information. Reading their work and adding their books to your personal research library will bring you many benefits in the years to come as it has for me.

These are not the Ten Commandments. These are not the only ways to do things, but they will provide you with a good foundation. You should know the rules before you think of breaking the rules, and it really isn't necessarily to reinvent the wheel.

Take what works for you and makes sense and leave the rest for others or for some time in the future when the little light goes on over your head and you are ready to process that information. Remember, this is just guidance and advice based on their own personal experiences.

I have kept their essays in the manner in which they submitted them. They were not told to follow a parallel structure but to write what they felt in the way they felt most comfortable doing so. The result is a conversational, sometimes anecdotal tone.

Each chapter should be read individually as a self-contained tutorial, not as part of a continuing flow but in any order you would like. I arranged the contributions alphabetically and not by topic. I also included some of their Disney-related books and their websites so that you can add them to your resources.

Michael Barrier

This essay was originally written in 2010 and was revised by Michael Barrier on July 21, 2015, for inclusion in this book. The "new" books he discusses were new when they were issued in 2010.

The Disney-Approved Narrative

I have wanted to see the Ford plant for a long time. To me, the main point of interest was the assembly line. There is a strong similarity between the Ford assembly line and our animated picture business. We have hundreds of workers all helping to assemble the cartoon that you see in continuity. Of course, it's somewhat different to run an assembly line with temperamental artists.

—Walt Disney, speaking to a *Detroit Free Press* reporter on April 12, 1940, after a visit to Ford Motor Company's huge Rouge plant in Dearborn, Michigan

It occurred to me, when I was reading the impressive new books about Disney animation by J. B. Kaufman and John Canemaker, that what might be called "independent" historical writing about Hollywood animation, of the kind I have practiced, is all but impossible for anyone starting out now, especially when the subject is the Disney Studio.

Disney has always been touchy where copyrighted illustrations are concerned, but back in the 1990s the Walt Disney Archives was open to serious researchers, and I spent countless hours there, often in the company of other outsiders. By then, Milt Gray and I had already interviewed hundreds of the veterans of animation's "golden age". Many of them were still alive and reasonably well throughout that decade, and they were willing and sometimes eager to be interviewed by other researchers.

How things have changed. The Disney Archives has been firmly sealed to almost all outsiders for a decade and more. Most of the animation veterans I interviewed, from Disney and other studios, are dead, their personal archives typically lost or scattered. Other important resources—the RKO archives, for instance—that once were open to researchers are now difficult or impossible to access.

There are compensations. Many more interviews are in print than was true in the 1990s, thanks to diligent compilers like Didier Ghez and Don

Peri, and the internet has made it easier to locate and use other sources, public records especially. Most important, the films themselves are much more accessible. But such gains are not enough to make up the difference. The prospects of any really independent new writing based on extensive research into Hollywood animation's "golden age" have all but vanished.

That is, I'm sure, perfectly fine with many people, and not just The Walt Disney Company and the other proprietors of the cartoons. I think a great many Disney fans in particular are satisfied with books that embody what I've come to think of as The Approved Narrative: the familiar story of Walt Disney's struggles and triumphs, supplemented now by a gingerly handling of the decline after Walt's death, glowing praise for the revival in the Eisner-Katzenberg period, and hosannas for Pixar.

J. B. Kaufman's book *South of the Border with Disney* is perhaps the strongest possible argument for the new dispensation under which, as a practical matter, serious books about the Disney animated films can emerge only if they bear the Disney imprint. (Kaufman's and Canemaker's books were both published by Disney Editions, a division of The Walt Disney Company. Kaufman's is copyrighted by the publishing arm of the Walt Disney Family Foundation, which runs the Walt Disney Family Museum in San Francisco; Kaufman is a member of the foundation's staff.)

South of the Border with Disney is an account of the Disney Studio's involvement with the federal government's Good Neighbor program just before and during World War II. Kaufman has made excellent use not just of the Disney Archives but also of Disney's Animation Research Library, a repository of production art and related documents that was off-limits to most outside researchers even when the Archives was open. He has also mined interviews, the U.S. National Archives, and a variety of other outside sources.

I was still living in the Washington, D.C., area in March 2003, when I gave Kaufman free run of my own files dealing with Disney films like *Saludos Amigos* and *The Three Caballeros*—interviews, clippings, meeting notes, and so on. As that date indicates, his book has been in the oven a long time, and I'm sure he used the years to make it better.

It's hard for me to imagine that *South of the Border* will ever be challenged as the most comprehensive, detailed, and accurate account of an exceptionally interesting period in the Disney Studio's life. The book's errors, if there are any, are too small to have any significance.

What *does* bother me is what I might call the book's lack of a distinct authorial point of view. *South of the Border with Disney*, like any book that is not simply a phone directory or a similar compilation, is necessarily selective in what it tells us; when I say that the book lacks a point of view, I'm saying that it's not clear to me that the author's basis for that selection extended beyond the requirements of The Approved Narrative.

In keeping with those requirements, the book treats everything that Walt touched as being of exceptional interest and, usually, merit, but the man himself is only intermittently present, as in a striking quotation from a 1944 interview with Dorothy Kilgallen about *Three Caballeros*. Kaufman is for the most part a clear and engaging writer, but his commitment to The Approved Narrative sometimes leads him astray. When, for example, he describes at length what went into the making of bare-bones educational films for Latin American audiences, the detail about trivial quarrels grows oppressive; most of that chapter belongs in an appendix.

When I was reading the chapter on *The Three Caballeros* I couldn't escape the feeling that Kaufman was bearing down on the technical aspects, especially what was involved in combining animation and live action, as a way of minimizing the larger questions about the film. No other of Walt's features, except possibly *Fantasia*, has met with so much skepticism and puzzlement. To condescend to the doubters, as if they simply couldn't see as far ahead as Walt, is less than satisfactory as a response, especially considering that such combination work never played the major role in the studio's filmed output that Walt briefly hoped that it would.

To take an opposite tack, I think it's unfortunate that Kaufman's treatment of an Ub Iwerks innovation that greatly facilitated the combination work—an innovation that I don't think has been described in print before— seems so truncated. After reading those paragraphs on pages 203–204 several times, I still couldn't make sense of them. I was reminded of the passages about Pixar's innovations in Amid Amidi's *The Art of Pixar Short Films*. In both cases—and perhaps this is a reflection on the editors at Disney Editions—a fear of boring the reader seems to have resulted in cutting back an explanation until it is incomprehensible, and thus *really* boring.

In the same vein, I was disappointed by the vagueness in Kaufman's references to the cost and box-office performance of *Three Caballeros*, in particular, so much in contrast to his specificity elsewhere. Maybe the Disney people have decided that such financial data must be muffled, although I can't imagine why.

What I see as a deficiency in Kaufman's book, the lack of a distinct point of view, may be owing in part to his choice of a subject. His earlier books on the Disney films have been about the silent cartoons and the Silly Symphonies, and I have no doubt, from what I've read, and from what I've heard in conversation with him, that his sympathies are heavily weighted toward the pre-war Disney films (as are my own).

John Canemaker has always cast his net wider, and in his book *Two Guys Named Joe: Master Animation Storytellers Joe Ranft & Joe Grant*, he spans seventy years of Disney/Pixar history—that is, almost the entire period embraced by The Approved Narrative—as mirrored in the lives of the two Joes. Both men died in 2005. Ranft, who was a story man for Disney and then for Pixar, died much too young, at only 45, in an auto accident. Grant, whose Disney career began in the 1930s, left the studio in 1949—temporarily, as it turned out—and returned part-time in 1989 and then as a full-time employee in 1991. He died at age 96.

Like Kaufman's book, Canemaker's has been heavily researched, often to excellent effect. The chapters on Joe Grant's pre-Disney years are wonderfully detailed, in both words and illustrations, reflecting not just intensive use of the internet resources for such research but also in-person examination of the relevant Los Angeles documents by Canemaker's partner Joe Kennedy. Like Kaufman, Canemaker draws on some of my own research, including interviews with Ward Kimball and Joe Grant himself.

Canemaker's is a warmer and more personal book than Kaufman's. It's evident throughout that he not only knew both Ranft and Grant well, but regarded them with the greatest affection. Canemaker slips into the first person occasionally, and he should have done so throughout. The book cries out to have been written as a memoir. Possibly Canemaker simply didn't see Ranft and Grant often enough to feel comfortable writing in that form (he has lived in New York most of his life, whereas Ranft and Grant lived in California).

Perhaps Disney Editions wasn't interested in publishing such a book. As it is, it seems to me that Canemaker, from the most sincere of motives, has inflated the importance of both men, presenting them as "unique influences on storytelling at two major studios during important periods in the history of animation" when it is doubtful that either was really such.

I'm less certain where Ranft is concerned, since I was never interested enough in Pixar to try to meet Ranft (or his colleagues) or learn the dimensions of his contribution. Surely, though, it is John Lasseter who has always dominated Pixar and is most responsible for its increasingly queasy mix of the sanctimonious and the morally incoherent (as exemplified by *Cars*, which Lasseter directed). I don't see anything in *Two Guys Named Joe* to suggest that Ranft did more than make the Pixar features a little livelier and wittier than they might have been otherwise. His comic sensibility seems to have been a better fit for Tim Burton (Ranft's name is in the credits for *The Nightmare Before Christmas*) than for Pixar.

Canemaker presents Grant as "Walt Disney's right-hand man and most trusted confidant from mid-1933 through 1949"—a striking overstatement, given that it has Grant becoming Walt's "right-hand man" as soon as he was hired and remaining in that position even as his rapport with Disney shriveled in the mid-1940s.

"Walt Disney discovered in Grant a storyteller extraordinaire; he was a unique, intellectually rich resource of new ideas and possibilities for the art of animation and inspiring others. Both he and Grant had creative minds and a shared passion for this new medium of storytelling. Kindred spirits, they were simpatico in energy, drive, and ambition." Canemaker acknowledges that Grant's awareness of his own talent provoked the hostility of some of his colleagues, but as he presents it, their hostility was overdrawn, sometimes descending to crude anti-Semitism.

Grant was certainly talented, and he certainly provoked hostility, but far from being uniquely important, he was one of a cluster of Disney people whose responsibilities were generally similar and whose careers followed comparable arcs.

Grant came onto the Disney staff as a caricaturist and story sketch artist—not an inconsequential position, but not all that important, either— and rose in the ranks rapidly, ultimately forming and heading the studio's character model department, sharing story direction of *Fantasia* and *Dumbo* with Dick Huemer, and producing *Make Mine Music* before his fall from grace. Compare his Disney career with that of Perce Pearce, who started even lower, as an inbetweener, then moved into story work on *Snow White and the Seven Dwarfs* and wound up directing part of that film, thanks to his talents not as an artist—Grant's strong suit—but as an actor who could impersonate the dwarfs for the benefit of the animators.

Like Grant, Pearce moved on to other significant projects after *Snow White*, heading story work first on "The Sorcerer's Apprentice" and then on *Bambi* and *Victory Through Air Power*. (He also shared Grant's reputation as a skilled manipulator of Walt Disney himself.) Then his career took a major turn: he began working in live action, serving as Walt's associate producer on *Song of the South* and *So Dear to My Heart* before moving to England to shepherd Disney's first entirely live-action features (*Treasure Island*, *The Story of Robin Hood and His Merrie Men*, *The Sword and the Rose*, and *Rob Roy the Highland Rogue*) onto the screen. In other words, Walt repeatedly chose Pearce to act as his surrogate where his interest was strongest. Joe Grant, in the meantime, made his exit from the studio.

There may have been a bit of typecasting when Walt sent Pearce to England—he was the son of English immigrants—but what was undoubtedly more important was Pearce's adaptability and his willingness to respond to the demands Walt made on him. Throughout the 1940s and '50s, people who had joined the Disney staff to work on animated cartoons followed similar paths, moving into live action or, later, into television or designing attractions for Disneyland.

Ben Sharpsteen was an animator, then a director of short cartoons and feature sequences, and ultimately the "supervising director"—that is, Walt's man on the ground—of *Fantasia*, *Dumbo*, and other features. But then, as Walt's interest turned toward the True-Life Adventures and the

People and Places series, he took Sharpsteen away from animation and put him in charge of those live-action films. Likewise, the director James Algar moved from animation into directing the True-Lifes.

Keeping up with Walt's demands could not have been easy; Ben Sharpsteen, when I first met him in 1976, still seemed a little shell-shocked when he talked about Walt. From all appearances, Perce Pearce adapted well to his life in England—in stories about him that I turned up during work on *The Animated Man: A Life of Walt Disney*, he sounds like a true English eccentric, particularly in his devotion to a battered hat—but he occasionally crossed the Atlantic with Walt on an ocean liner, and as much as I wish I'd met Walt Disney, I balk at the thought of being confined on a ship with him for four or five days. Talk about stress! There's no telling if such stress contributed to Pearce's early death in 1956, but it couldn't have helped.

For the most part, the people who accepted Walt's assignments and stuck with him did so with no regrets. Others resisted in some way, and they were soon gone. Dave Hand was evidently one such casualty, although the exact circumstances of his fall are still murky. In Gerry Geronimi's case, there's no room for doubt: after years as an animation director, he balked at directing live action in Europe for the Disney TV show. Goodbye, Gerry, and don't let the swinging door hit you on your way out.

Such departures weren't always so abrupt: Wilfred Jackson, a meticulous soul who had suffered a heart attack and felt sure that directing live action would kill him, was sent on a trip around the world and allowed to retire gracefully. But if you worked for Walt, and he thought you could fill a job you'd never done before, you'd better give it a try, or you'd better leave. More often than not, Walt's assessment was correct.

Joe Grant ascended at Disney when the studio was making films that played to his strengths as a graphic artist: films with a rich pictorial emphasis, like *Pinocchio* and *Fantasia*. *Dumbo* was different, a true cartoon, and it's not at all clear how important a role Grant played, compared with Dick Huemer. It's impossible to say, in the absence of meeting notes and other such evidence, whose ideas might have dominated, but the long *Dumbo* treatment that Grant and Huemer submitted to Walt in 1940, a chapter at a time, is more in Huemer's mock-serious voice than in Grant's.

Grant and Huemer collaborated on a handful of wartime shorts before Grant produced *Make Mine Music*, conceived as a sort of pop-music *Fantasia* and thus a natural assignment for one of the principal creators of the earlier film. In the meantime, the character model department, the base of Grant's strength, had disintegrated under the pressures of the 1941 strike, the war's demands, and the studio's financial difficulties.

Grant was involved with *Cinderella* for several years. As early as 1943, according to an October 29 memo from Hal Adelquist to Walt, Grant and

Huemer had worked out a "talking plan" for *Cinderella* but had put nothing in writing. In meetings on *Cinderella* early in 1946, before Walt placed that story in other hands, Grant spoke enthusiastically about the Alice Duerr Miller version, a book that is in verse and is, compared with the eventual Disney film, a tad precious. Grant also spoke of the "old Vogel books" as a promising source for settings, but Hermann Vogel's elaborate nineteenth-century illustrations could not be further removed from the Mary Blair designs actually used in the film.

Grant's Disney career sputtered out in 1949, for predictable reasons when that career is measured against the careers of his contemporaries: Grant wanted to do what he wanted to do, rather than what Walt Disney wanted him to do. Canemaker quotes Grant quoting Walt, evidently in the postwar years: "You know, I can't figure you out, Joe." It was, I'm sure, a highly practical observation: if the studio wasn't making films of the kind that Joe Grant wanted to work on—films like a *Cinderella* that was not at all what Walt had in mind—how was Walt to justify keeping Grant on the payroll? Having known Joe fairly well, I can't imagine that he could ever have followed a career path like that taken by Perce Pearce or Ben Sharpsteen. Could Joe Grant ever have been, say, a producer of live-action hours for the Disney Sunday show? Not possible.

So, one might regard Joe's exit from the Disney Studio as evidence of his integrity, or, alternatively, evidence that he recognized his own limitations and didn't want to fail Walt and himself by accepting responsibilities he couldn't fulfill. But if you love Joe Grant and want him to be regarded as one of the seminal figures in Disney animation's history, you can't settle for describing him in such restrictive terms.

And so Canemaker has Grant being hounded by lesser talents at the Disney Studio, pygmies jealous of the great man's genius: "He was a figure of authority, a studio manager with unique access to Walt Disney, who relied on and trusted his advice regarding films, story, design, and personnel. This did not sit well with those who did not enjoy similar privileges, such as the animators. Envy was inevitable." He goes so far as to present the animator Ward Kimball as something like a villain because his hostility to Grant never cooled over the years. Kimball wasn't just critical of Grant, he "fumed" about him, in "sulfurous interviews", and there was the odor of anti-Semitism in his characterization of Grant as a conniving "Sammy Glick".

It's unfortunate that Canemaker, so earnest in his admiration for Grant, descends into pettiness in his characterization of Kimball, who was, to my mind, a considerably more significant figure in Disney animation's history than Joe Grant. As Canemaker notes, Kimball made only one long trip with Walt, to the Chicago Railroad Fair in 1948, in contrast to Grant, who traveled east with Walt on a number of occasions. But other people made long trips with Walt, too, people like Emile Kuri, the set designer, whom no one would confuse with a major figure in the studio's life.

Walt traveled with people who were good company, and he traveled with people who could be useful to him on a particular trip, as with Kimball on the Chicago trip—since Kimball was a fellow train buff—and as with Grant and Huemer when they accompanied Walt to Philadelphia in April 1939 for the recording of the *Fantasia* soundtrack. What Walt never did, as best I can tell, is choose traveling companions as a way of bestowing his favor.

When he visited New York and Detroit in April 1940, on a *Fantasia*-related trip, Ben Sharpsteen went with him, and both men were accompanied by their wives. Did Joe Grant's wife, Jennie, ever travel with Joe and Walt on their trips to the East Coast? Not so far as I know. Does that fact have any significance? Almost certainly not.

Canemaker quotes at length from my 1976 interview with Kimball, in which he described Grant's efforts to bring animators like Kimball under his control while they designed characters for *Cinderella*; that episode may have occurred in 1946, but, as I've indicated above, it could have been earlier. As Canemaker does not say, I asked Grant about that episode, and he told me that nothing like it ever happened. I'd still put my money on Kimball.

So far from Kimball's being jealous of Grant, it may have been the other way around; it was, after all, Kimball who in the 1950s was allowed to make cartoons (*Toot, Whistle, Plunk and Boom*; *Mars and Beyond*) that were much more to Kimball's taste than to Walt Disney's, precisely the sort of liberty that Grant was not allowed.

Grant and then his posthumous reputation have thrived for two reasons: he outlived most of his colleagues (and his critics, like Ward Kimball) and he returned to the Disney Studio and worked there for the last fifteen years of his life. To Canemaker's credit, he makes clear that some of Grant's co-workers in those last years found his presence annoying and his work less than useful, but more of them seem to have regarded him as an astonishing emissary from the studio's golden age, a good-luck charm in the new digital era. If his ideas often were flimsy, to the point of being frivolous—like many of the sketches Canemaker reproduces—that would not have mattered much.

In old age, as Canemaker notes, Joe had not lost his talent for charming people who could be helpful to him. Canemaker has most of Grant's former colleagues warming up to him, even when, like the animators Frank Thomas and Ollie Johnston, they had expressed reservations about him before; but such mellowing was encouraged, no doubt, when those colleagues saw Joe enjoying the patronage of the likes of Roy Edward Disney and Howard E. Green, a Disney vice president.

(The Kaufman and Canemaker books both heap praise on Howard Green, Canemaker going so far as to dedicate his book to Green and identify him as "a patron saint to animation historians". Just for the record, not *all* animation historians. Howard is a nice fellow, and he once saved me some money when the Disney licensing vultures were trying to charge me an exorbitant fee for reproducing a few old publicity stills, but if I ever had anything like a "patron saint" at the Disney Studio, it was Dave Smith, the recently retired archivist.)

Two Guys Named Joe is the culmination of the approach Canemaker has taken in all of his books about Disney animation, each book consisting mainly of biographical sketches—typically well researched and highly sympathetic to their subjects—of members of the Disney staff. Grant himself was the subject of such a chapter in *Before the Animation Begins: The Art and Lives of Disney Inspirational Sketch Artists* (1996). Because Hollywood animation has always been such a collaborative medium, I've never been persuaded by the biographical approach, although it can be justified most easily when the people in question, like those profiled in *Before the Animation Begins*—Albert Hurter comes immediately to mind—worked in greater isolation than most Disney artists.

There's a larger problem, one bound up in that word "artist".

Although Canemaker's focus has always been on the Disney films of earlier decades, his books extend to the present day; for instance, there's a concluding chapter on the sketch artists of the '90s in *Before the Animation Begins*. His biographical approach is, I'm sure, highly appealing to many people who work in today's Hollywood animation, because in its close attention to the individual it in effect validates their own status as artists. But most of the people working on Hollywood animated films, whether in the "golden age" or today, have been "artists" only in the most limited sense, as people who draw or paint or otherwise work with the materials of the visual arts.

They are for the most part not true creative artists, that is, people who determine the essential nature of a film, but rather craftsmen who carry out the wishes of others. Their work may have a great deal of art in it—it often does—but only the people in control of the films, the people whose vision (or lack of it) determines what winds up on the screen, can legitimately claim that title.

When Walt Disney spoke in Detroit about the similarities between the Ford assembly line and his own studio, he wasn't being facetious—and like Henry Ford, he wasn't inclined to let his employees determine how they went about their jobs.

Certainly, there are many people working in animation today who are unquestionably artists, John Canemaker himself being one; his Academy Award-winning film *The Moon and the Son: An Imagined Conversation* is intensely personal, as Hollywood animated cartoons never are. And there are others, like Michael Sporn and Bill Plympton. But they are much more likely to be found working away from Hollywood, in New York and elsewhere, and to be working on films very different from the Hollywood product.

In Hollywood, in the "golden age", it didn't much matter whether you thought of yourself as an artist, because artists were in charge: if you were working for Bob Clampett or Chuck Jones or Tex Avery or John Hubley, you were contributing to a work of art. Today, the reverse is more nearly true: a lot of Hollywood people, especially those who have worked at the Disney Studio, think of themselves as artists, and they flock to shows like the Motion Picture Academy's Milt Kahl retrospective, projecting back onto dedicated craftsmen like Kahl their own self-perception.

The reality is that not only are they not artists, they're carrying out the wishes of someone who is also not an artist but is instead a John Lasseter or a Jeffrey Katzenberg or a faceless corporate master. Perhaps that discrepancy, between what's wished for and what is, accounts at least in part for what I've come to think of as today's default "Disney personality": a compound of naïveté, sycophancy, and seething rage.

Of the artists making animated films in the "golden age", the most important was Walt Disney. In reading John Canemaker's new book, as in reading his earlier books, I can never escape the feeling that he doesn't quite approve of Walt, who was always determined to have his own way, often at the expense of people, like Joe Grant, whom Canemaker finds more sympathetic.

There's never any direct criticism of Walt, and that's a pity; how much more enjoyable (if wrongheaded) the book might be if Canemaker's sympathy for his protagonist were given free rein, as it could not be without violating the rules implicit in The Approved Narrative. And so Walt remains a shadowy but faintly ominous presence.

Me, I find Walt Disney boundlessly interesting and entertaining. One of the sad ironies of the triumph of The Approved Narrative is that Walt's place in it will almost certainly become more shrunken and diminished over time. Writing about him in anything but the most conventional terms will be too difficult, given that The Walt Disney Company and the Walt Disney Family Foundation will be peering over the writer's shoulder. And that's a pity, because there are so many aspects of Walt's life and work that still invite close attention.

By way of illustration, let me touch the third rail of Disney studies: the claim that Walt was anti-Semitic.

Roy Disney was born in 1893, a few years after my grandparents; his younger brother, Walt, was born in 1901, about fifteen years before my parents were born. All of those people grew up in the middle of the country, a few hundred miles apart, when bigotry of many kinds was the air everyone breathed and racial slurs were a normal part of conversation. My parents and many other members of their generation eventually purged their speech and, I'm sure, their thoughts of most such prejudice, but I don't think my grandparents ever did.

So, when in research for my own books I found an occasional trace of prejudice in letters and interviews by Roy Disney, and interviews about him, I wasn't surprised or offended—it would have been amazing if none were there. More important, I found plenty of evidence that Roy enjoyed warm and mutually respectful relations with Jewish motion-picture executives, in particular. He simply wasn't a bigot, in any meaningful sense of the term.

Where Walt is concerned, what was truly amazing was that even the traces of prejudice were absent. In reading thousands of pages of documents at the Disney Archives, I can recall only one instance in which someone—not Walt— spoke disparagingly about a race or ethnic group in the notes from a story meeting, and the notes do not show Walt responding favorably, or at all.

In *The Animated Man*, I quote Roy Disney as saying, "For an artist that had delivered, Walt didn't care how he combed his hair, or how he lived his life, or what color he was or anything. A good artist to Walt was just a good artist and invaluable."

So I was surprised, to say the least, when I ran across this passage in *Boffo! How I Learned to Love the Blockbuster and Fear the Bomb*, a 2006 book by Peter Bart (then the editor-in-chief of *Variety*, earlier a reporter for *The New York Times*), in a chapter devoted to the Disney Studio:

> The moguls (except for Darryl F. Zanuck) were Jewish guys whose manner and tastes were still tied to their Eastern European roots. Disney remained something of a hick from the Midwest who thought of Jews as accountants and merchants. I once made the mistake of asking Walt a question that had business implications (we were having lunch in the Disney commissary at the time) and he replied by saying, "Let me check that with my Jew." He started to summon a financial aide nearby, but I quickly changed the subject.

Bart's book (which was, ironically, published by Hyperion, a Disney publishing imprint) appeared after I'd finished writing my Disney biography, so I couldn't mention it in my own book. But I wasn't sure what I would have said about it, anyway. I don't think what Bart wrote attracted much attention on the web, except for a piece on Jim Hill's site. What a curious episode!

What *did* Walt mean when he referred to "my Jew" (assuming that's what he actually said, as opposed to saying something like "Let me check that with Montague")? Was a reference to "my Jew" actually a relic of 1920s Kansas City? Or was it an in-house joke of some kind? Did some Jewish staff member, aware of the mutterings about Walt's supposed anti-Semitism, refer to himself (in Walt's presence, and for his amusement) as "Walt's Jew"?

It would be good to know what was going on at that lunch table. I don't foresee any startling revelations; we already know too much about Walt for any such passing remark, however awkward, to acquire great significance. But still, it would be good to know. With The Approved Narrative dominant, we never will know, I'm sure, and there's a great deal more about that very interesting man Walt Disney we'll never know. That's too bad, for us and for his memory.

© 2015 Michael Barrier

● ●

MICHAEL BARRIER [michaelbarrier.com] is a renowned historian whose pioneering work opened countless pathways for many others. His publication *Funnyworld* is still regarded as one of the earliest and most accurate periodicals about animation and Disney. Barrier was responsible for bringing attention to the work of comic book artist Carl Barks among many other achievements, including writing *Building a Better Mouse—Fifty Years of Animation* catalog for the 1978 Library of Congress exhibition.

His Disney-related books include:

- *Hollywood Cartoons: American Animation in Its Golden Age* (2003)
- *The Animated Man: A Life of Walt Disney* (2008)

In addition, he has written *Funnybooks: The Improbable Glories of the Best American Comic Books* (2014), *Carl Barks and The Art of the Comic Book* (1982), was coeditor (with Martin Williams) of *A Smithsonian Book of Comic-Book Comics* (1982), and coauthor (with Harvey Kurtzman) of *From Argh! To Zap! Harvey Kurtzman's Visual History of the Comics* (1991).

For links to Michael Barrier's books, visit:

themeparkpress.com/historians

Alberto Becattini

Confessions of a
Disney Comics Historian

How does one become a Disney historian? I guess it is a very subjective path, depending on your roots, experiences, personality, and sensitivity. In my case, it all began in the late 1950s, when I learned to read. Or rather, even before I learned to read, short-sighted as I was, it became evident that I had what you might call a "keen eye".

My parents told me that at three years old I could tell one type of car, or truck, or train, from another. As comics were in the house from the start, I learned to read more thanks to them than to what I was taught in school. And, of course, some of the first comics I read were Disney comics, which I could find in the weekly *Topolino*.

I guess I was lucky to have been born in Italy, because Disney comics, and American comics in general, appeared in almost every publication when I was a kid. In fact, I especially refined my art-spotting ability on such King Features newspaper strips as *Flash Gordon*, *Mandrake the Magician*, *The Phantom*, and *Secret Agent X-9*. This happening during the early-to-mid-sixties; there was very little fandom at the time, but a fanzine existed called *Comics Club 104* that opened my bespectacled eyes.

It was founded and written by young Alfredo Castelli, eight years older than me, who was also enthusiastic, and sounded knowledgeable, about US comics—and Disney comics. I consider Alfredo one of my inspirations (I tell him that every time we meet). In a special Disney issue of the fanzine that he published in 1966, there were the names of hitherto-unknown artists—Carl Barks, Al Hubbard … a true revelation! Now I was able to match the different drawing styles I had spotted with the respective artists' names.

Another lucky break was to have been born in Florence—not the largest Italian city, but one of those whose newsstands were literally flooded with US comic books in the sixties and seventies. So, I started buying and collecting them in November 1967 (DC Comics first), and have continued since. Thanks to them, by the way, I learned a lot of the English that I'm still teaching in high school. But I digress.

As for Disney comic books, I started buying them on a regular basis in 1971, and immediately after I set out on compiling my personal chronologies and checklists—rigorously handwritten on recycled paper—of who-did-what-when. That proved useful when I was consulted by the authors of an essay on Carl Barks (*Introduzione a Paperino*, 1974) as regards original publications of Barks' stories. This was seven years before Michael Barrier's *Carl Barks and the Art of the Comic Book* was published (another eye-opener!), but of course I was familiar with his articles and checklists in *Funnyworld*, as in the meantime I had also started buying US comics fanzines.

As years went by, my passion for identifying artists and for cataloging their works did not wane. Another epiphany of sorts happened when I bought the four volumes of Jerry Bails' and Hames Ware's *Who's Who of American Comic Books*. Unbelievable. They listed the names and credits of most US comics writers and artists—including Disney, of course. Again, the matching game started, and eventually I was able to tell that Gil Turner was the great *Li'l Bad Wolf* artist I'd been trying to identify, or that Ken Hultgren had drawn *Bambi's Children*.

I was still much of a fan, though, and little else. As I felt the need to spread the knowledge I had acquired, my friend Stefano Piselli and I eventually gave life to our own fanzine, *Funnies*, which featured typewritten articles and checklists of—guess what? Disney characters and artists. Since then it's been a long way. I have written hundreds of articles for fanzines, pro-zines, and newsstand periodicals published in Italy, the US, France, and Norway, as well as essays and books about scores of Disney authors—starting from Floyd Gottfredson and Carl Barks (my personal gods) and encompassing the "minor" ones, who I felt deserved credit and recognition, too.

Eventually, I decided that my personal checklists, largely based on the huge Disney comics collection I'd been building up, also deserved being published. From 1984–1992, three limited-edition print volumes of my *Disney Index* appeared, which I'm proud to say were the basis of the I.N.D.U.C.K.S. website, to which of course I've been directly contributing, as well as to the online version of the *Who's Who of American Comic Books* and the Grand Comics Database.

Now back to the main question. How does one become a Disney historian? Well, it depends on what field, or fields, of Disney history you want to deal with. In my case, it has mainly been comics. Since the visual approach is essential, I would say that you have to have innate skills to tell an artist's or a writer's style from another's. Of course you have to enhance your knowledge of Disney comics, from the very first *Mickey Mouse* strip in 1930 to the latest comic book stories or graphic novels, by reading, and reading, and reading … but someone could read forever and not be able to tell Bradbury from Buettner, or Toth from Tufts.

I am talking about intensive reading, or rather, "alert reading"—which means scanning a strip, or a story, panel by panel, balloon by balloon. Anything can be revealing—even the lettering style, or (as regards Disney newspaper strips) the way the "Walt Disney" signature was made. This is probably the most time-consuming activity a researcher will have to do, but it is also the most fascinating and in the end it may be the most rewarding, if you finally identify who did what. Eureka!

I am sorry to say this, but I am pretty sure that not everybody can become, or should become, a Disney historian. And even if you become one, you should exploit your skills but not go beyond what you are actually good at. I, for one, am not very good at identifying writing styles. Guys like Joe Torcivia and Christopher Barat are much better than me in this region. But again, I guess that is in part due to that I have always concentrated on the art rather than the script.

Do not misunderstand me. I am, of course, an avid reader, and I am convinced that a good comic is a perfect blend of good art and good story-telling. I guess it's just that I'm not as gifted for telling who-wrote-what as I am for telling who-drew-what. In my line of research, you have to have a very good photographic memory, and you have to have a lot of patience and dedication.

I really don't know if young people today could stand sitting at a table, or in front of a computer screen, for hours and hours just to check, triple-check, counter-check, and cross-check. They will indeed sit at the computer for hours, playing games or chatting on social networks—but that is a different story. Memory, then, can be elusive. For instance, it often happens that when you are pretty sure about a publication date, you get it wrong. So never trust yourself completely; always double-check even if you may think it is unnecessary.

As much as you should not trust yourself or anybody else completely, you should never take "outer sources" for granted either. I started my research when the internet did not exist, and whereas I have to say that the net has been manna to researchers like me, I'm still using books for reference, too. On the other hand, what you find on the internet is not gospel truth. Sometimes it is misleading to say the least, and it's up to you to separate the wheat from the chaff.

One good piece of advice, banal as it may sound, is to always base your assumptions and identifications on actual documents and comics pages. I spent hours and hours in the Disney Archives warehouse, supervised by Dave Smith, leafing through US, British, and Argentine comics magazines I had never seen before, frantically making notes in my notebook. (By the way, I still have that notebook, and time and again I find myself checking the information I wrote in it.)

It is always advisable to exchange opinions with other researchers—although in the end you may disagree with them. And if that happens, you can reconsider and go over the comic you have been analyzing again, but if after this process you still think that you are right, it probably means that you are right. I don't want to sound conceited, but there are four, maybe five people in the world I trust when it comes to identifying who-did-what. And even when I ask for their opinion, it's always me that has the final word.

A Disney historian is primarily a researcher, but of course, as I said before, there comes a time when he feels the need to share his knowledge. At this point the intensive reader-researcher will necessarily turn into a writer. Writing is another skill, a very personal one. I know of people who have a great knowledge of Disney comics, but who can't just communicate it properly. I've read essays which were rambling, hard to read, and uninformative.

As Oscar Wilde said, "There is no such thing as a moral or an immoral book. Books are well written, or badly written. That is all." That goes for articles and essays, too. A good command of language—whatever the language may be—is a primary element. Differently from your innate flair for art spotting, the ability to write well can be acquired, or at least improved.

Silly as it may sound, you learn to write—by writing. Now this seems to be a real problem with young chaps today, as they don't write that much any longer. Text messaging speed won't help—sorry. Neither will verbosity, because you will be usually asked to write an article within a limited number of pages.

A good article must be concise, straightforward, and yet does not have to sound cold or soulless. Within the limitations of the space you're given, you should be able to clearly provide interesting information (better still, if it's brand-new or little-known), possibly seasoning it with anecdotes or statements by the author, if any are available, on a specific character or story.

Don't waste any precious room reveling in useless lucubration that you might be the only one to appreciate. Get to the point; tell readers what most of them don't know in a way that may not only be understood by the "elect". Always bear in mind that you are writing for a general public, even when you are handing out specialized and specific information.

Also, be sure not to neglect the "human element". Analyzing strips and stories is fascinating, but a good deal of the charm consists in creating a connection between the storytelling and artwork on the one hand, and the people—men and women of flesh and blood—who created them. So a good article or essay should also tell the readers about the creators—how they worked, how they lived.

Researching about the authors, their beginnings, their hardships, will tell you a lot about their personality and about their artistic choices. And it will open new doors—through their relationships you will find yourself researching on other creators, in a sort of spiral approach which you will eventually have to reorder and make proper use of.

Such books as *Who's Who in America*, *Who's Who in American Art*, and Graham Webb's *The Animated Film Encyclopedia* have been veritable treasure troves of information, as have been such online resources as the *Internet Movie Database*, *FamilySearch*, *Social Security Death Index*, *California Death Index*, and *The National Archives* (NARA).

As regards authors, interviews are, of course, essential. During the last 35 years I have interviewed scores of writers and artists—in person, by mail, and by email. And I have learned a couple of things. Some clever authors used to write down everything they did, thus creating invaluable records of their works for historians to make use of; others could offer precise memories of their careers, even in their very first phases.

Yet I have also met, or corresponded with, authors who remembered very little about entire periods of their long careers. And, mind you, one of the most frustrating things is when you say to someone who doesn't remember, "But you *did* draw that story … I *know* you did" … which creates embarrassment for both the author and you.

Also, even when you are told facts quite clearly and believably, you should always double-check to make sure that the chronology is correct. Sometimes even a good memory will play tricks, and it is easy for facts and dates to overlap and get misplaced. So it's often up to you to put the whole jigsaw puzzle together.

As I said before, interviews are essential, and a serious Disney historian should interview as many people as possible—before it's too late. I regret having delayed some interviews which will never happen because in the meantime the author has passed away.

More generally, the existence of a Disney historian is characterized by regrets. Very often I'll have a look at my past works and cringe when re-reading what I've written, because in the meantime I've come up with more reliable information. But then I tell myself that when I wrote that, I couldn't do any better. And I am determined to correct it when I'm given a chance to. After all, the true spirit of research lies in research itself—and when you think you've finally got hold of the Holy Grail you'll find out that it's slipping away. Undaunted, get ready to go on a new quest.

So far I have said that Disney comics are my main field of interest, but I wouldn't want someone to think that what I research and write about is only comics and comic artists and writers. One of the features of a serious Disney historian should in fact be to have a good level of general knowledge. Comics are a form of art which very often intertwines with other forms of art such as the cinema, visual arts, and literature.

I think it's impossible to write about the history of Disney comics, or even about a single story, if you don't know anything about animation, for one thing. Because most Disney characters originated in the animated cartoons, and because most Disney comic artists previously, concurrently, or subsequently worked in the animation field, you need to know about Disney animation to write about Disney comics.

Thus, besides reading tons of Disney comics, you will have to watch (and hopefully enjoy) scores of Disney animated shorts and features. It will be useful to make connections, but also to point out the differences, for instance, between a movie and its comics adaptation. Movies in general, then, will be an inspiration. If you have a good knowledge of the cinema, you will be able to find implicit or explicit references in almost every single story. "That's Hitchcock's *Spellbound*!" I remember exclaiming while reading Romano Scarpa's classic Mickey Mouse story, *The Chirikawa Necklace*.

A good knowledge of literature will also help make your writing more attractive. Many Disney comics stories (and movies) are partly based on literary works. In Italy there is a long tradition with "Great Parodies", stories in which the Disney characters play the roles of famous literary characters.

Last but not least, each story should always be analyzed considering the historical period when it was created. Floyd Gottfredson's *Mickey Mouse* newspaper strip continuities are a case in point—chock full of references to the facts and fashions of the years in which they were released. But even if you are not so much into history, art, or literature, do not fear. As a serious researcher, you should still counter-check what rings a bell in your mind, as it seems to mirror something that happened, was written in a book, or appeared on screen.

Even a minor character, his name, or what he says might evoke some movie actor, singer, musician, or politician you may have but a vague memory of. Just check. If you find a match, that may provide an original addition to what you're going to write.

Even if you have what it takes to succeed as a Disney historian, bear in mind that it won't be a full-time job.

Well, in my case it isn't. I am a high school teacher, and I guess that one of the reasons why I chose to become a teacher was that it would give me precious time to devote to my passion. Let's say that teaching has allowed me to combine duty with pleasure. But I couldn't have been a full-time Disney historian, or a comics historian, anyway.

The only paying jobs I've done in this field have been with Disney-Italy and with their current licensee as regards publications, Panini Comics. The rest—all the rest, which means hundreds of articles and thousands of written pages—I've done for free. And I had a kick out of writing most of them. So don't expect to make much money as a Disney historian.

Find yourself a good, steady job. Then you will be able to devote most or all of your spare time to researching Disney stuff, as I've been doing for over forty years. Other than the skills I have written about before, you have to have an ardor, a real compulsion that has nothing to do with greed.

© 2015 Alberto Becattini

ALBERTO BECATTINI [alberto-s-pages.webnode.it] is a high school teacher of English who has been writing about comics, illustration, and animation for over forty years. He was born in Florence, Italy. He has been a contributor to Italian Disney publications since 1992, and has also written for *Alter Ego*, *Comic Book Artist*, *Comic Book Marketplace*, and *Walt's People*, among others. An indexer for the Grand Comics Database and the I.N.D.U.C.K.S. project, he has written books about Floyd Gottfredson, Romano Scarpa, Alex Toth, Bob Lubbers, Milton Caniff, Alex Raymond, and Matt Baker.

His Disney-related books (in English) include:

- *Profili Album: Paul Murry—Mice, Ducks, and Cheesecake* (2004)
- *Disney Index: Dell Comic Books Volume 2* (1994)
- *Disney Index: Dell Comic Books Volume 1* (1992)
- *Disney Index: Syndicated Strips* (1984)

Disney-related books in Italian include *Topolino—60 Years Together* (1993; the history of the popular Italian magazine featuring Mickey Mouse comics), *Disney Comics—The History, The Characters: 1930–1995* (the "bible book" of Disney comics), *Don Rosa and the Disney Renaissance* (1996) (the only biography written about Don Rosa, but in Italian), *Floyd & Mickey* (1998), *Seventy Years of Animate Fables: Silly Symphony* (1999), *Romano Scarpa: Calidornia Dreaming* (2001), *Carl Barks: The Duck Man* (2001), *Fantastic Walt* (2001), *Disney in Italy: The Illustrated Books—1932-1975* (2012), *Italian Disney Comics* (2012), and many other non-Disney books about comic art and artists.

For links to Alberto Becattini's books, visit:

themeparkpress.com/historians

Jerry Beck

How I Got Started—And Ten Tips
I Learned Along the Way

More and more these days I get emails from younger people (usually in high school about to enter college) asking me what courses did I take to become an animation historian. This is a career path they wish to pursue. They ask for advice to follow my line of work.

I smile and flashback to a time (circa 1973) when I had just graduated high school and there were no career possibilities to become a professional "animation historian". Simply considering such a vocation would get you laughed out of the room. No one took the field seriously.

It was a different time. Cartoons were "kid stuff". Bad prints of the old ones were rerun on TV puppet shows, the new ones were low-budget cheapies on Saturday morning. There was no internet, no DVD compilations of restored classic cartoons, no YouTube, maybe one or two books on the "Art of Disney", one lone fanzine, and little else.

I was lucky. I lived in New York City and could cultivate my interest in animation history by attending occasional screenings and festivals at Lincoln Center, the Museum of Modern Art, and other venues where like-minded folks would meet. That also included art institutes like the School of Visual Arts and the New School For Social Research which pioneered the teaching of cartoon history by incorporating such lectures into their existing film or animation courses.

At some point in my teenage years, I had rediscovered how funny and "artistic" the classic Warner Bros' cartoons were due to their constant presence on weekend morning and weekday afternoon TV. During one Saturday morning I had missed the opening of a cartoon that I had become quite fond of, and had a desire to know the name of it so I could quote it to my friends. At that fateful moment, I realized I had nowhere to look up this simple piece of information. No books. No references.

I realized then there was only one way to know the name of that one cartoon—I would have to actually watch *The Bugs Bunny Road Runner Hour* each week, pencil in hand, and write down the titles and plotlines of each cartoon myself—until that elusive title showed up again! (Thirteen weeks later I had my answer: "It's Hummertime" from 1950, directed by Robert McKimson).

This set me off on a path to document ALL the Warner Bros' cartoons. It was something I wanted, something I needed. But why stop there? How many other cartoons were there? Who directed them all? When did they start, when did they stop? So many questions...

First stop: the public library. I found a book called *The Great Movie Shorts* (Leonard Maltin, 1972) and fell in love with it. It listed all the Our Gang/Little Rascal shorts and the Laurel and Hardy and Three Stooges films which were still run as kids programming on weekday afternoons. A book like this, but devoted to animated cartoons, was exactly what I was looking for. Did such a thing exist?

Let's stop here for a moment. Here are the first two "tips" you need to begin a career as a historian—or to conceive a book project.

- **Tip #1**: The personal need and desire for a piece of research that apparently doesn't exist.

- **Tip #2**: Research if such a book or research already exists.

If you have such a desire for a particular slice of historical information and it does not already exist—you have the beginning of a research project.

One day, around this same time, I was waiting at a bus stop and began looking into store windows on the block. One store was a book shop and in the window was a brand-new book—*The Disney Films*, by that same fellow, Leonard Maltin ("author of *Great Movie Shorts*", as it said on the cover). I can still vividly recall my going into the shop and thumbing through the book. I couldn't put it down. Less $9.95 later (which was big money back then), I was home reading this book cover to cover.

A few weeks later I discovered that this same Leonard Maltin would be teaching a class at the New School on the history of animation! Despite my modest finances at the time, nothing was going to stop me from enrolling in this 14-week college-credited course and meeting the guy who wrote and researched these books.

The tuition was huge and the class was small. Leonard and I became immediate friends and soon enough, colleagues. In reality, Leonard became my mentor. He had already done major research on Hollywood shorts, movie comedians, and Walt Disney films. He was writing/editing a fanzine (*Film Fan Monthly*), had published several books (with more on the way), and was a working professional writer.

We bonded with a common interest in championing the fringes of classic movie history. Leonard had a broader interest in all Hollywood movie-making; I was focused on a narrower slice of the pie: animated cartoons. But through Leonard I came to learn a valuable lesson.

I learned that things didn't just happen in a vacuum. They happen for a reason. Or several reasons. A novice can simply write "Paul Terry created Mighty Mouse in 1942" and that could be taken as a true statement, but a thorough historian knows there are many factors left out of that sentence and should be understood—even if some information is left on the cutting room floor, it's important that the writer know it.

Mighty Mouse was created as a parody of the popular Superman character (which had debuted in 1938, and on screen in cartoons in 1941). The character was initiated in the Terry story department by Isadore Klein who conceived the character as a fly. Paul Terry changed him into a mouse—and the first several cartoons bill the character as "Super Mouse" in a red-and-blue super-suit. Pressures from National Comics (Superman) and Pines Comics (Super Mouse—published the same year) led to Terry changing the name and costume to Mighty Mouse in 1943.

- **Tip #3**: To properly research and comprehend your subject, you must learn much more than the basic answers you desire. You must know more about the time period of your subject, the pop culture of that era, the national and world events that shaped that period, and the events of the period leading up to it.

Leonard's class gained in popularity as the 1970s wore on. I asked him why, with his knowledge of animation history, he hadn't attempted writing a book like *The Great Movie Shorts* devoted to animation. Leonard told me he did not want to compete with Michael Barrier who had just announced, in his fanzine *Funnyworld*, his intentions to write such a book..

I, on the other hand, could no longer wait to answer the burning questions I still had. How many cartoons were made, who made them, what were the titles, release dates, etc.? I asked my mentor how he compiled the filmography in the *Great Movie Shorts*. He advised that I start at the library. But not just any library—in Manhattan there was a special public library at Lincoln Center, the Library of Performing Arts. The library there had bound back issues of several motion-picture trade newspapers and magazines; these alone were a treasure trove of interesting information, with release charts of shorts listed in every issue.

I slowly began the meticulous process of hand copying ALL the information I needed from these magazines. Sound easy? It wasn't. The bad news: it literally took three years of almost daily visits to the library. The good news: I picked up an assistant to help with this work. Will Friedwald was a teenager who was taking history classes at the New School and who was equally crazy for classic cartoons as I was. He agreed to assist me with this Herculean task.

A few years went by, and still no book from Barrier (it would take another twenty-five years—in 1999—for Barrier's excellent *Hollywood Cartoons* to emerge), so Leonard decided to take the plunge.

- **Tip #4**: If possible find an assistant or a collaborator. It will make the work go faster and will keep you focused on the importance of the project.

But he would need help. And he knew I was independently compiling a horde of information from the Hollywood trades. This was 1976 or so. We worked together on what became the still-in-print book *Of Mice and Magic: A History Of American Animated Cartoons*. Leonard Maltin wrote the book, I was credited as his research associate.

I tagged along on interviews, compiled the filmography, screened films, did all sorts of research, and generally became immersed in the history of the Hollywood cartoon. Some of us thought, with the 1980 publication of *Of Mice and Magic*, that the story of the Hollywood cartoon was now written— and done. No more to know. On the contrary; it was only the beginning.

Will Friedwald and I felt that, like *The Great Movie Shorts*, Leonard should have included a one-line plot synopsis for every cartoon in the filmography. The publisher felt to do that would add too many unnecessary additional pages to the book. Leonard wasn't sure that getting all those synopses was even possible to compile.

We decided to take on this challenge, and to head back to the library— and to the libraries of several film collector friends (video tape collecting had not taken off yet)—to screen, re-screen, and take notes on every car- toon we could watch. Eventually, we narrowed our focus to concentrate on our favorite cartoons—the Warner Bros' cartoons and that became the basis of our first book, a filmography entitled *The Warner Brothers Cartoons* (Scarecrow Press, 1981).

From that point on, I continued my cartoon research writing numerous articles, books, and blog posts … it's never really ended. There is always some- thing new to discover, and there are more unanswered questions than ever.

Why do I keep doing this? Because I love it. I love the medium of anima- tion and the artists involved with it. And its history is endlessly fascinating. You must have that passion for your subject to be a good (or great) writer.

So what else can I tell you? What other tips do I have for an aspiring writer and researcher based on over thirty-five years of experience?

Well, for one—I'm a self taught writer. So learning how to write and communicate effectively is very important. So what did I do?

- **Tip #5**: Find a writer (or two or three) you admire and study how they construct their sentences, their paragraphs, and analyze how they compose a whole chapter (or article).

I studied Leonard Maltin's earlier books like *Movie Comedy Teams* and his essays about the individual Disney films. I noticed Leonard always began in a clever way—and usually ended on an "up note"; always finding something positive to say about a subject, even if that subject was not particularly appealing. This is something I've adopted in my work.

For examples, check what Leonard says about Terrytoons in *Of Mice and Magic*; or about "The Mis-Adventures of Merlin Jones" in *The Disney Films*. He is not a fan of either, but of Terry he ends by admiring the studio's popularity and longevity, and of *Merlin*, he concludes by noting the film's box office success.

- **Tip #6**: Write about what you are personally enthused about. Tell us why this subject touched you or entertained you—then tell us how it came to be.

If I have no opinion of what I'm writing about, then I simply cannot write about it.

It helps that I love doing research. Research is like doing a jigsaw puzzle—and all the pieces are scattered everywhere, some are buried, some are right in front of you. You must become Sherlock Holmes and dig out what you are looking for.

When I moved to Los Angeles in the mid-1980s, a whole new sandbox opened up for me to play in. LA has the Academy of Motion Pictures Margaret Herrick Library, open to the public four days a week; this library holds the key to much of Hollywood's movie history mysteries.

However, for the information you seek, no librarian there will have all the answers you need. Let me rephrase that: the librarians and staff at the academy library are extremely helpful—but it will be up to you and your knowledge, and diligent detective work, to find what you are looking for. The answers are there somewhere. You have to be clever to find it.

That is not the only resource of primary information in Los Angeles. There are motion picture libraries of great depth at USC and UCLA, the American Film Institute, and numerous private collections. Much of the information contained in these libraries is not on the internet.

- **Tip #7**: The internet does not have all the answers. Don't expect any one source to provide you with all the answers you need. You must talk to a lot of people and do physical research on your own.

Use common sense. Be skeptical of any claims of something being labeled "the first". We now know that *Steamboat Willie* was not the first sound cartoon. (Van Beuren's *Dinner Time* was released a few months before *Steamboat Willie*, and Max Fleischer did a series of synchronized DeForrest Phonofilms in 1924). We now know that *Flowers and Trees* was not the first three-strip Technicolor cartoon. (Ted Eshbaugh's *Wizard Of Oz* was made earlier in 1932).

- **Tip #8**: Interview witnesses, survivors, relatives, and other historians to get the full picture.

Everyone has their particular point of view. Like Rashomon, one person's recollection of an event can be contradicted by another. Having multiple viewpoints will clarify the story and reveal the proper history.

A few final tips:

- **Tip #9**: When interviewing a person, have the most important questions you want answered written down in front of you—BUT, do the interview in the most casual, conversational way that you can. The looser it is, the more open the interview subject becomes—and the more information will come out.

- **Tip #10**: Transcribing interviews is the worst part of writing and researching. It IS worth paying someone to do this for you.

Once I established myself as an animation historian, work eventually came to me. Understand, I had day jobs for the first half of my career as I wrote and researched animation history at night and on weekends. I wrote fanzines, and when the internet emerged, I began writing blogs.

I wrote for magazines, wrote VHS package copy, and had the good fortune to write several more books. I used my emerging reputation and expertise to curate animation programs for venues like the Museum of Modern Art and the Annecy International Animation Festival.

I've even had the opportunity to appear on several TV shows (PBS' *History Detectives*, Joan Rivers, etc.) and numerous DVD bonus material documentaries. My proudest moment came in 2012 when I co-hosted with Robert Osborn six hours of animation on TCM.

These days I teach animation history to student animators at Woodbury University in Burbank and at Cal Arts in Valencia. That there are now actual full-time jobs for animation historians is very gratifying.

My path to becoming a professional writer was unique and personal—yours will be completely different. The good news: researching cartoon history is no longer a laughing matter.

© 2015 Jerry Beck

JERRY BECK [cartoonresearch.com] is an American animation historian, author, blogger, and video producer. He is also an authority on modern animation and a frequent researcher and commentator for DVDs and BluRays. Early in his career he collaborated with film historian Leonard Maltin on the book *Of Mice and Magic* (McGrawHill/Plume, 1980). He was instrumental in founding the international publication *Animation Magazine* and continues to be a popular lecturer and teacher. He is currently teaching animation history at Cal Arts.

His Disney-related books include:

- *The Animated Movie Guide* (2005)
- *The 50 Greatest Cartoons* (1994)
- *Of Mice and Magic* (1980) (Research associate to Leonard Maltin)

Other books include *Animation Art* (2004), *Not Just Cartoons: Nicktoons!* (2007), *The Flintstones: The Official Guide to the Cartoon Classic* (2011), *The Hanna-Barbera Treasury: Rare Art Mementos from Your Favorite Cartoon Classics* (2007), *The SpongeBob SquarePants Experience: A Deep Dive into the World of Bikini Bottom* (2013), *Pink Panther: The Ultimate Guide* (2005), and *Looney Tunes and Merrie Melodies: A Complete Illustrated Guide to the Warner Bros. Cartoons* (with Will Friedwald, 1989).

For links to Jerry Beck's books, visit:

themeparkpress.com/historians

Greg Ehrbar

How Do You Get to Wonderland?

My favorite song is "Alice in Wonderland" by Sammy Fain and Bob Hilliard. It is the main title tune from Walt Disney's 1951 animated feature, a magnificent ballad with a solid melody and—like most truly great songs—deceptively simple lyrics.

Like "Over the Rainbow", it posits the existence of a magic land and ponders the possibilities of reaching such a place. It could be far away or "just behind the tree". That lyric is especially thought-provoking, as it suggests the Rabbit Hole—a fantastically impossible passageway to a place where there is an apparent sky, yet there isn't one in the logical or design sense (thanks to the genius of Mary Blair and the other Disney artists).

There have always been Disney records in my life. Before I could walk, talk, or sing along, my father bought his trusty Silvertone stereo system from the Sears store in White Plains, NY, complete with two speakers disguised as Shakespeare volumes. For years afterward, I challenged friends to find the living room speakers and delighted in their startled faces when they realized that the music was coming from the books.

Dad bought several LP records to play on his shiny new Silvertone. Two-channel stereophonic records were all the rage in the early 1960s. Most stereo albums devoted much of their cover space to huge opposing arrows and undulating sound waves alongside such lofty terms as "Stereo-Rama" and "Living Stereo". Album liner notes explained this wondrous technology in meticulous, unfathomable detail.

The soundtracks of our lives

Also purchased at Sears were Disneyland Records soundtrack albums to Walt Disney's *Pinocchio, Peter Pan,* and *Snow White and the Seven Dwarfs.* While they were not stereophonic, it didn't matter as each golden note permeated my psyche and made my soul soar.

Much as I love those early albums (and lots of others in my library), one record continues to play a special place in my life: the musical score album of *Alice in Wonderland.* This spectacular recording has been in print somewhere in the world since its 1957 release, and is still available on iTunes.

It is my all-time personal favorite record album, even though it does not feature music from the original motion picture soundtrack (such an album would not exist until 1997). Rather, it presents songs and score material arranged and conducted by composer and Disney Legend Tutti Camarata. Alice's solos are movingly performed by Mouseketeer Darlene Gillespie, a recipient of Walt's "Mousecar" award along with most of her fellow Mouseketeers at the 2015 D23 Expo in Anaheim.

Walt Disney's *Alice in Wonderland* (DQ-1208) was the first album I owned outright—as a reward for a good report card—but it was far from the last. I continued to seek out Disney records as well as those released by other labels.

My collection became a library. As I listened to the discs, read the album notes, took note of the label credits, I began collecting all the data I could find on index cards and cross-referencing the information that linked them. No one asked for (or needed) this documentation; I genuinely enjoyed gathering and expanding upon it (and this was before home computers).

The more I discovered, the more I wanted to keep discovering. I was soaking up knowledge, always finding new inspiration within the beguiling wonder of superb recordings (and even some that were less than superb, but still entertaining).

Much of the material could be connected with Disney in a number of ways. I looked for additional records featuring the same vocalists, voice actors, writers, arrangers, and musicians. That led to more discoveries. Still more records featured alternate or completely different interpretations of songs and stories. If something had a resemblance or kinship to a Disney product, I wanted to find it and listen to it.

Interest in such Disney-linked material led to new worlds of discovery. Soon, whether there was a strong Disney connection or not, I gained enthusiasm for non-Disney works that had been released as records and later tapes, compact discs, and digital downloads. In addition to their recordings, I greatly admire the projects and history of many other studios, such as Hanna-Barbera, Rankin/Bass, Warner Bros Animation and Filmation, as well as countless films, music, and TV shows.

Disney is still the "family homestead", but it is not the sole object of my expertise on the entertainment landscape. Why limit yourself if something else comes along to delight and intrigue you, too? Keep that in mind if you numbered Marvel, the Muppets, or *Star Wars* among your interests just a few years ago. Who could have dreamed that all of them would become part of the ongoing Disney history?

Sehh-renn-dipa-dipa-dipa-tee...

Being a Disney historian is not something I sought out. It just happened as a result of years of joyfully compiling and enjoying Disney materials, information, and experiences. Each historian has forged his own path through this enchanted forest of Disney history, a legacy that repeatedly influences countless lifetimes and subsequent works.

There is simply nothing else that fully compares to the infinite scope of Disney subject matter, be it classic or modern day. As Donald Novis sang over the main titles of Walt Disney's *Bambi*, "love is a song that never ends". Nobody knows everything. New generations of Disney historians will explore our paths and discover new highways.

There is no singular formula or procedure. You might start by becoming fond of a specific aspect. Next comes a desire to look further into a given topic, just out of curiosity. Deeper knowledge intensifies the appreciation, and often the enjoyment, of a given Disney work and those surrounding it.

Let's say, for example, you sit down to watch *Mary Poppins* for the first time, or the 100th time. At some point, you might focus on the music: the writers, performers, what they did before and after the film, etc.

You might read that the film was actually Walt Disney's second "book" musical. Every source tells you a fact that lights a fire in you to investigate more about that fact and more—about the animation artists, the on- and off-screen actors, the music, the narrative structure of the film, and so forth.

Like a reflex action, you could find yourself probing into these films, songs, attractions, historic periods, and artists with greater frequency, gaining understanding with every new revelation. Though there is really no point at which you are "anointed" a Disney historian, it just might happen somewhere along the way.

The sky's no longer the limit

Blogs, social networks, online videos, renting, buying, and borrowing material are accessible for checking—and more importantly, cross-checking what others have discovered about Disney subjects and exploring varied opinions. You might compile a list of "Holy Grail" Disney materials that relate to the subject.

You might find yourself going to events and presentations; soon you might create essays and presentations of your own. All the while, you keep exploring your favorite Disney "lands", contacting interview subjects, digging through information resources, reading, discussing, and commenting.

Historians relish the opportunity to watch, read, and listen to their cherished works over and over again. Countless Disney enthusiasts can instantly name the book (or books) that most influenced them, one that they read and memorized totally or in part. For me, as well as others, the book was Leonard Maltin's *The Disney Films*. Many a Disney or Pixar artist will tell you that they were almost surgically attached to Bob Thomas' *The Art of Animation*. Every subsequent read only widens the mental expanse.

Readin', 'ritin', and reorganizin'

Writing skills are crucial. In this era of online as well as print communication, you already know how easily the simplest messages can be misinterpreted and verified facts scattered to the four winds. Faulty information can spread like an internet virus, leading people to believe—and even cite—this information as correct. The hope is that there will always be those who are dedicated to getting accurate information wherever it is needed.

Organizational skills are also important. You don't have to be obsessive about creating cubbyholes and buying Tupperware to secure each and every item. But if you find yourself telling others, "I know it all looks messy, but I know just where to find everything," maybe it's time to sift, sort and store. If not, you'll be frantically searching for something needed immediately as time runs out and frustration mounts.

To fully understand all things Disney, it's advisable to gain some under-standing of the business contexts. You don't have to read the *Wall Street Journal* (unless you want to), but Disney history is one of business as well as entertainment. Every year, you can stream the audio portion of the Annual Walt Disney Company Stockholders Meeting without going to the event or buying Disney stock.

Most other aspects of popular culture, whether Disney or not, can and often should be taken into consideration by historians. Disney creations have never existed in a vacuum. Countless people, events, and organizations crossed Walt's path, just as they intersect with the Disney organization today.

Simply watching a classic Disney film alone does not convey the social and pop culture context surrounding it. But you need not have lived through the 1940s or the 1960s to gain this knowledge; it's accessible through documentaries, video bonus features, books, articles, solid internet posts, and other sources

You're also likely to have lived through the time period in which a Disney film or park attraction premiered. You can recall how it was received—either positively or negatively—or how time has altered the public perception. Many Disney projects were not appreciated in their initial release, yet over time they've become beloved classics and/or gained their own loyal followings.

"I've learned that I've still got a lot to learn."

— Albert Mouse (Tammy Grimes), Rankin/
Bass' Twas the Night Before Christmas

To not know everything is to be alive and learning. In a sense, everything I write is unfinished. Endless tweaks and additions beg to be added. Published books are frequently revised. On my web posts, the comments from readers are a treasure trove of information from people generous enough to share what they know. Times change, perceptions vary, and facts are brought into greater focus—or take on more complexity—with each passing year.

Are you pursuing the title of "historian" or the pastime? A little of both? That's fine. To be a Mouseketeer, you just had to watch *The Mickey Mouse Club* TV show. No purchase was necessary, though the series was a business endeavor as well, since you also watched the commercials.

Of course, not everyone "gets" why someone would be into "that stuff". Hopefully these well-meaning folks also have things in their life that bring them happiness. How sad if they do not. Just remember that *you are allowed to like Disney stuff*. You are fortunate to have such enjoyment in your life.

The designation of "Disney historian" may or may not be attributed to you along the way. It can take years, even if it does. Either way, enjoy the ride. A life of ongoing discovery, magic, and excitement from something as uniquely extraordinary as Disney is a great way to live, even with its occasional challenges. May these endeavors only become more enriching, pleasant, and fruitful for you in the years ahead.

© 2015 Greg Ehrbar

• •

GREG EHRBAR [mousetracksonline.com] is a founding member of the Hyperion Historical Alliance. A two-time Grammy-nominated and Addy-winning writer/editor/producer, Ehrbar is in his 30th year at The Walt Disney Company. Currently a staff writer at Disney's Yellow Shoes Creative Group, Ehrbar has thousands of credits, including national advertising campaigns for Disney Parks and Resorts, as well as print, network television, and publications enjoyed by millions worldwide.

Ehrbar continues to create concepts and copy for Disney Parks Merchandise product lines, such as the top-selling Wonderland Tea and Mickey's Diner products. He adapted major films into books and produced numerous best selling recordings. As an entertainment historian, Greg appears regularly on TV, home video movie releases, the official Disney Parks Blog, animationscoop.com, cartoonresearch.com, mousetracksonline. com, gregovision.com, wonderlandcompany.com, and syndicated radio's *TV Confidential*.

His Disney-related books include:

- *Inside the Whimsy Works: My Life with Walt Disney Productions* by Jimmy Johnson (2014) with Didier Ghez

- *Mouse Tracks: The Story of Disney Records* (2006) with Tim Hollis

He is also a contributor to *The Cartoon Music Book* (2002) by Daniel Goldmark and Yuval Taylor.

For links to Greg Ehrbar's books, visit:

themeparkpress.com/historians

Jim Fanning

Disney Historian or Disney "Distorian"?

Not too long ago I emailed a friend of mine who I don't know all that well aside from our association at our church. When I saw him in person afterwards it became apparent he had visited my website because he asked with an incredulity he could not conceal, "You're a *Disney historian*?" As in, "You can make a living doing *that*?" Or, "That's a job? That's a career?" Or more typically, "What in the world is a *Disney historian*?"

Well, I'm used to it. Very few people understand what a Disney historian is supposed to be. Including some Disney historians. Including me.

Truthfully, I really don't care for the term "Disney historian" as applied to myself. I use the term as shorthand in explaining my specialty as a writer, as more of a marketing term to editors who might potentially hire me for a writing gig. I use the appellation advisedly, as a way to say that I'm a writer who explores the behind-the-scenes creativity that results in an animated feature, TV show, theme park attraction, etc.

I have always written more than about Disney (although that is by far my emphasis) and more than history—I have written creative content in the form of stories, books, and comic books. And also if I wrote about *Beauty and the Beast* and *Aladdin* before they were released (and I did) or write about *Frozen* or *Big Hero 6* (and I have), is that really *history*? Maybe a better term would be Disney journalist, as I try to report the facts and weave them into an accurate account, to tell the story of how a Disney project comes to be.

Another reason I am not overly fond of the term "historian" is that particular concept seems to imply I can answer any question off the top of my head. An additional reaction I sometimes get when people discover that I am a Disney historian is that they ask me questions, usually to test me. Sometimes these pop quizzes are on the easy side. (When a friend asked me if I knew the middle name of Donald Duck, I replied that while I knew the answer— Fauntleroy—I was impressed that *she* knew the answer.)

However, I am often unable to answer such questions on the spot. I do have quite a bit of Disney knowledge in my memory, but there is much more information that I don't know off the top of my head. I recall that Walt Disney Archives founder and former chief archivist Dave Smith once told me he wouldn't do well on the trivia challenges that he himself created because he simply doesn't have a lot of trivia-type answers in his head. But he certainly knows where to look up answers and how to find information. Dave and retired Walt Disney Archives manager Robert Tieman both asserted that a historian knows where to find things and where to look things up.

The mention of Dave and Robert, certainly among the best of Disney historians, should serve as a reminder that the use of the term, whether by me or someone else, is audacious. Considering those who are truly worthy of the name, one should proceed with caution before daring to put themselves in such esteemed and accomplished company. I have been honored to know, and in some cases to have worked with, the best of those who can truly be considered Disney historians. Certainly among the tops in the historian game was the late Bob Thomas, the veteran Hollywood journalist and the author of what is still the best biography of Walt, *Walt Disney: An American Original*, even though it was published 40 years ago.

Also at the top of the heap is author, filmmaker, and educator John Canemaker (the best of the best of Disney historians), prolific author/host/moderator and commentator Leonard Maltin, and ace Disney Studio publicist Howard Green (considered the "patron saint" of Disney writers and historians, Howard has assisted innumerable Disney historians, including me). A good friend and supporter, author and commentator Jeff Kurtti maintains the highest principles of writing and historical reporting. And of course there's the archival triumvirate, the aforementioned Dave Smith and Robert Tieman as well as former archivist Paula Sigman Lowery. This trio, headed by Dave, has set standards that the rest of us can only strive to meet.

Invoking theses names and the level of quality they represent reminds me of another question that I am sometimes asked, especially by those who think they might want to enter the field: What are the hurdles in being a Disney geek for hire? The challenges for a Disney historian or journalist in today's world are the same for historians or journalists of any stripe.

That is, the de-emphasis and growing disregard for magazines and newspapers has led to a de-emphasis and disregard for standards of excellence. The internet has made it possible for anyone to write about anything, regardless of actual knowledge, scruples, or wherewithal. This has widened opportunity—if you want to write and be read, go ahead and do it. You don't need an editor or a publication. Your writing can be up and out in the time it takes you to write it.

People have even scored paying writing gigs and book deals based on their online writing. However, the other side of that internet coin is that ease in publishing means there is no filter, no fact-checking, no criterion. And that might be okay (though it really isn't) when writing about other subjects, but if one is calling themselves a historian and then beyond that a Disney historian, both those terms—"Disney" and "historian"— demand a higher standard of excellence.

The internet has also elevated opinion to a state equal to or surpassing fact. If you doubt this statement, you aren't reading the comment section of fan forums or even perhaps the comments on your own Facebook page. One unfortunate aspect of the whole "just because you have a thought doesn't mean it's true" syndrome (in other words, there are plenty of internet writers who have many expressed thoughts that contain a minimum of truth) is that non-fiction is trumped by some loose cannon's version of the facts. This extreme paraphrasing has led to distorted versions of reported facts.

A recent non-internet example is someone telling me as straight fact that Walt hated (their word) the spaghetti-eating scene in *Lady and the Tramp*. The truth is more complex than that (the internet with its Twitter-fueled obsession with oversimplification abhors complexity and encourages shallow understanding). According to Disney Legend Frank Thomas who animated that scene, Walt indeed had misgivings about the spaghetti-eating scene in storyboard form; he thought two dogs eating spaghetti would be distasteful, and had in fact replaced it with other material.

Frank believed he could pull the scene off with charm, personality, and appeal. (Perhaps he was emboldened by a similar experience: the ice-skating scene in *Bambi*.) The result made Walt a believer, and he changed his mind, adding the scene ot the film. To the person who told me in such reduced terms how Walt felt, this somehow translated to Walt hating the scene.

I deliberately if obliquely dealt with this distortion in an article I wrote for the Disney Music Emporium website by including a Walt quotation from Bob Thomas: "Some of the things in *Lady and the Tramp* topped anything we had done until then, especially ... the dinner at the Italian café." So, in an era with more challenges than ever before—in a time when we ironically have more Disney historians (in name only, at least) than ever before—those who seek to be Disney historians need to be on guard lest they become "Distorians".

All of this leads me back to those who truly have earned the title of Disney historian. There are an additional three who truly inspire, who have not only recounted Disney history, but were instrumental in creating what Disney is, working closely with Walt himself in doing so. As they proved in their authoritative books, master animators Frank Thomas and Ollie Johnston had a flair for not only recalling behind-the-scenes incidents, accounts, and personalities, but also how it all fits in the development and meaning of Disney. Additionally, aside from having interviewed Frank and Ollie, I heard them speak many times. They said something new, something I had never heard recounted before, every time.

In the same way, Richard M. Sherman—the rightly acclaimed composer who along with his brother Robert set the insights and philosophies behind the Disney "magic" to music—has demonstrated in interviews, presentations, and writing his incredible knack for both recalling a lived history in which he actually participated and also understanding the way in which it works in what makes Disney *Disney*. It was a great pleasure and honor to tell Richard in person that he is my favorite Disney historian.

So take note, would-be Disney "historians": this gives you some sense of the standard to which you are held. Thanks to those worthy of the term, the bar is incredibly high.

© 2015 Jim Fanning

• •

JIM FANNING [jim-fanning.com] is an internationally published writer, historian, editor, blogger, lecturer, and researcher specializing in Disney. In a career dedicated to celebrating and exploring the work and life of Walt Disney and his colleagues, as well as those who carry on their creative legacy, Jim has authored books, magazine articles, online pieces, TV documentaries, and comics.

A regular contributor to *Disney twenty-three*, the magazine of D23, the Official Disney Fan Club, and the D23 website, as well as *Disney Fan*, published in Japan, Fanning has written for and consulted on officially commissioned projects for many departments of The Walt Disney Company, including Publishing, Consumer Products, Educational, Home Entertainment, Imagineering, and the Walt Disney Archives. He has also contributed writing and research to the Walt Disney Family Museum in San Francisco.

His Disney-related books include:

- *The Disney Book: A Celebration of the World of Disney* (2015)
- *Finding Nemo in the Disney Theme Parks* (2009)
- *Disneyland Challenge* (2009)
- *Walt Disney Classics: The Making of the Jungle Book* (1997)
- *Disney's Sing-A-Long Book* (1997)
- *Walt Disney's Masterpiece Cinderella* (1995)
- *Walt Disney (Pop Culture Legends)* (1994)
- *The Making of a Masterpiece: Walt Disney's Pinocchio* (1993)
- *The Disney Poster* (1993)

For links to Jim Fanning's books, visit:
themeparkpress.com/historians

Sam Gennawey

When Worlds Collide:
Finding Your Point of View

"Be good at something, it makes you valuable. Have something to bring to the table because that will make you more welcome." Those are the words of Dr. Randy Pausch celebrated on a plaque alongside the Mad Tea Party attraction at the Magic Kingdom. For the aspiring Disney historian, it is good advice.

When I look at my Disney bookshelf, it is hard to imagine there is anything left to be said on the subject. Not only are there hundreds of books but also dozens of websites, podcasts, and new stuff that The Walt Disney Company is constantly pumping out to satisfy what seems to be an insatiable demand. With that said, there is always room for one more voice but only if you bring something to the table.

First, let us take a reality check. Sad to say, there is not a lot of demand for full-time Disney historians. The only people who make a lot of money writing about Disney are Disney. For the rest of us, this multi-layered and flexible topic should be great fun and a stimulating intellectual pursuit.

Another piece of advice came from the incredible Yogi Berra. He said, "You got to be careful if you don't know where you're going, because you might not get there." It has always been my feeling that the best books are written because the author could not find another book that met their needs and they decided to write it for themselves. That is how I was motivated.

During the day I am an urban planning consultant, urbanist, and educator. I work with communities to create great big beautiful tomorrows. Ever since I was a young boy, I have always been fascinated by the changing physical landscape of Disneyland. As I grew older I began to appreciate just what Walt Disney had done. Then I got into the planning field where my training prepared me to better understand the historic and aesthetic building blocks that make up the urban (and theme park) experience.

As an example, I learned that in 1965, architect Charles Moore called the park "the town square of Los Angeles" and the "most important single piece of construction in the West in the past several decades". Town builder James Rouse told an audience of planners and architects at Harvard in 1963 that "the greatest piece of urban design in the United States today is Disneyland".

Urban sociologist Mark Gottdiener said in 1982, "Disneyland definitely establishes a contrast to the surrounding urban life. That kind of environment is all but lost in the Los Angeles area." He noted, "It's always been the case that the best examples of urban design have come from visionaries who occasionally have been given the opportunity to produce environments that make people happy. Disneyland is an example of that."

Most recently, architecture critic Beth Dunlop said, "Urban planners study Disneyland to understand ideas of proportion and perspective and to learn, more technically, about the flow of pedestrians and the placement of public spaces. Disneyland simply changed the way we think." It certainly changed the way I thought.

Walt Disney's interest in urban planning was a topic where my two worlds could collide. It became the foundation for everything I write. It has become my niche. It became my seat and has led to wonderful opportunities to speak before interested audiences.

What is your passion?

Maybe you could base your research on your professional life or a special expertise that you have acquired over the years. Were you a former cast member, Disney executive, or an Imagineer? Do you have a background in the entertainment industry, real estate, or the financial markets? Breaking down complex topics such as engineering and technology is a welcome addition to the existing literature. Virtually any topic can be reflected in some way with Walt Disney, the man, or the Disney brand. Upon reflection, in some ways that is kind of creepy, but it does make for an awesome party trick.

Each of us brings a certain point of view. That is our greatest strength as researchers and authors. The public has grown wise and is looking for books that add value to their visits, provide historic context, or express a distinct editorial point of view. Remember; ask yourself what are you bringing to the table?

In my first book, *Walt Disney and the Promise of Progress City*, I followed the example of other authors who have used the life of Walt Disney or the activities of The Walt Disney Company to explore other topics. In my case, I was able to illustrate best practices in urban design by referring to spaces familiar to most Disney fans. Using this same technique, many others have successfully explored a broad range of topics such as customer service, business leadership skills, and issues of faith.

The Disneyland Story: The Unofficial Guide to the Evolution of Walt Disney's Dream was a very different challenge. Although I had this life-long interest in Disneyland's history, many other authors had already covered the topic. Instead, I thought I would write about *The "E" Ticket* magazine. This was the resource that deepened my interest in the park.

Leon and Jack Janzen were the publishers, writers, graphic layout artists, and distributors of *The "E" Ticket*, a magazine dedicated to Disneyland, along with glimpses at other historic southern California amusement areas. From 1986 to 2009, I would rejoice when I found a new edition in my mailbox. Their brilliant work, which remains available today through the Walt Disney Family Museum, is the inspiration behind my obsession in trying to understand why Disneyland has become something greater than the sum of its parts.

Then came *Jazz: A Film by Ken Burns*. While watching the mini-series, I realized that Burns had successfully crafted a biography about an ever-changing idea. He found the narrative balance between the story of the forest and the trees. Why could I not do the same for Disneyland?

A biography provides rules, limitations, and boundaries. The focus would always be on the internal and external forces that shaped the outcome. I would stick to the physical changes and avoid topics such as entertainment or backstage gossip. Other authors could tackle those projects. The book quickly came together after that epiphany.

Write what you know. Write what you are passionate about. Tell a story. That is how you get a seat at the table.

© 2015 Sam Gennawey

• •

SAM GENNAWEY [facebook.com/sam.gennawey] is a contributor to *Planning Los Angeles* and other books as well as a columnist for the MiceChat website. His unique point of view built on his passion for history, his professional training as an urban planner, and his obsession with theme parks has brought speaking invitations from Walt Disney Imagineering, the Walt Disney Family Museum, Disney Creative, the American Planning Association, the California Preservation Foundation, the California League of Cities, and many Disneyana clubs, libraries, and podcasts. He currently is a senior associate at the planning firm KPA.

His other Disney-related books include:

- *Walt Disney and the Promise of Progress City* (2014)
- *Universal vs Disney: The Unofficial Guide to American Theme Parks' Greatest Rivalry* (2014)
- *The Disneyland Story: The Unofficial Guide to the Evolution of Walt Disney's Dream* (2013)

For links to Sam Gennawey's books, visit:

themeparkpress.com/historians

Didier Ghez

The Lucky Disney Historian

"You must be very lucky!" I hear that sentence often when I explain to outside observers that I have just "stumbled" upon the diaries of Disney concept artist Ferdinand Horvath, the autobiography of story artist Homer Brightman, or the lost memoir of Disney animator Eric Larson. In reality, to paraphrase Edison, those discoveries are really one per cent inspiration and ninety-nine per cent perspiration.

There is a disciplined method behind those lucky breaks, a few "tricks of the trade" without which you cannot expect to significantly further our knowledge of Disney history.

Here are a few critical rules that will get you started. Day in, day out, for the last twenty-five years, they have served me well.

Learn everything there is to know, then start digging

If there is one rule that trumps all others, it is this: if you want to contribute meaningfully to Disney history research and make interesting discoveries, choose a well-defined Disney-history topic which fascinates you, focus on it, learn all that has been written about it, discuss it with some experts, look for holes in the existing research, then start digging. This is when you might start to stumble upon gold nuggets. The funny thing is that the gold nuggets may not be directly related to the subject you are researching.

Serendipity is a serious historian's friend. To share a few examples from my own experience:

You were looking for biographical information about Disney's first merchandising guru, Kay Kamen. By following the trail you end up uncovering a treasure trove of documents about the early days of Disney in the Nordics and Latin America (the Robert Hartman papers). They barely mention Kay, but fill a large gap in Disney history.

You were trying to find out a little more about a photograph of Walt and French cinema pioneer Louis Lumière. You end up finding out whether Walt actually met Mussolini in 1935 and discovering when Disney's subsidiaries were first established in the UK and France, not to mention writing a full monograph about Walt and Roy's trip to Europe before World War

II (*Disney's Grand Tour*).

You went searching for more stories about Bill Evans and unearthed the diaries of Disneyland's forgotten "chief landscaper", Ruth Shellhorn.

And on it goes. Serendipity seems to act as your dearest friend.

However, for serendipity to act as a friend, you need to be able to know when you have stumbled upon a treasure trove when you see one, even when that treasure trove is not part of your core area of expertise. And for this to happen, two conditions need to be met: you need to have at least a rough knowledge of the fields of expertise closest to yours (Disney parks, Disney comics, or Disney merchandising, if you are a Disney animation expert, for example; Disney in the '40s, '50s, and '60s, if your key focus is the '30s). You also need to be able to tap into a network of experts in those other fields.

In other words, the more you know about your field of expertise, the more bridges you have built with other ones, the likelier you are to make significant discoveries.

Follow all the leads in a timely fashion

Having learned all there is to know about a subject and having studied the research already conducted by other Disney historians, you are bound to find virgin trails that need to be followed. When you do, follow all of them and follow them quickly. You will soon understand why.

When I was starting to conduct research for my new coffee-table book series about Disney's concept artists, *They Drew As They Pleased*, the first thing I did was to get access to Disney historian John Canemaker's files, which are stored at New York University. I knew they would contain some great interviews with Disney concept artists and their families. Those interviews had been conducted by John when he was researching his book *Before the Animation Begins*.

While checking the interview transcripts carefully, I stumbled upon a sentence that gave me a jolt: one of the interviewees was talking about the diaries of Ferdinand Horvath which had been sold to a Los Angeles dealer a few months before the interview was conducted. Diaries, correspondence, memoirs, and photographs are the treasures good historians are passionately seeking, which explained my excitement. That interview, however, had been conducted more than 20 years ago. And John Canemaker had clearly not located the diaries at the time of the interview. Was the lead worth following? Surely the trail would be cold by now.

I would not respect myself as a historian, however, if I did not follow *every* trail. I did, and thanks to a good friend I managed to locate the dealer. As you guessed, that dealer still had the diaries and a whole pile of letters, which I did not know existed. Part of the material was in Hungarian, part in German. All of it was utterly fascinating and helped me write a chapter about Horvath filled from start to finish with brand-new information as shared by Horvath himself.

Following all the leads is not enough, however. You have to do so in a timely fashion. A few days ago, I sent an email to a fellow animation enthusiast. For close to ten years I had been trying to locate the memoir of a Disney story artist from the 1950s, and I thought that this animation enthusiast might be able to help. I asked him if he knew how I could contact the granddaughter of the artist (since both the artist and his daughter were long gone). He told me to contact him in three months since he was too busy to help at the moment. That was a Thursday morning.

On the Friday morning he emailed me again, this time to ask me to call him right away, which I did … in a heartbeat. He had stunning news for me: a few hours after he had first emailed me back, he had heard from the granddaughter of the Disney artist, who called to have breakfast with him on the Sunday morning in Los Angeles. He had not heard from her in three years and she lived in Rome, Italy. If I had emailed him just a few days later... Well, if I had emailed him just a few days later, we would probably still have located the memoir, but would have missed a great story.

In the case of my interview with Disney artist Ray Aragon, however, the consequence of waiting would have been a complete disaster. I interviewed Ray Aragon for the first time on February 23, 2009. At the end of that first session, I knew I needed a second session to complete the interview. I was very busy at that time, though, and was tempted to postpone for a few weeks. Fortunately, I did not listen to myself, and I interviewed him again on March 5. Ray passed away on March 15.

Follow all your leads and do not wait to do so!

Be persistent

A year ago, while conducting research on the second volume of *They Drew As They Pleased*, I contacted the son of animator and story artist Retta Scott. I wanted to know if he had preserved any documents related to his mother's Disney career. He mentioned that he only had a few autobiographical notes written by Retta.

That was excellent news, but I wondered if that was really all he had. I kept insisting and he kept mentioning that he had nothing else. While reading the notes, I noticed that Retta, after 30 years out of the business, had come back to animation in the '80s, at the end of her career and right before her death. I decided to track down artists who had worked with her at that time.

While interviewing one of them, I learned that Retta had once shown that artist the mock-up of a book called *B-1st* that she had designed with fellow Disney artist Woolie Reitherman in 1941. I emailed Retta's son right away to find out if he knew anything about that book, and he emailed back letting me know that he actually had the book!

If he had that book and had not mentioned it, what else did he have? I spent the next few weeks insisting politely, and after a while, he realized that he had a few documents that might be of interest to me … as in over a hundred pieces of never-seen-before Disney concept art by his mother. In other words: be polite, but be persistent!

Check even "known" facts

In all the biographies of Walt and Roy, their 1935 trip to Europe is only briefly mentioned. The authors usually state that Walt met with Benito Mussolini and that he received a gold medal from the League of Nations. Bob Thomas, in his biography of Roy Disney, having had access to Roy and Edna's diary, adds a lot of details to these sketchy accounts.

And yet, while conducting research for my book *Disney's Grand Tour*, when I started looking more closely at what appeared in those other books, I quickly realized that there were a lot of issues with the stories they told.

Take the meeting with Benito Mussolini. The main "proof" that the meeting happened appeared in a newspaper dated July 20, 1935. But to be released in that newspaper, that day, the article had to have been written on July 19. Since the Disneys arrived in Rome on July 20, this meant that the newspaper reported the meeting before it actually took place. In other words, that "proof" was worthless.

What about the medal of the League of Nations? The first question I asked myself is whether there was such a thing as a medal from the League of Nations. Not so, unfortunately. So who gave Walt the medal that both he and Roy firmly believed, even at the time, came from the League of Nations?

Study of the French newspapers from June 1935 quickly led me to a committee called C.I.D.A.L.C. (in English, the International Committee for the Diffusion of Arts and Literature Through the Cinema). The question became: was C.I.D.A.L.C. controlled by the League of Nations? The surprising answer was found in the Archives of the League of Nations preserved by the UNESCO and does not match any of the accounts released until the publication of *Disney's Grand Tour*.

Even Bob Thomas' more detailed story of the trip, based on Edna's diaries, proved to be full of incorrect information. At some point Thomas writes: "[The Disneys] took the *Sterling Collander* train to Edinburgh, where they sat near the King's Box and watched the Duke of York review the troops at the Tattoo." Unfortunately, there is no train called *Sterling Collander*. There are however, two cities called Stirling and Collander in Scotland, and the Disneys did drive through them. But what was more puzzling is that, based on Edna's diary, I knew that the Disneys were no longer in Scotland on June 22, when they attended the Royal Tattoo. So how did Bob Thomas deduct that they had been in Edinburgh to see it?

The answer is an easy one, but also shows why I had to recheck absolutely every fact: today the Royal Tattoo does indeed take place in Scotland. However, when one carefully checks newsreels and newspapers from the 1930s, one finds out that, at that time, the Tattoo took place in a city close to London called Aldershot. Things started to make more sense.

Connect the dots

Now that I had identified and corrected some key mistakes, I had to start connecting the dots, and that's when things started becoming really, really fun. Let's take a few examples.

On his trip by train from Los Angeles to New York, where he would board the *Normandie* to Europe, Walt stopped in Chicago and met with his childhood friend Walt Pfeiffer. We knew that Walt Pfeiffer worked at the Studio in later years, and I wondered if... By checking an interview of Pfeiffer I had released a few years back in the *Walt's People* book series, I confirmed my suspicions: during that short meeting in Chicago, Walt Disney convinced his friend to join the Disney Studio, and, close to forty years later, Pfeiffer still remembered that meeting fondly.

In England, Walt met with famous science-fiction author H.G. Wells. When I read this, I remembered that several Disney artists, including Mel Shaw, Maurice Noble, and Dick Huemer, had described a joint visit of the Disney Studio in the 1930s by H.G. Wells and Charlie Chaplin. I wondered if there was a link between the two events. There was, and finding that link also answered the question of how and when Walt and Charlie Chaplin were officially introduced. One more connected dot.

Another key source of information, aside from Edna's diary, was the correspondence of Roy O. Disney from June and July 1935. While Edna's diary focused on the most entertaining parts of the trip, from social events to the monuments toured in each city, Roy's correspondence was mostly focused on the business end of things. In letters dealing with the Italian part of the trip, Roy is clearly disturbed by the business practices of several local Disney representatives—Andry Veglianiti, Robert Bennett Martin, and Pierre de Beneducci—but gives very little details about them or about the issues Disney had with them.

This is when being able to read in several languages, including Spanish and Italian, became critical. The recently released book *Eccetto Topolino* ("Except Mickey Mouse") answered my questions about both Andry Veglianiti and Robert Bennett Martin, and I found some background information about Pierre de Beneducci in an unpublished manuscript in Spanish about the history of Disney in Spain and Portugal. But the real breakthrough about de Beneducci and his unsavory practices came from an extremely little known book called *Edmundo*.

Our "friend" de Beneducci was mentioned in it in passing. By contacting the author, I managed to unearth a long memo about de Beneducci, written by the English Disney office in the 1940s, a memo which was not preserved at the Disney Archives and which gave all the keys to the situation Roy was going through at the time with the three Italian crooks.

Focus on the smallest details

When you connect the dots, one of the important lessons you need to keep in mind is that no historical detail is too small to lead to big discoveries.

The content of one of the letters from Roy which was sent from the Disney office in Paris was full of details about the business he and his brother were conducting in the French capital. Interestingly, however, the most important clue was not to be found in the body of the letter but in the letterhead, in the guise of a cryptic inscription: "R.C. Seine 262.816 B". When I saw this, my heart raced. I understood I had found a critical piece of the jigsaw puzzle.

I knew almost instantly that R.C. stood for "Registre du Commerce" (French for "Register of Commerce") and that the number that followed must be the official registration number of the French company "Walt Disney—Mickey Mouse S.A.". With that small information in hand, I knew I would be able to get access to the official records of Disney's French subsidiary, finally understanding when it was founded, who was on its board of directors, etc. Mind you, even with the R.C. number, this was not an easy task.

The records were stored in the Archives of Paris, an archaic place where none of the documents are digitized and which only allows access in person with a pen and paper. Since I was based in Spain at the time, I asked my mother, who lives in Paris, to pay a visit to the Archives. She did, had to spend more than six hours there, and finally came back with information that answered all of the questions I had pondered for more than two decades. One of the names on the mid-'30s board of directors, Richard Joseph, was totally unknown to me and led to even more discoveries.

Another example of the importance of focusing on small details: in Edna's diary, which was preserved only as a transcript, in one or two instances words are missing. In one specific case, the missing word was particularly frustrating. During the sojourn in Italy, Edna wrote: "Walt went to see [word missing] who gave him the rights to use their music." Who did Walt meet? I thought there would be no way to tell.

And then I discovered an Italian magazine from August 1935 which I decided to pick up on eBay. I doubted it would contain any information I did not already have. When I received it, I read the article quickly and found nothing new.

But then, a few months later, I decided to re-read this article and others, line by line, to make sure I had not missed anything. And there it was, hidden in plain sight in an innocuous sentence, the company that Walt had met while in Milan: the Italian music publisher Casa Ricordi, owner of the music rights of such great classic artists as Rossini, Verdi, Bellini, and many others.

Do not neglect what is hidden in plain sight

Treading the same paths over and over again in many different ways more often than not leads to new discoveries. But what is more puzzling is that you often also locate new information when you are looking for something totally different … and what you uncover was often hidden in plain sight.

At some point during the project, I was trying to identify an English Disney artist who had drawn several of the most beautiful Mickey Mouse books from the 1930s. That artist had also provided artwork for the Disney licensee Happynak, which produced sand toys at the time, so I decided to check out a little-known book called *Comic Character Metal Sand Toys* by Pat and Doug Wengel. I had had that book in my library since its release in 2008.

While I did not find the name of the artist in that book, I discovered two stunning photographs which had been hidden in plain sight for all these years showing the head of Disney merchandising for Europe, George Kamen, in his office in England. In other words, I had just located the only two known photos of the English Disney office in the 1930s. Paydirt!

Use new technologies

Historians of the twentieth century are bound to envy us: the tools we have at our disposal today to conduct research are mind-blowing when compared to what they had access to just ten or twenty years ago. We would be unforgivable if we did not use them and if we did not use all of them.

One of the key breakthroughs in finding out if Walt Disney and Benito Mussolini had actually met came from an email sent by an Italian historian to the director of the Disney Archives, Rebecca Cline, who forwarded that email to me almost straightaway. Becky is based in Los Angeles, I am in now in Miami, and the Italian historian Roberto Dulio is in Italy. Roberto found the "smoking gun" in less than two weeks in the guise of scans from Mussolini's official agenda. Needless to say, all of this would have taken months before the internet.

But it is the combination of old and new tools which struck me as even more exciting. When I found out if the meeting with Mussolini had or had not happened, I still had to make a few other odd pieces "fit". In order to do this, like a detective in a criminal TV series, I had to understand if Walt and Roy, in the span of just a few hours, could have visited the Ministry of Propaganda in Rome, then gone to Mussolini's private residence, back to their hotel, and finally to the Barberini cinema.

One of the addresses was missing—that of the Ministry of Propaganda—and it was not easy to find. Whether for security reasons or otherwise, the address was not made public in the 1930s. To find it, I had to use three very different tools. I first checked out some newsreels from 1934 posted on the website of the Italian Istituto Luce, which showed the newly inaugurated ministry. Unfortunately, the newsreel did not mention the address ... but it showed the façade of the building. Then, on an online forum, I found a post that mentioned that according to a book from 1936 the ministry was located on the Via Veneto. With that bit of information in hand, I ran to Google StreetView and went down Via Veneto, checking each façade carefully. Fortunately, Via Veneto is a fairly short street and the façade is still exactly as it was in 1934! I found the building and its address.

If the Mussolini mystery was the most obvious one to solve, another one had been bothering me for more than twenty years: who was the first head of Disney in France in the 1930s, and how was the Parisian company structured? Based on rare archives from the Disney representative in the Nordics, Robert Hartmann, which are stored in Knoxville, Tenneesse, and also based on Edna's diary, I was starting to suspect that the company was headed by a woman called Helen Werner.

Who was Helen Werner, was she really the person in charge, and how did the company operate under her guidance? Once again, relatively new internet tools helped answer those questions. Through Ancestry.com, I was able to find out not just Helen's birth date, where she was born, etc., but I also located a physical description thanks to her passport application. But I still had not answered the other two key questions, just two months before the planned release of the book!

And then luck struck: I attended a professional event in France and came upon a recent issue of the entertainment trade magazine *Variety*, which contained an ad for the *Variety* "archives" website. *Variety* had some online archives!? A few hours later I had located a fairly long article from 1935 which not only confirmed that Helen Werner was in charge, but which also discussed the way the business was set-up. That was the last discovery of the *Disney's Grand Tour* project, and it was a major one.

Credit your sources

The first rule I mentioned in this chapter is "learn everything there is to know, then start digging". Learning everything there is to know, and knowing what ground has already been covered by previous Disney historians, is made immensely easier when those historians take the time to credit their sources. From my standpoint, this is the golden rule: whatever you write, credit your sources very clearly with detailed end notes.

There are three key reasons for this: first, by forcing yourself to do so, you will quickly identify the gaps in your own research; second, your readers will know that what you share is based on carefully checked information and will be able to recheck that information themselves; third, and even more importantly, as you probably realize by now, Disney historians do not operate in a vacuum and it is vital to share your leads and research insights with your fellow historians. This will allow them to make new discoveries which will help with your own discoveries, which will help with their discoveries, etc., etc. You get the idea.

I have a feeling that if you follow those rules, you will soon make some fascinating Disney history-related discoveries and often hear the words: "You must be very lucky!"

© 2015 Didier Ghez

• •

DIDIER GHEZ [disneybooks.blogspot.com] has conducted Disney research since he was a teenager in the 1980s. His articles about the parks, animation, and vintage international Disneyana, as well as his many interviews with Disney artists, have appeared in such magazines as *Disney Twenty-Three*, *Persistence of Vision*, *Tomart's Disneyana Update*, *Animation Journal*, *Animation Magazine*, *StoryboarD*, and *Fantasyline*. He serves as managing editor of the prestigious *Walt's People* book series that are an essential part of every Disney historian's personal library.

His Disney-related books include:

- *Walt's People: Volumes 1–17* (2005–2015)
- *They Drew As They Pleased: The Hidden Art of Disney's Golden Age* (2015)
- *Disney's Grand Tour: Walt and Roy's European Vacation Summer 1935* (2014)
- *From Sketch to Reality: Disneyland Paris* (2002) with Alain Littaye

In addition, he has edited *50 Years in the Mouse House: The Lost Memoir of One of Disney's Nine Old Men* (2014) by Eric Larson, *Inside the Whimsy Works: My Life with Walt Disney Productions* (2014) by Jimmy Johnson with Greg Ehrbar, and *Life in the Mouse House: Memoir of a Disney Story Artist* by Homer Brightman (2014).

For links to Didier Ghez's books, visit:

themeparkpress.com/historians

J.B. Kaufman

Thoughts on Becoming a Disney Historian

I'm thankful and flattered that Jim Korkis has invited me to contribute my thoughts to this collection—but I'm humbled, too. I've published some books and articles on Disney history, but frankly I still feel that I'm learning this craft, and am more inclined to seek advice than to hand it out. Accordingly, I'm not going to get into specifics. Instead, I'll offer some more general thoughts—and some of these points may *also* have been addressed by other writers, but I'll take the chance.

To anyone considering becoming a Disney historian, the most important single piece of advice I can offer is this: *take it seriously*. We all start out in this field as Disney fans, but if you're going to take it upon yourself to document Disney history, it's time to move beyond fandom. Whether your subject is Walt himself, one or more of his films, or some other specific aspect of his life or career, you're dealing with a *highly* significant piece of cultural history.

Your account of your subject is likely to be absorbed into the literature, and may well be adopted by posterity as the definitive account of that particular subject. That's a tremendous responsibility! It's also a tremendous privilege, of course, but most great privileges do come with great responsibilities, not to be taken lightly.

To live up to that responsibility, my experience (so far) is that it's helpful to follow two major principles:

Be thorough

My guess is that anyone conducting *any* kind of historical research will tell you to seek as much documentation as you can find, from multiple sources. One source is good, two are much better, and if more than that are available, by all means pursue those, too. It's often very difficult to state with certainty that a given historical event occurred in a particular way—but the more eyewitness accounts, written records, and other sources you can find to corroborate that event, the more certain you can be. Of course that makes research more difficult—but, luckily, research is the fun part! My experience is that the more effort you put into this phase of the work, the more enjoyable it is.

This idea of pursuing multiple sources is especially important when you're dealing with interviews. Over the years I've interviewed a fair number of Disney veterans myself, and recently more such interviews, conducted by others, have become publicly available, especially with the advent of Didier Ghez's *Walt's People* series. Needless to say, these personal accounts by participants and eyewitnesses are a precious, invaluable resource—*when they're used properly.* There's nothing like direct quotes from "Walt's people" to bring events to vivid, immediate life on the page and to give them a rich historical context. At the same time, the historian needs to be *very* careful about taking the interviewees' statements at face value. Human memory is of course fallible when recalling events that occurred (in some cases) decades earlier—and, in addition, some interviewees are inclined to put their own spin on those events. Many of them have spent the better part of their lives engaged in creative pursuits, and when they sit down with an interviewer, their creativity is still at work!

With this in mind, I think it's a great idea to quote directly from Disney veterans—simply in the sense of reporting their words—but in forming my own picture of events, I always try to check their accounts against other sources. These can include production records or other written materials, or sometimes, other interviews. It's not uncommon for two eyewitnesses to describe the same event in radically different terms.

And sometimes this Rashomon effect can be a valuable historical sidelight in itself, providing a more fully rounded *sense* of some key event in Disney history. But in any case, I think we serve history best when we draw our information from as many different sources as possible.

Follow the trail

This point is directly related to the other one, but in a particular way. In my experience, learning about some aspect of Disney history *always* leads, sooner or later, to learning about some other subject outside the immediate Disney universe. That's a gift—take advantage of it! In my own case, my interest in Disney history overlaps with, but is distinct from, my interest in American film history, in general, during the Golden Age.

My various Disney book projects have afforded me many excuses to extend my research to the Academy's Margaret Herrick Library, the Library of Congress, George Eastman House, the Museum of Modern Art, and other established film-history research facilities. Time after time, that extended search has led to fascinating discoveries. Walt Disney didn't live or work in a vacuum; he was a human being who lived in a particular time and place and engaged with his world in a highly individual and remarkable way.

To see his classic films, in the context of other Hollywood films of his day, is to more fully appreciate both. (Not to mention enjoying an even more extensive banquet of classic film!) And I'm sure that other historians who have a particular taste for early television, or the world of theme parks, or other specialized interests can find similar connections for later phases of Walt's life and career.

But this principle goes far beyond my own comfort zone, or anyone else's for that matter. In the course of Walt Disney's life, his restless spirit of curiosity led him into a wide variety of interests and activities. For that reason, the historian who follows the Disney trail will often find it leading into unexpected territory. Here again, that means both extra work *and* an enriched experience.

I once wrote a book on the Latin American-themed Disney films of the 1940s—initially just because I was fascinated with *Saludos Amigos* and *The Three Caballeros* and wanted to know more about them, but what a learning adventure that turned out to be! The films had been produced in cooperation with the U.S. government's Good Neighbor program during World War II, and in order to understand that context I wound up learning a great deal about the government's home-front activities during the war.

That involved reading some standard historical accounts of the period, but I also benefited from researching primary documents at the National Archives in Washington and (since the agency that commissioned the films was headed by Nelson Rockefeller) at the Rockefeller Archives Center in New York state.

And, since producing the Good Neighbor films required the Disney artists to broaden their knowledge of the various Latin American cultures, I had the opportunity to learn about those cultures myself, particularly their musical traditions. Ultimately, that book became one of the most exhilarating learning experiences of my life. My initial desire to learn more about *Saludos* and *Caballeros* was satisfied, more abundantly than I had ever expected.

Today, my enjoyment of those films (and the many other Disney Good Neighbor films)—enhanced by these additional layers of historical and cultural resonance—is far greater than it was before.

Other books have involved similar voyages of discovery. *Snow White and the Seven Dwarfs* was, of course, produced by the Disney Studio without any input from outside agencies, and my research into its production was drawn almost entirely from internal documentation (and, given that film's vital role in the studio's history, there was *lots* of internal documentation). But it was based on a folk tale that had existed, in many cultures, for centuries beforehand. The tale's history was an important part of the film's history, and in following *that* trail I wound up getting a crash course in folklore—another vast and fascinating discovery.

Pinocchio had a back story of its own, this time based not on a multicultural oral tradition but on a specific work of literature, steeped in Italian culture. That provided me with a great excuse to delve into the Italian traditions surrounding *Pinocchio*—and, in addition, the production and release of the Disney film coincided in a peculiar way with the events of World War II, so once again I found myself considering the film in the context of a wartime perspective. I don't think this principle ever fails: when we set out to learn in depth about a Disney subject, we ultimately gain a broad, fresh, comprehensive view of that subject *and* of the larger world surrounding it. And I think Walt himself would be very happy to see that!

Let me stress again that I set out these thoughts not as a wise old know-it-all, but as someone who is gradually figuring these things out himself, by trial and error. But they seem to be working so far, and they're affording me a thoroughly enjoyable experience into the bargain, so I offer them here in case they're helpful to anyone else.

In recent years there's been an explosion of Disney books, articles, and posts; but even after all of that, I feel the surface has only been scratched. There's still a vast realm of Disney history just waiting to be explored in depth. And I really believe that the more meticulous, conscientious effort the Disney historian puts into his work, the more he will enjoy it—and the more we will all benefit in the long run.

© 2015 J.B. Kaufman

• •

J.B. KAUFMAN [jbkaufman.com] is an author and film historian who has published and lectured extensively on Disney animation, American silent film history, and related topics. Kaufman has presented programs at festivals including the TCM Classic Film Festival, the San Francisco Silent Film Festival, and Le Giornate del Cinema Muto, the distinguished annual silent film festival in Pordenone, Italy, where he contributed to *The Griffith Project* and other retrospectives.

His Disney-related books include:

- *Walt Disney's Silly Symphonies: A Companion to the Classic Cartoon Series* (2016) with Russell Merritt
- *Pinocchio: The Making of the Disney Epic* (2015)
- *Snow White and the Seven Dwarfs: The Art and Creation of Walt Disney's Classic Animated Film* (2012)
- *The Fairest One of All :The Making of Walt Disney's Snow White and the Seven Dwarfs* (2012)
- *South of the Border with Disney: Walt Disney and the Good Neighbor Program, 1941–1948* (2009)

- *Walt in Wonderland: The Silent Films of Walt Disney* (1993) with Russell Merritt

In addition, he has contributed essays to several Disney related books including *Funny Pictures: Animation and Comedy in Studio Era Hollywood* (2011), *50 Years in the Mouse House: The Lost Memoir of One of Disney's Nine Old Men* (2015), *Walt Disney's Mickey Mouse Color Sundays Volumes 1 and 2* (2013), as well as other books including ten volumes of *The Griffith Project* (British Film Institute).

For links to J.B. Kaufman's books, visit:

themeparkpress.com/historians

Jeff Kurtti

Disney Scholarship

We live in a remarkable age of information. We have at our fingertips the collective knowledge and data of centuries. One might think that this access would breed a higher standard, and somewhat more competitive scholarship in any given field. But for students of Disney and other popular culture, a peculiar inverse is the norm. In the age of the internet, "Disney historians" are a dime a dozen.

Much as might be imagined in an auditorium with an open microphone, whoever can get to the mike and speak convincingly (whether accurate or not) captures the discourse. There's a conventional wisdom that if you like something, and can cobble some cohesive sentences together, and post them for people to read, some degree of expertise is inherent, or at least implied.

Nothing could be further from the truth. The internet has bred lazy scholarship, celebrity historians, and armchair experts who would be laughed out of any typical scientific or academic enterprise. I recently spent far too many hours on a web site trying to pull the plug on yet another Disney myth being put forward as "truth" by an overly enthusiastic—and quite ill-informed—fan. (Seriously, his resource was that "a bartender at [the location being discussed] told me".) And don't get me started on the bogus "Walt Quotes" and memes that people excuse with, "Well it *sounds* like something he'd have said."

In their eagerness to be a part of the community, too many people don't treat their own scholarship with gravity, and don't start from the beginning.

In many ways, I think becoming a "Disney historian" is not due to intent as much as a natural inclination. I didn't set out with a goal of being a writer, researcher, author, or scholar on the subject, it just "happened", slowly, and over the course of 30-plus years.

To me, scholarship *follows* characteristic behaviors and attitudes. I'm not sure how much, if any of it, can be taught or learned. But I do have some thoughts about Disney scholarship that I'm happy to share, for those who are inclined to follow such a path.

Examine your motives

Recently, many areas of cultural history have become beset with "fanboi experts". It's easy to see why. Like so many glamorous vocations, the public perception of this life is one of endless Disney Legends ceremonies, movie screenings, D23 Expos, and theme park events. Those things can certainly be a part of the ultimate reward, but they are not a part of the proficiency or discipline required to get there.

I counsel many young friends who claim to be actors. What I come to find out is that fewer than half of them actually are actors. There is a line in a movie called *My Favorite Year* where the swashbuckling hero cries out, "I'm not an actor; I'm a *movie star!*" This is a key and crucial idea that I find in my young thespian pals. They desire fame, or money, or attention. That's someone who wants to be a movie star. Actors need to act just as artists need to paint or musicians need to play. It's *in* them, and needs to be made manifest.

You don't *want* to...

It's the same with Disney, or any kind of cultural or intellectual scholarship, I think. You do it not so much because you want to (although you do, every waking minute); it's more because it's simply a characteristic of your personality and personal culture. You *have* to.

If the study and communication of this subject matter is about your own fame or your own public identity, that is not sufficient—either as a means, or in the final analysis, as an end. Scholarship is *work*. Lots of it. Work that never really stops. I have been reading, researching, interviewing, strategizing, and producing Disney scholarship pretty constantly since about 1977. You will not get rich from it. You will not likely make a living at it.

It means looking through file boxes in library collections and other repositories where you don't exactly feel welcome. It means reading obscure books that no one has checked out for a decade. It means talking to a lot of people. It means dead ends, seemingly wasted time and effort, disappointment, and expense.

It means going to places and examining things, and developing an innate sense of critical thinking about the people, places, and projects; an internal compass that guides your study and your conclusions. It means remaining humble about your knowledge, because the amount you do *not* know about something will *always* exceed what you have been able to learn.

And if your scholarship is sound, all of the above will bring you varying degrees of joy.

If you feel ready to commit to the idea, and are looking for some guidance in the mechanics, read on. Disney scholarship is a lot like any form of creatively-based study, and you'll find the same ideas apply across subjects and interests of many kinds.

Research and sources

As a researcher, the internet is your best friend. It is not, however, your *only* friend. An internet search can be most useful as a kind of road map or infrastructural aid to an overall research strategy. By searching and reading blogs, lists, databases, and wikis, you can gain a general sense, "take the temperature", if you will, of the subject.

A lot of standard information and general resource can be drawn: names, places, dates, and opinions. But each of these elements may be most useful as a starting point for further research.

Taking the recurring and apparent material as a base, and expanding outward, yields the true riches in research. This is background that helps guide you to archives, libraries, books, files, and human beings who can then begin to inform and enhance your understanding and context of a subject.

It is during this process that you should keep a Velcro mind (aka "sticky thinking") to pay attention to repetitions, echoes, overlaps, redundancies, and complete contradictions that will even further develop and enrich your research.

Because the internet is a more accessible and vast *vox populi* than any other resource for research—it is also the most unreliable. Other, older, more established, and more verifiable sources are highly desirable. As in any journalistic effort, multiple sources bring credibility to any information.

And about sources—identifying sources is all-important when looking at things. Of course, books have footnotes and bibliographies, but when using blogs, websites, and the like, it's vital for the researcher todetermine if these sites cite sources—and then the researcher can go find those sources, and further explore.

In addition, the alchemy and algorithm of perception, deduction, and critical thinking by the scholar must constantly come into play; a perpetual cross-reference and cross-check of all the apparent information is imperative.

Start with what's come before

There is a lot of solid Disney scholarship out there, dating from Robert D. Feild's *Art of Walt Disney* in 1942. It's important to learn from all of those who have gone before. Bob Thomas. Pete Martin. Christopher Finch. Frank Thomas and Ollie Johnston. John Canemaker. Brian Sibley. J.B. Kaufman. The collected works of Didier Ghez and his colleagues. The documentary films of Ted Thomas and Kuniko Okubo.

Magazines are a frequently-forgotten research tool, but were, in their time, weekly or monthly treasure troves of contemporary voices. (The caveat being that, as typically commercial material, the messages and information may have been crafted to conform to an acceptable corporate view or specific promotional need of the moment.)

The advent of home video, and especially DVDs, created a profusion of documentary material. Although much of it is no longer readily available, a wealth of it has migrated to YouTube, Vimeo, and other online locations. Frequently, this offers rare opportunities to see and hear firsthand information on a given subject, or examine historic material that had heretofore been almost impossible to see. (And the same caveat as above applies.)

Information needs to be weighed in an overall balance, contextualized, and perpetually cross-referenced, checked, and confirmed (or denied). Too much scholarship is left by the wayside as people rush to publish without seeking *proper* sources. Even eyewitness accounts are often questionable, altered by time, "enhanced" for retelling, and requiring context and corroboration. "That's one of the reasons historians have to be careful," as scholar and author Jim Korkis says, "even if they are getting the information from a first-hand source."

Interviews

First-hand interviews are an amazing resource, and whenever possible, participants and eyewitnesses are highly desirable. As a scholar, it is vital that, prior to conducting an interview, you have done as much research as possible, and are as well-versed on the given topic (and the interview subject) as you can possibly be. Interview subjects know immediately if you are prepared or on a "fishing expedition". It is disrespectful in the extreme to arrive for an interview unprepared.

In conducting the interview, you must allow a certain amount of fluidity. Interviewing is about *listening* carefully, and helping guide memory and detail. Have a "road map" for your interview—but do not be needlessly rigid. Keep the discussion as on topic as possible, but allow your subject to go on tangents, or provide unrequested detail or additional thoughts.

In most cases, I even avoid asking direct questions. Instead, I set a brief scenario, and then ask, "*Tell me about* [that person, that incident, that idea]." Freed from the restriction of the question mark, the subject is then able to reminisce more naturally.

Some basic ideas when interviewing:

- Speak to first-hand sources whenever you can. People who were "in the room" tend to offer the most veracity.

- Trust everyone—and doubt everyone. Because of their age, stature, or accomplishment, you may feel the need to believe as fact every-thing an interviewee offers. You don't have to. As Elizabeth Loftus, a psychologist at the University of California, Irvine, puts it: "Just because someone says something confidently doesn't mean it's true."

- Don't trust everyone's memory. Sometimes firsthand accounts are memories of something told to them rather than experienced by or witnessed by them. In some cases, due to a previous need, a subject may have formulated a compelling memory that didn't happen as they tell it.

- Be wary of people polishing their own legacy. Either by evolution or intent, mighty oaks grow from tiny acorns. I've seen this happen in the course of my career. Over thirty years' time, a sweet, intimate anecdote, fundamentally true, is embellished and re-crafted into the imparting of a legendary event. Over the years, a one-time, sec-ond-hand compliment becomes an oft-repeated pronouncement; one quick sandwich at the Commissary becomes a weekly private luncheon in the boss' private dining room.

- An in-person interview gives you something no amount of document study and file flipping can truly give: tone, inflection, body language, and personal context. You must be able to identify and use this to verify, find connections between ideas, factor in personality and professional position and career context, etc., in order to utilize an interview to its fullest potential.

- Whenever you can, interview more than one person about a subject—especially one that might be murky. There is a *Rashomon* effect to every human memory of a shared or group event. (This is a contradictory interpretation of the same event by different people. The phrase derives from the film *Rashomon*, where the accounts of the witnesses, suspects, and victims of a rape and murder are all different.)

Context

If Disney is your field, it is by no means a narrow one. In order to create for yourself a thorough basis for understanding Disney, the breadth of your knowledge should at least include a fundamental understanding of Hollywood history and culture (and, biographically and culturally, the men and women who created it), art history and techniques, animation principles and history, and the history of world's fairs, amusement piers, and county fairs.

Any subject that Disney touched in any medium, and any technique he used to communicate, is a valid and substantive field of study. I owe my knowledge of Abraham Lincoln and understanding of the golden age of nautical piracy to interests created by my Disney fascination.

What this background provides is an ability to contextualize. Facts and data are thought-provoking only to the degree that they have meaning, derived from the act of placing the context that makes facts interesting. The element of greatest fascination often is not *when* or *where*, but *how* and *why*.

By the same token, a lack of proper context undermines your authority. A recent documentary on Walt Disney's life suffered from a frequent lack of contextual relationship. Several of the generalist "media experts" and "historians", due to their superficial knowledge, missed critical connections between Walt's life, personality characteristics, and the resulting work; conversely, they freely took the zeitgeist of past eras (warts and all), placed a 21st century sensibility over it, and held Walt Disney responsible for the disparity. This is poor scholarship, plain and simple.

Different eras, different projects, and different personalities all carry different and intertwining *context*. You role as a scholar demands an examination and communication of these manifold complexities and their relationship to your subject, in order for your reader, viewer, or student to process and understand the importance of its meaning.

Connections and conclusions

As I mentioned earlier, scholarship is an alchemy and algorithm of perception, deduction, and critical thinking by the scholar; a perpetual cross-reference and cross-check of all the apparent information is imperative. A good historian will make connections, highlight ideas, point to (but not draw explicitly) conclusions.

Engaging your audience in acts of analysis and critical thinking makes them not only more informed about the subject, it enriches their sense of entertainment, excitement, and discovery as they make a learning journey alongside you. Where possible, take your own persona, and particularly your first-person voice, *out* of your work. It will help ensure that your own identity is absent from the discourse, without removing your expertise or scholarship.

Avoid making definitive statements of fact when there is not sufficient evidence, personal experience, or erudition to support them. A recent biography, brimming with factual detail and rich with erudite context, undermined its entire reliability by making broad absolute statements about its subject's personal life. These statements were not based on first-hand evidence or eyewitness accounts, or even informed observation or assessment of the evidence that was present.

Surviving relatives and colleagues, in fact, *refuted* these opinions and assessments. But apparently in an effort to draw some element of salaciousness to the proceedings, the author instead called every other conclusion in his work into question by offering sweeping declarations of personal (and unsubstantiated) opinion as fact.

Gain a storehouse of knowledge

You must gain and nurture a storehouse of ready knowledge, a fundamental understanding of the timeline, people, places, and projects of the subject of your expertise. *Time* magazine recently reported:

> The ready availability of search engines is changing the way we use our memories, reported psychologist Betsy Sparrow of Columbia University in a study published in *Science* last year. When people expect to have future access to information, Sparrow wrote, "they have lower rates of recall of the information itself and enhanced recall instead for where to access it". It's good to know where to find the information you need—but decades of cognitive science research shows that skills like critical thinking and problem-solving can be developed only in the context of factual knowledge. In other words, you've got to have knowledge stored in your head, not just in your computer.

It's not a contest

Like any field of scholarship, there is often a sense of hierarchy, jealousy, and competition among Disney historians. This will not change, but it is certainly not good for anyone, or the discipline itself.

Certain individuals have become acknowledged experts in particular areas of Disney scholarship, and that specialization tends to be respected and used as a resource by others across this academic field. But there is no real "officialization" or "certification" of Disney historians, except the trust of The Walt Disney Company or the Disney family.

The only other "official" evidence is a body of work, a compendium of projects, writings, presentations, or other similar evidence of responsible expertise and erudition. This commendation is only gained over time, and with profuse effort.

The wonderful thing is that the community of serious Disney scholarship is a collegial and munificent one, and those within it are extraordinarily enthusiastic and generous with other historians. If you are earnest and committed to this field, seek out those whose work you have consumed and admired, and ask for their guidance and input.

Most of all, Disney historians are like ministers of faith. They want nothing more than to put forward the word, celebrate the culture, and share their passion for the subject.

© 2015 Jeff Kurtti

• •

JEFF KURTTI is the author of more than 25 books, a prolific documentarian, and a curatorial and themed experience director. He worked for

Walt Disney Imagineering, the theme park design division of The Walt Disney Company, and then for the Corporate Special Projects department of Disney. He was creative director, content consultant, and media producer for the Walt Disney Family Museum. Now entering his third decade of such work, he continues to consult for several divisions of the Disney company on a variety of projects.

His Disney-related books include:

- *The Art of Walt Disney World* (2009) with Bruce Gordon
- *Walt Disney's Imagineering Legends and the Genesis of the Disney Theme Park* (2008) with Bruce Gordon
- *The Art of Disneyland* (2005) with Bruce Gordon
- *Disney Villains: The Top Secret Files* (2005)
- *Since the World Began: Walt Disney World The First Twenty-Five Years* (1996)
- *Disney Dossiers: Files of Character from the Walt Disney Studios* (2006)

Other books include *A Bug's Life: The Art and Making of an Epic of Miniature Proportions* (1998), *The Art of Mulan* (1998), *Dinosaur: The Evolution of an Animated Feature* (2000), *Treasure Planet: A Voyage of Discovery* (2002), *The Art of the Princess and the Frog* (2009), and *The Art of Tangled* (2010).

For links to Jeff Kurtti's books, visit:

themeparkpress.com/historians

David Lesjak

I became interested in Walt Disney back in 1981, when I purchased and began collecting *Walt Disney's Comics & Stories* comic books at the local comic shop. A year or so after selling that collection, I started to collect all forms of what was referred to at the time as Disneyana—Disney collectibles from the 1930s through the 1960s. I didn't have a focus; I just collected what appealed to me. Soon after I caught the collecting bug, two significant things happened that affected what I bought and how I approached the hobby.

Revelation #1

One day, a friend who ran a comic book/toy shop bought a great reference book for me at a thrift store. The title of the book was *Disneyana: Walt Disney Collectibles* and it was written in 1974 by Cecil Munsey. When I opened the book for the first time and began thumbing through the pages, my eyes lit up like the proverbial Christmas tree. I was in awe. Hundreds and hundreds of great vintage, pre-1945 Disney collectibles were showcased, along with some of the related background information.

Looking back, I can now say Munsey's book was the spark that ignited the rocket that shot me into the hobby at the speed of sound—those great-looking Disney items from the 1930s—the toys, books, premiums, school supplies, food products, figurines, and much, much, more. All of the items were exceptionally pleasing to the eye.

I loved the graphics. Mickey and Minnie Mouse, Donald Duck, Dippy Dawg (aka Goofy), Horace Horsecollar, Clarabelle Cow, and Pluto, with the little triangular sliver of white in their eyes, (known as pie-cut eyes because the missing piece of the pupil looks like a piece of pie), appealed to me in a way I cannot explain even today. I was hooked.

After reading Munsey's book, I decided I had to find a focus—I was spending too much on too diverse a selection of items. I decided pre-1938 Disneyana with a preference to the 1930s Mickey Mouse Club and Christmas-related items, as well as anything connecting the Walt Disney Studios to World War II would be my main areas of focus. I decided to collect the former items because I love the graphic designs of the 1930s characters, and the latter because as a teen I had always been interested in World War II history.

Revelation #2

The second thing to happen was the 1983 Victoria Cartoon Festival. The friend who bought me the Munsey book asked if I wanted to go with him to that convention. Having never been, I said yes. While I was wandering the sales room in one of the hotel's cavernous ballrooms, I came across a gentleman who was showing other conventioneers a large portfolio of original Disney art. "What was this?" I asked myself.

As I inched forward to within earshot, I heard the gentleman giving those gathered in the semi-circle around him the history of the art he was offering for sale. I was caught in his spell. I had never seen animation art in person before (remember, this was before the general availability of the internet). I couldn't believe you could buy a production drawing from *Snow White and the Seven Dwarfs*, conceptual art from *Fantasia*, or even the art from a 1940s Disney comic book.

Disney collector friend #1

After members of the crowd purchased some of the art and others finished asking questions, I was the only one left standing in front of the man and his portfolio of beautiful things. He asked me if I had any questions. I had plenty.

Where did he find the art he sold? Did he have more art for sale? Did he own a store or gallery? How did he know the history of the art he was selling? How did he know so much about the different types of art? Was he friends with the artists who created the art? How long had he been selling cartoon character art and was he a collector as well as a dealer?

The gentleman, it turns out, was Dennis Books, the owner of the Comic Character Shop, which at the time was, in his words, "the oldest continuously run cartoon collectibles store in the United States". As we parted company later that day, Dennis told me to visit him at his shop in Pioneer Square the next time I was in Seattle.

Several months later I took Dennis up on his offer. That led to an invitation to visit him at his house. The shop was amazing. His house? Well, there are no words to describe what I saw when I entered the front door for the first time—it was like I had entered the three-dimensional version of Munsey's book. Rooms filled with display cases loaded with literally hundreds and hundreds of pre-1945 Disney items. And the walls—literally every square inch of vertical space was covered in framed artwork, all from the 1930s and 1940s.

The night of my first visit Dennis pulled literally dozens and dozens of pieces of animation art from storage. He explained the significance of each piece in the realm of Disney history, and he even knew the names of the artists who created many of the pieces. I was hypnotized by the beauty of each piece of art: drawings, conceptual art, storyboards, backgrounds, production drawings, animation roughs, publicity and presentation art, film promotional art, and comic book art. It was all there.

Dennis also let me thumb through dozens of archival binders filled with rare paper items and he allowed to me to look through bookshelves loaded with every type of vintage Disney publication you could imagine: there were pristine copies of the *Mickey Mouse Magazine*, *Walt Disney's Comics & Stories*, and rows and rows of books—actually, there were lots and lots of books.

Dennis claimed to own every Disney book published from 1930–1945, including story, coloring, paint, activity, paper doll, humor/joke, and give-aways. And how could I forget the foreign Disney books: over a hundred and fifty 1930s British books alone, along with dozens of other foreign editions from France, Germany, Italy, Russia, and several South American countries.

Since the chance encounter at the cartoon festival, the visit to his shop and then his house, Dennis has become not only one of my best friends but a mentor as well. He is a wealth of information and a source that is unrivaled. Dennis not only introduced me to the "Who's Who" of Disney artists—from Carl Barks to Gustav Tenggren and everyone in-between—but because he met many of them in person, he was able to share stories with me about those great animators and illustrators.

Dennis and I have been friends now for over thirty years, and every time I visit with him at his home I see something I have never seen before or I learn something new about a vintage Disney item or piece of art. He has graciously let me use his vast archive for research purposes and he's let me photograph rare and wonderful items for inclusion in articles I have written.

While Dennis was Disney friend number one, I have since accumulated a collection of other Disney friends. Some are casual collectors, while others are more serious. Some are writers, while others just like to research Disney history.

I even have one friend who doesn't collect any Disney merchandise, new or old—he tells anyone who asks that his collection is composed of friends who collect Disneyana. It doesn't matter which category my friends fit into. They all enrich my life and many have assisted me at some point in time with my research and writing.

Cracking the market

I graduated from a technical college with a diploma in Broadcast Communications, in 1985. I landed a job right away working in the newsroom of one of the local radio stations. I worked that job for maybe one year before I decided I wasn't enjoying my chosen profession. I didn't like that you could only spend a limited amount of time researching and writing a story that was no more than twenty or thirty seconds in length, before you moved onto the next one. I decided I was more a print journalism type of guy. I liked to spend time researching my topic and then writing a lengthy piece revealing all the great information I had discovered. I quit my radio job and got hired by a telecommunications giant. While I still wasn't writing professionally, I enjoyed the work I did at the telco much more than I had the radio gig.

My father told me early in life to turn my hobby into a business. He said I'd enjoy the work and I might get paid to do it. He was definitely right on the first account. I followed his advice. In 1987, I decided I would try and get my first piece of Disney-related writing published. It wasn't easy landing that first gig. No one wanted to go with an unpublished author. But I persevered and succeeded in convincing Keith Kaonis and his wife, Donna, who were the editors of a magazine called *Collector's Showcase*, to run a story I had written on *Snow White* collectibles that also tied-in with the 50th anniversary of the film. I can't tell you how excited I was to finally see my first Disney article in print and the byline near the article's opening paragraph.

Since that first magazine article, I have written dozens more for a wide range of publications including *Disney News, Collector's Eye, Inside Collector, Toy Trader, Antique Weekly, Antiques and Collectibles, Military Trader, America in World War II*, and Primedia's number-one rated *World War II*, where I not only wrote cover and feature stories but had my own column as well.

A couple of the publications paid a decent amount, but in most instances the pay wasn't the greatest. That was okay, though, because I wasn't writing for a living. The telco job paid the mortgage and put groceries on the table. The satisfaction I received from writing about Disney came with sharing my knowledge with others, and of course, the coveted byline.

The first book

Over the years I amassed a large collection of Disney reference books. Some are well known, while others are obscure. The one thing I noticed in pretty much all of those books was the lack of material related to Walt Disney's role in World War II. I knew the studio produced some training films and combat insignia and I knew Walt took a hit financially because the war closed foreign markets to his films. Other than one chapter in Munsey's book, however, most Disney reference books glanced over this topic with just a couple of pages or a few scant paragraphs. Surely there was more to this chapter in Disney's history.

Then I discovered Richard Shale's book *Donald Duck Joins Up*. The book was the culmination of Shale's research and was in actual fact his university thesis. The thesis was a great resource, but I still wanted more. I had a large collection of Disney war-related memorabilia by this time and none of the reference books I had, including Shale's, really addressed or provided background on any of the artifacts I owned. I decided the time had come for me to write a book on the topic and become the source for that information.

I approached The Walt Disney Company to see if they would give their permission for the book. I was told by one executive there was no market for the book I wanted to write. Undeterred, I contacted Disney's Legal Department. They said I couldn't self-publish the book and I needed to have a publisher for them to consider authorizing such a venture.

Given that the genre I was writing about had a limited audience, I knew no large publishing house would be interested. I didn't think there would be a big enough market for a mainstream publisher to get the type of return they would be looking for. So, with some trepidation and the fear of a cease-and-desist order from the House of Mouse, I decided to self-publish with the mindset that whatever would happen, would happen.

The driving force behind my book was that I had information to share and I wanted to share it. I had no delusions about becoming rich or even making my costs back. I just wanted to share my knowledge and get others interested in this amazing time in Disney history.

Research

The first thing I did was inventory and take photographs of all the artifacts in my collection. Not only did I want to cover Walt's wartime studio contributions, but I also wanted the book to be a visual guide to all the wonderful items that were produced in support of those serving in the military, and those contributing on the home front. I wanted to produce a reference book where other Disney history enthusiasts and collectors could learn about the history of the items they may have seen previously or owned or wanted to own.

For every item in my collection I noted the artifact's dimensions, copyright notation, the name of the manufacturer, year of production, number of items if they were part of a set, and any background information that was available.

My sources for background information on the artifacts were varied. Some information came from print media articles and advertisements, while other useful bits were provided by friends. Dennis was one of several who gave me access to his material. For example, he owns a great brochure loaded with details about all of the Stensgaard Disney war bond posters. The brochure listed all fifty-four of the posters the company produced as well as the method used to produce them, along with publicity material giving examples of how the posters could be used on the home front. Through Dennis' generosity, the Stensgaard material made its way into the book and now, for the first time, readers would know the history and background of those items.

The advent of the internet has been a boon to collectors. Auction sites like eBay, Heritage, and others have provided many great items for my collection, while lightening my wallet in the process. I have also used these auction sites as an information resource. I have a definite budget when it comes to collecting and there have been a few occasions where I have not been the successful bidder on an item I have wanted.

Before the auction ends, I always make a copy of the photo of the item and the corresponding description. I record the information for research purposes only. I have never used an image in my books from an online source without first asking permission. That said, I have used the information obtained in auction listings in my book. I may not own the item, but that doesn't mean I can't alert others to the existence of that piece.

One great war-related cache I purchased at auction was a series of scrapbook pages from the war years that had belonged to a member of Disney's Ink and Paint Department. The former owner hadn't just pasted one or two items onto the scrapbook pages. She had pasted literally dozens of items on each page. The memos, inter-office communications, and bulletin board announcements were glued along their top edges, one above another. This trove provided a lot of interesting background that I included in the second edition of my war book. None of the information contained in that scrapbook had ever been published before and appeared in my book for the first time.

Recently, I have been purchasing items that belonged to Bob Jones, a member of Disney's Model Department at the Hyperion location of the Disney Studio. These artifacts are being sold piecemeal, but they are rare and provide great information on the department and the projects they worked on. These photos will be included in another book I am writing.

Other internet sites have also provided resource information. I located details about some matchbook covers featuring Disney insignia designs on a matchbook collector's webpage, while a comic book dealer's website provided some background related to a series of bubble-gum cards featuring Disney insignia designs. Remember, though, just because material is published on the internet doesn't make the information true.

In both the aforementioned examples, I used the information from the collector's sites to search for and ultimately locate related newspaper ads for both products. Always try and corroborate new information from multiple sources, if possible.

Another source of great information for this project was The Walt Disney Company staff newsletters from the war years. I was able to review almost every single issue of *The Bulletin* through the generosity of several friends who have copies in their collections.

I also belong to several Facebook groups and internet collector groups. Members of those communities have provided information to me as well. In one instance, Les Hughes, a friend from one of the military collector sites I belong to, sent me copies of correspondence related to the insignia Disney created for the OSS (Office of Strategic Services—they were the precursor to the CIA). Not only did Les send along the information for me to use, but he also sent a photo of the related patch.

Other friends, including Dave Kaufman and Sam Grabarski, sent along images of their authentic Disney combat insignia patches for me to use. I sent a request out to all of my collecting friends. Many responded with information and photos of items from their collections.

After cataloging all of the items I owned, and other artifacts I knew about but didn't own, I assigned them to the various chapters. I decided my book was going to be broken down into six chapters that included topics like The Studio, The Home Front, Insignia, and so forth. I envisioned the book as having a chapter filled with information about each one of the particular topics, followed by a section with details about all of that chapter's related artifacts.

The format seemed logical and I think worked wonderfully. In the chapter related to The Studio, for example, the reader could read about what was happening at the studio when war broke out, and then in the pages following that particular chapter they could learn about all the related artifacts like memos, ID badges, staff newsletters, etc., that were produced at the studio during the war years.

As I mentioned previously, I use a wide range of sources for gathering information including both free and pay newspaper and magazine sites. I've found the free sites just as good as and sometimes even better than the ones that ding your wallet.

Just the other day I counted-up the number of digital magazine, newspaper, technical, and trade journal articles I have downloaded from various sites over the years. I was astounded by the final tally: the number was close to 4000! And to think these articles only cover the years 1923–1945. This number doesn't include the physical magazines and newspaper articles I have purchased over the years.

Some of the articles I've downloaded contain no new information, but if you search long enough and look close enough, you can and will find useful material no one else has discovered or written about previously. Sometimes a lengthy article might have nothing you're looking for at that particular moment. Other times there might just be one or two sentences of new and useful material. And sometimes you'll hit the motherlode and the whole article is crammed with the new information you were looking for.

You just have to be patient and persistent.

Some words of advice regarding research. Make sure you properly note all of your resources. I always create footnotes as I write the manuscript. The footnote I create at that point in time might not be in the proper format with all of the pertinent details, but I record enough information at the time to know where to get the rest of the citation when I have the time to do so.

If you create files on your computer containing research or print off paper files for your filing cabinet, make sure you note your sources at that time, be it an auction or article or online archive or whatever. What you think is useless information today might be useful to you or a fellow researcher you're helping at some point in the future. I have gone back into my files and have actually pulled material for friends that I had discovered years prior but never used.

Your friends will love you because you'll not only be able to provide them with great information they can use, but you'll be able to provide them the proper source citation, too.

One thing I've found useful when conducting research is to look at the sources other authors have used. Sometimes I'll review the author's source material before I actually read their book. I have discovered several new institutions and archives by seeing where they've gotten their information. And what's also interesting about this is that particular author may have used only one tiny bit of material from the source document they referenced in their manuscript, and they could have left out a whole lot more that may be useful to you at some point in time.

One person I need to tip my hat to and thank again publicly is researcher Paul Anderson. He has the largest archive of Disney research material outside of the Disney Archives. While writing my war book, he graciously invited me to his house to conduct research. I came home from that trip with dozens and dozens of pages of useful and important information.

It pays to cultivate friendships in the Disney history community. Most members of that group are more than willing to help out and share information. A lot of us have been at this hobby for a very long time and have huge archives of material.

Writing

I live in a very busy house with several children and pets. During daylight hours there is a lot of hustle and bustle under our roof and it can get quite noisy. I cannot write in a noisy environment. I have to be in a quiet space so I can concentrate and not lose any thoughts or ideas as I bang away at the keyboard. Because of this, I do the majority of my writing at night after the kids are in bed.

When I started writing the manuscript for my war book, I created headings for the different chapters in a Word document. Then, I went through all of my research and transcribed, copied, or pasted that information into the related chapter. I don't worry about the flow of a chapter until much later in the writing process. I don't set out to write a pretty-looking manuscript from the onset.

At the start, I just transfer the research material into the chapter and then I go back later and add, delete, and edit the material as necessary. My work starts off quite jumbled, but the text is refined as I go through the different iterations. What is important to me is to get the source material into the chapter of the book it needs to be in, and then once the material is there, I can manipulate the words as needed.

I've also developed a habit of reading my work out loud as I edit the text. This probably relates back to my training as a broadcast journalist. I guess I've always figured if the text sounds good when read aloud the words will make equal sense when someone is silently reading them.

Here's a neat trick I picked up from another Disney researcher a long time ago. As I write, if I can't remember a fact or a name or some other bit of info, I type the letters "asdf" as a marker where the information will eventually need to go. That way I can carry on with whatever text I am writing and I am not distracted by information I would need to go searching for.

I find this keeps the text flowing from my brain to my fingers. Later that night or the next day or even two weeks down the road I do a search in the document for "asdf". The computer will take me to all the instances where the notation appears in the text. I can then do whatever further research is necessary to complete that particular sentence or paragraph.

Stay away from using the word "it" over and over. I've always considered "it" the lazy way out. Describe whatever "it" happens to be. Your readers will be grateful and your text will be richer and more interesting to read. I've always disliked the words "thus" and "that" as well. Personal preferences.

And please, please remember to back up your manuscript. Every week I save my research to multiple devices: my desktop hard drive, a standalone hard drive, and recently I have also started to save any projects to their own flash drive as well. And as you sit in front of your computer writing, make sure you hit the save button frequently. You never know when the power will go out or your computer will crash.

Getting paid

When I wrote the first edition of my war book, *Toons at War*, my good friend Mike Sturba did the layout for me in Pagemaker. Mike ran a desktop publishing company at the time. Once the book was laid out and proofread and ready to be printed, we agreed on the printing cost per book. Mike printed up the books and spiral bound them. We ran the operation as a print-on-demand venture. That way I had no inventory to worry about.

I would order ten books at a time. When I needed more, I just emailed Mike and he'd have additional copies to me within a week or so.

I sold copies of the book at Disney collector meetings, through one of my blogs, and on eBay. I sold over 1000 copies of the book. Not bad for a little side venture that one Disney executive said there was no market for. I look back on that first edition of the book with pride. It may look a tad amateurish, being spiral bound and all, but the book received overwhelming positive feedback. The only complaint was related to the binding—but at the time it was the only option available to me. And the mice in the Disney Legal Department never pursued action against me. For that I am grateful.

The book has since undergone a revision, a second printing, and a title change. *Service With Character. The Disney Studio and World War II* continues to do well, both in print and e-book formats. I have since released another book, *In the Service of the Red Cross. Walt Disney's Early Adventures 1918-1919*, and I have three more in the works.

I'd be remiss not to include one more shout-out. Bob McLain, the owner of Theme Park Press, has been a godsend to us Disney history geeks. He has published both of my books. His company has published many other worthwhile Disney-themed books that no other publisher would have taken on because of the limited reach most of these books have. Bob is easy to work with and he pays a great royalty. If you have an interesting Disney topic, send him an email. He can be reached by at bob@themeparkpress.com Nothing ventured, nothing gained, as the cliché goes.

The last chapter

Write about Disney history because you're passionate about the topic. Don't expect to become rich, because you won't. Don't even expect to get paid very often. Compared to the glory days of the late 1980s and early 1990s, the internet has virtually wiped out all of the specialty magazines and trade papers that used to be interested in Disney history articles.

Be inspired by others. If you want to research and write about Disney history, read books written by other writers in that genre. My favorite Disney authors are Michael Barrier, John Canemaker, Didier Ghez, JB Kaufman, Jim Korkis, Tim Susanin, and Bob Thomas. Their work is always interesting to read and their research is impeccable.

Publicize yourself and your work. Join Facebook groups and pages. Start your own blog. Become a podcaster. I'm a co-administrator of the Facebook page Friends of the Walt Disney Family Museum and I'm the administrator of the Facebook page Disney and the War. I also moderate a Disney section on the USMilitariaForum.com website.

Cultivate contacts through these ventures. I receive emails all the time because of my involvement with these communities. I've had the children and grand-children of former Disney staff members email me because they saw a post I created or a comment I've left somewhere on the internet. These contacts are great sources. Once you've established a rapport with them, they'll usually share all the material they have with you.

I was given access to a huge cache of material because one of artist Hank Porter's children contacted me about some material they had. Porter worked in the Publicity Department from 1936–1951. Walt Disney referred to him as a "one man art department". The three Porter children had a lot of material, which they generously shared with me: family photos, studio photos and memos, letters, original art, magazine and newspaper clippings, and more. The material was so vast and interesting, and the two surviving Porter children gave such great interviews, I decided to write Porter's biography.

And finally, write about topics no one else has covered. Try not to repeat the same old stories. Bring something new to the table. Be different. Be engaging. Be helpful. Contribute. And most importantly, have fun.

I hope you've found this piece interesting. If you ever have any questions, feel free to drop me an email: WaltDisneyResearch@yahoo.com.

© 2015 David Lesjak

● ●

DAVID LESJAK [vintagedisneymemorabilia.blogspot.com] has been writing about the history of Walt Disney and his studio since the mid-1980s. In 2007, Walt Disney's daughter, the late Diane Disney Miller, asked Lesjak to join the staff of the Walt Disney Family Museum as a consultant, special projects. He loaned the museum items from his collection for display in the museum's war gallery, conducted personal research for Diane, and has lectured at the museum's *Fantasia*-inspired theater.

Lesjak owns one of the largest collections of Disney WW II-related material in the world and a large collection of vintage 1930s Disneyana. He also maintains an extensive archive of original Disney research material from the 1930s and 1940s as well as a Facebook page (Friends of the Walt Disney Family Museum) and Facebook group (Disney and the War).

His Disney-related books include:

- *In the Service of the Red Cross: Walt Disney's Early Adventures 1918-1919* (2015)
- *Service with Character: The Disney Studios and World War II* (2014)
- *Toons at War* (2000)

For links to David Lesjak's books, visit:

themeparkpress.com/historians

Todd James Pierce

Preparing for the Interview

I should probably start with this story: the first formal interview I conducted many, many years ago was with Buzz Price, the man who did much of the original SRI land use and feasibility reports for Walt Disney when he was looking to build an amusement park in southern California. Buzz's research would place the park in Anaheim and his economic projections would prove useful in attracting lessees and sponsoring companies into an unproven venture.

When I was growing up, my grandmother had worked for The Walt Disney Company, so I knew my way around company history—or at least I thought I did. During that first interview, I discovered that, though I had a good general understanding of company history, I didn't yet have a strong enough specific understanding of Buzz Price's involvement with Walt Disney to manage a good interview.

In short, with many questions, I embarrassed myself. I felt more like an amateur than someone thoughtfully trying to explore and preserve the history of The Walt Disney Company.

I should also point out that this was before the wonderful explosion of useful books and websites and open archival materials in the early 2000s. This was before the *Walt's People* series, before Buzz published his memoirs, and before Buzz's papers were archived at the University of Central Florida.

I thought I'd done a good job in preparing for that interview, but in truth, I hadn't done nearly enough. And Buzz let me know it more than once.

It would be a few months before I did my next interview (with art director Bill Martin), but in those intervening months I started to think long and hard about how to effectively prepare for an interview, a process that I keep updating. So in writing up my entry for this book, I'm listing some practical steps that may help you in preparing for an interview.

Realize that your interview is one piece of the puzzle

Most lead animators, art directors, engineers, architects, and cast members have been interviewed many times. As best I can tell—in magazines, newspapers, video, and so forth—Ward Kimball was interviewed about 150 times. Realize that your interview will be more valuable if you ask unique questions. Ward Kimball, for example, told the story of attending the *Snow White* premiere in at least twenty interviews. In virtually all of these, Kimball focuses on the audience's emotional reaction to the film. If your interview simply records another version of the *Snow White* premiere story, focusing on the audience's reaction, it doesn't add anything new to the historical record.

Perhaps you want to include familiar stories in your interview, especially as a starting point, but in terms of historians collectively preserving the larger scope of history, look for ways to branch off from the familiar story into areas not yet covered in other interviews or books. Again, using Ward Kimball's experience at the *Snow White* premiere as an example, possible good questions to branch off from the familiar story might include: Did you, Mr. Kimball, notice a difference in Walt's mood before and after the premiere? What did other animators say about the screening once it was over? Can you describe how the premiere changed the studio in the day's following its success?

In each interview, I always try to expand the historical record in some way, to find information, experiences, anecdotes that haven't yet been recorded. I may go down familiar avenues with an interviewee, but during the interview, I'm always looking for ways to help our discussion move into stories—or new aspects of familiar stories—not yet preserved.

Conduct research

Back when I first started interviewing art directors and animators, we didn't have the wealth of digital databases and electronic resources available today. When I first started interviewing, I used to mark up each book I read, each copy of the *E-Ticket Magazine*, each old Xeroxed newspaper article with yellow sticky notes that indexed information in a way that allowed me to easily find key topics. Today the process of researching a potential interviewee is much easier.

Here is a list of resources that I regularly use in preparing for an interview. Keep in mind that my research interests are in mid-century activity (1940s–1960s). If you're interested in, say, Pixar, some of these resources may not work for you, but you'll get the general idea of how the process works.

Let's say that I'm going to interview Animator X about his work in the 1950s.

- **Existing interviews**

  The first thing I do when preparing for an interview is to track down all interviews that my subject has already given. These may be published or collected in an archive. I will usually track down interviews with friends who were close associates of the person I want to interview as well. If Animator X's two best friends at the studio were Animator Y and Z, I'll track down interviews with Y and Z.

- **The *Walt's People* series and other interview books**

  The *Walt's People* series is an extremely valuable resource in terms of collecting raw information about individuals who worked at The Walt Disney Company. At the time I'm writing this, the series has seventeen volumes, probably around 5,000 pages of interviews. My friend Didier Ghez has assembled this unequaled resource. For each of the books in the *Walt's People* series, I own both a paper and a digital copy. I will read the paper copy, sometimes making notes. But I'll use the digital (Kindle) copy as a type of searchable database. In this, I'll look for Animator X's name in each volume, perhaps the films on which he worked as well.

  Along with the *Walt's People* series, I'll also look for Animator X's name in electronic (Kindle) copies of other interview or interview-centered collections, such as the *Vault of Walt* series and the *Working with Disney* series. I will also search electronic versions of major Disney biographies, such as those by Michael Barrier and Neal Gabler. To the best of my knowledge, the Bob Thomas biographies are still only available as physical books, but on Amazon, if you use the "Search Inside This Book" function, you can locate any inclusion of Animator X's name. You will likely need the physical book to check the information in context. You can also use Google Books to perform many of these same "Search Inside This Book" tasks.

  I will repeat this process with other books—sometimes purchasing new electronic titles—until I feel that I've exhausted the book resources that strongly speak to the life and work of Animator X.

- **Google search**

  Books, generally, are the best source of information in pretty much any field. Books are edited, usually, by multiple people. Sometimes books are fact-checked by experts, particularly those books published by large, commercial houses. A person writing a book will often spend years on the subject and likely have a strong insider's view of his or her material. Once I've assembled the book-related material on my subject, I will turn to the internet. The internet has some highly-reliable resources, such as Michael Barrier's website, but also some less-than-reliable resources, such as various fan discussion forums. I'd usually want to see what was out there on the web before assembling my interview topics and questions. But with the web,

I proceed carefully, understanding that internet sources can have a lower level of reliability than other published sources.

In preparing a simple Google search, I'd likely use quotation marks to capture a phrase, such as "Animator X" (in quotation marks) to ensure that the search results include only entries with the exact phrase Animator X. I'd also likely exclude words that produce unhelpful results. For example, I'd likely include "-pin -pins" to remove any entry that has either the word "pin" or "pins", as no doubt Animator X has inspired a number of trading pins and the pin sites won't help me better understand the work or personal life of Animator X.

- **Newspaper databases**

There are two main Newspaper databases that I regularly use: ProQuest Historical and Newspapers.com

ProQuest is a digital database that collects major newspapers, such as *New York Times, Los Angeles Times, San Francisco Chronicle,* and so forth. It is searchable by target words, date range, and article type. For example, you can narrow down your search to pull up only reviews of *Snow White* from 1938. You can also search any inclusion of "Animator X" (using quotes, again) in the history of a newspaper. ProQuest subscriptions are likely too expensive for most individuals. But many colleges and universities have institutional subscriptions. Often you can use these databases for free at public computers in a university library. ProQuest manages about forty historic newspapers. Universities will likely not have subscriptions to all ProQuest titles. The two most important for Disney-related research are *Los Angeles Times* and *New York Times.* The next three would probably be *San Francisco Chronicle, Wall Street Journal,* and *Washington Post.*

Newspapers.com is one of a few databases that collects historical material from local papers. In specific terms, *ProQuest* has *Los Angeles Times,* but Newspapers.com has the small city papers from Pasadena, Long Beach, and Pomona. The regional papers are far more likely to carry personality pieces (i.e., interviews) with local artists.

- **Google Books**

For me, Google Books is hit or miss. It collects scanned copies of published books and old magazines. Sometimes—particularly in the magazine listings—I come across interesting material that will help in developing topics for an interview. But almost always, Google Books will only offer a "snippet" preview of the material (for reasons of copyright), and I'll need to track down a physical copy of the book or magazine that interests me, through interlibrary loan.

- **My own database**

  If you're just starting out with your own interviews, you probably don't have a wealth of unique information to feed into a personal database. I know I didn't, back when I first interviewed Buzz Price. But over the years I've collected typed manuscripts, old magazine articles, letters, inter-office correspondence, company newsletters, unpublished interviews from friends, and so forth. With most of these materials—and honestly, this is still an ongoing process—I've created searchable PDFs of the material so that my own hard drive becomes a personal database. It's fairly easy to create searchable PDFs. You will need to scan paper documents into PDF form. You'll also need to use a program to make the documents OCR (optical character recognition) readable. To do this, you will likely need Adobe Acrobat Pro. It's a fairly easy process. But as with the ProQuest databases, Acrobat Pro is an expensive resource, one you may not wish to own personally. But also like the ProQuest databases, Acrobat Pro is often loaded on computers in university libraries that are available to the public.

Prepare the interview topics

Usually I'll order my topics or questions with a general chronological organization. That's an easy way to focus an interview. But with that, I might pull some questions, either to the beginning or the end of the interview. For example, if I knew that Animator X had a lot to say about *Alice in Wonderland*, I might start with that as a means of creating interview space in which the answers have a fullness to them, a sense of story defined by the details. If I wanted to ask about a sensitive topic, I might also hold off on that until the end of the interview. For example, if I knew that Animator X spent a year developing *Chanticleer*, a Disney project that was never produced, I might wait until the end of the interview to approach that topic in case Animator X has some strong, negative feelings about the experience of working on that film.

Along with ordering the topics, I will almost always bring visual or auditory aids with me. Photos are a fantastic way to help situate an interview subject into the past. I might also use audio. For example, if I had previously interviewed Animator X's best friend, Animator Y, I might bring along a two- or three-minute audio clip of my Animator Y interview. It's been my experience that people respond strongly to the voice of a friend, even if that person is not physically in the room with them.

Sometimes I just prepare a list of topics, to keep the conversation open. Other times—particularly if I'm talking with a person who has been interviewed many times before—I'll prepare questions, primarily to make sure that our session cuts into new ground. If I prepare questions, I make sure that they are open ended. Usually a question that requires a yes/no response does little to advance the preservation of history. Generally, I try to craft questions that invite the subject to tell a story or at least discuss an event with concrete details. Again, with Ward Kimball as an example, I might ask: Can you tell me how *Snow White*'s success changed how you thought about animation, how it changed how you approached later feature assignments?

Review your subject's work

One of the things I enjoy doing, especially the day before an important interview, is to review my subject's work. That may be films, photographs of attractions, visual art, and so forth. One of the reasons I like to review a subject's work is that I can never tell where an interview might go. I want to be prepared and have this person's body of work fresh in my mind.

Be focused on the day of the interview

A couple of last things that probably go without saying.

- Arrive on time. If I'm meeting an interview subject at his house—especially if the house is many miles from where I live—I arrive in their neighborhood at least an hour early. I drive by their house, check the address, then I usually relax in a nearby Starbucks until our appointment time. There's nothing worse than being late for an interview.

- I always allow a subject to tell any story that they want preserved on tape. Even if I have a detailed interview outline, I let the interview expand in an organic fashion, going to topics that the subject wants to explore as well as those I want to cover.

- Finally, I try to let my subject speak without interruption. You have no idea all of the ways that your interview will be used. Maybe you'll pull a story from it for a documentary or a podcast. Maybe you'll pull an audio segment for some other purpose that you haven't yet imagined. It's helpful to have small margins of silence (maybe only a second) around a subject's response, as that allows a story or an observation to be cleanly pulled from the recording, without untangling your own voice from the mix. In general, it's a good idea to not speak at the same time your subject is speaking.

Overall, I'd say my strategy is a simple one: be prepared. Or rather, be overly prepared. Well-known artists and Imagineers have stories that they've told many, many times—at parties, in presentations, to other interviewers. You will likely need to do significant research to help guide your interview subject into new or more complex material.

I've often found that when I've done my research the people I'm interviewing respond well. They recognize that I've put in some serious time to craft this interview, and in return, they're willing to do the hard work of recalling their life with specific details and concrete stories.

Lastly, if you have a bad interview experience, learn from it. My first interview with Buzz Price wasn't an *absolute* bust. But it certainly wasn't great. I discovered that I wasn't fully prepared, and that in the moment of the interview, I wasn't able to guide the conversation effectively. I also looked like an amateur. I didn't talk to Buzz again for, perhaps, a year.

But in those intervening months, I searched newspaper databases more carefully, I asked around and found some unpublished interviews with him, I also found audio of his presentations. The next time I interviewed Buzz I had better questions; I also knew how to navigate the intellectual territory I wanted to cover in the interview.

It was this interview that gave me some important information for a book I was writing; also, this interview allowed me to return to Buzz many times with new questions about the dozens of projects he worked on for Walt Disney in the 1950s and 1960s.

© 2015 Todd James Pierce

• •

TODD JAMES PIERCE [disneyhistoryinstitute.com] is the author of four non-Disney related books, most recently *Newsworld*, which won the Drue Heinz Literature Prize and was a finalist for the John Gardner Book Award and the Paterson Prize. His novel *The Australia Stories* (also published as *A Woman of Stone*) is regularly taught in high school and college literature classes. His work has been published in over 80 magazines and literary journals. He co-directs the Creative Writing program at Cal Poly University.

Pierce's *Three Years in Wonderland: The Disney Brothers, C.V. Wood and the Making of the Great American Theme Park* is scheduled for publication in early 2016 by University Press of Mississippi. Pierce conducted over one hundred interviews and referenced hundreds of source materials. He writes frequently for the Disney History Institute, and he edited the autobiography of Pinto Colvig, *It's a Crazy Business: The Goofy Life of a Disney Legend*, released in 2015 by Theme Park Press.

For links to Todd James Pierce's books, visit:

themeparkpress.com/historians

Russell Schroeder

My relationship with the enchanting worlds created by Walt Disney and his artists began in the mid-1940s, when I was about three or four years old. One of my earliest memories is coloring the pictures in a Mickey Mouse coloring book.

Of course I didn't realize it at the time, but the line drawings in that book were all based on Disney Studio publicity art created by such masters as Hank Porter and Tom Wood, and sometimes stills taken from the films. Publicity art was designed to capture potential moviegoers' interest and make them want to see the film.

Because of that objective, the characters were alive with action and placed in situations that were both engaging and humorous—and captivating to an impressionable youngster. And those drawings, no doubt crudely colored by me, made an indelible impression. And had a profound effect on my entire life.

My interest in Disney's animated characters continued throughout my childhood via comic books and other publications. In those days, before the prevalence of television and home entertainment film formats, the premiere or re-release of a Disney animated feature was an eagerly anticipated event that only happened once every year or year and a half.

By the time I was nine, I knew I wanted to be a Disney artist. I started to read every article or book about Disney I could find. And like any youngster who has discovered a subject that fascinates him, be it baseball statistics or the latest car designs, I found it easy to absorb and remember information about that field. It was also a learning process made easier because at that time the Disney company was primarily represented by animated films and merchandise, with the addition of the first few live-action films.

In December 1950, Disney's entry into television was in its earliest stages, first with two Christmas specials and an hour-long Ed Sullivan Show special and then, when I was eleven, weekly television programming. The change into the multifaceted entertainment company Disney has become was a gradual process, making it easier to follow the development of its components.

If this essay about being a Disney historian, beginning as it does with my connection with Disney art, had been assigned as a school project, you might expect a teacher to comment that I didn't understand the assignment.

But even though I have sometimes been referred to as a Disney historian, that title came my way because of my first having been a Disney fan and then having worked for the Disney company as an artist for twenty-nine years. If a role title within Disney is applied to me, I claim "artist".

For most of the non-fiction books I have written, the role of artist has played an important part, not only by the connections within the company it has afforded, but by the fact that I approach most projects as both artist and writer. In fact, I usually think about both the written and visual presentation simultaneously, fitting the one to the other.

An essential ingredient for me must be mentioned: the helpfulness of contacts that had been made through my years within the company. When the book *Mickey Mouse: My Life in Pictures* was being discussed, one page had been devoted to the story of "Mickey and the Beanstalk". We already had several color stills from the film, but I thought it would be effective if we could use an animation drawing, story sketch, or pencil layout of the growing beanstalk to anchor those images to the page.

I casually mentioned this idea to Dave Smith in the Walt Disney Archives one afternoon, but admitted I had been unsuccessful in finding something appropriate. With his encyclopedic knowledge of the treasures within the archives, Dave pulled out a folder of Dick Moores' pencil sketches for the Capitol Record Reader of the film and there was a drawing of the beanstalk.

Although its dimensions didn't exactly work from the lower-left corner of the page to the top right, as I had previously discussed with the book's designer, Janice Kawamoto, she was able to add it to the page, where it did form an interesting element in the overall design.

All during my employment I continued to read about Disney, simply out of interest, and through my role as artist was fortunate to have received wide exposure to the many departments and divisions that comprise the Disney organization, having worked at Walt Disney World and been involved in merchandising, publicity, the food division, theme park design, costuming, the resort hotels, attraction operations, and WDI.

In California, I was able to gain experience working in publicity, consumer products, publishing, and animation. And most important of all was getting to work with and meet within those and other divisions the many people whose talents have contributed to the legacy of Disney. Many more facts came my way simply through work-related or informal chats with Disney employees. A truly rewarding experience for a Disney fan!

Several of the non-fiction books I've been involved in came my way because they had tight deadlines and it was felt I could hit the ground running. A couple of these were the collector's editions relating to the then up-coming releases of *Mulan* and *Tarzan*. I was asked to write and select the art for the sections about the creation and animation process for each film.

This assignment was offered to me since at the time I had been on each film for almost a year, assisting the producers with the development of the many books that would need to appear simultaneously with the release of each film. On a daily basis, I was surrounded by and able to enjoy and appreciate the work of the many artists whose talents contributed to the ever-evolving movies.

I was also on the spot for the progression of each film's many components and witnessed when things changed within the storyline or presentation. And through frequent meetings with the producers I was able to learn why those changes were deemed necessary. The added understanding I gained about the creativity and commitment of all those involved in bringing Disney animation to the screen increased my appreciation of each film many times over.

Since I was able to approach these particular writing assignments with an intimate knowledge of each project, I already knew what pieces of artwork I would like to showcase. Knowing what the animation process involves, its early exploratory stages as well as finished elements, I didn't have to ponder the development of an outline; it was already in my head. I merely had to consider my approach to the subject matter in order to make it feel fresh or identify some particular idea I wanted to convey.

Working with the team on *Mulan*, I was impressed with the wide variety of disciplines required to make an animated film—and not all of these involve an ability to draw. So, in addition to following the many steps of animation in the book, I also wanted to convey to youngsters who might be interested in working in animation that many non-art roles are also essential.

As mentioned earlier, in developing a book I considered both art and text as a whole, so for *Mulan* and *Tarzan* I prepared rough layouts as to how I visualized the presentation of those elements. I then gave those rough layouts, along with the text and selected art, to the book's designer, who brought his own sense of art and creativity to the finished project.

The creation of the two books that are part of the *Disney's Lost Chords* series came about in a different way, although the initial impetus remained the result of being a Disney fan. But by their nature these projects required more traditional approaches to research and documentation.

In the late 1970s, I had become aware that a large number of songs had been composed for Disney films but not used in the final productions. Being a fan and collector of Disney music via recordings and sheet music, I was naturally intrigued by these forgotten songs.

My connections with the Disney Music Group allowed me access to the several storage areas where material from the group's decades-long history was preserved. The forms for the material are quite varied: full scores, as recorded for a film's soundtrack; rough hand-written manuscripts as the composer developed his compositions; hand-written lead sheets of music and lyrics that were sometimes transcribed in full arrangements, sometimes in vocal melody lines only, and occasionally in sketchy melody lines, for which the lyrics might be found by chance in unexpected locations.

Regardless of the completeness of these lead sheets, I was often able to sit at the piano and play the pieces. As expected, many of them were quite good from a composition standpoint, and as I speculated about why they might have been dropped from the films, familiarity with the films allowed some educated and reasonable guesswork.

Since I was enjoying this newly discovered music myself, I reasoned that other Disney fans would also be pleased to find out about them. But what would be the most effective way to present the material? Writing about them in text only would be rather frustrating; people would also want to know how a song sounded.

If the compositions were simply gathered together as songs in the format of a traditional sheet music folio, they would be lacking in placing them properly within the development of their intended film stories. And since, just as they had done with their musical heritage, the Disney Studio had preserved much of its art from the earliest days. So there was a good chance that artwork relating to these deleted songs might still exist.

Once having decided on the three elements of the book's contents, the creation of the basic outline followed the chronological order that feels most natural to me for this type of material. Arranged by film based on their release dates, each section consisted of text tracing the development of the film's story and song score, accompanied by relevant art, which was then followed by full arrangements of the selected songs I felt best illustrated the studio's creative process. Each song also included one or more illustrations, accompanied by captions where additional information might prove beneficial.

And so began a concentrated effort involving research within several departments of the Disney organization.

An initial location for my research was the Walt Disney Archives. Material located there is varied—and sometimes unexpected. The knowledge and resourcefulness of the staff always proved invaluable. Within their file folders, organized by film title, decades-old inter-department memos revealed comments about proposed songs.

There were story meeting notes that contained Walt's positive feelings about the value of a particular composer, and in the case of *Sleeping Beauty*, the moment when Walt decided to discard the entire original song score, stemming from a change in the film's art direction, came to light. A page from an early *Peter Pan* script had the lyrics for one of Wendy's songs. The music-only lead sheet for this song was in the Music Group's files, so I was able to unite the two separate song ingredients into a single composition. And in one of the folders for the shelved production *Rainbow Road to Oz*, there was a sketchy pencil composition for a song that had not come to light elsewhere.

As expected, the Walt Disney Feature Animation Research Library provided many visual complements to the deleted songs in story sketch, visual development, and character designs. Once again, the unexpected cropped up when early story synopses, storyboard documentation, and occasionally, lyrics for unused songs were discovered among the art.

As well as saving their original documents, the Disney Studio also made a photographic record of many items. The Walt Disney Photo Library thus became a source for material that had not been located elsewhere, sometimes taking the form of photos of sketches, photocopies of music, and even full storyboards.

Locating many of these images was made easier by the reference system begun years ago and by the organization and knowledge of the library's current staff. Whether in the Photo Library, the Walt Disney Archives, the Animation Research Library, or the Disney Music Group, the dedication and intimate knowledge of their respective areas and their willingness to assist those with questions enable research within those departments to be pleasurable and rewarding.

Being able to interview persons who were actually involved in a researcher's field of study is gratifying. Not only does it allow answers for specific questions or concerns, but often totally unexpected and revealing information comes to light.

I was sorry that most of the composers who are represented in my books are no longer with us. I was, however, able to contact people, such as composers Richard Sherman, Mel Leven, and Carol Connors, who were extremely helpful and enlightening.

One shelved production from the 1970s, *Tale of a Mouse*, had faded from the memories of folks at the studio; I couldn't even find out if the film had been planned as live action or animation. But here I was in luck, for Mel Shaw, who created the storyboard drawings for the entire film, still lived in the Los Angeles area, and he was able to clear up many things about the film.

One thing that an historical researcher cannot discount is the value of contact with others involved in a similar enthusiasm—and their delight in sharing their own discoveries. I have been particularly fortunate in knowing several individuals who have enabled me to enrich my own research through their own findings. Disney historians such as Stacia Martin and Les Perkins had uncovered demo recordings for deleted song material that became unique sources of reference for my projects. Even Stacia's visits to garage sales and antique stores brought to light art and music material that didn't exist elsewhere. "Fortuosity" should not be taken for granted.

Lastly, any researcher benefits from the achievements of those people whose research preceded his. Particularly now, many books have begun appearing that concentrate on a specific period or aspect of the Disney company's history.

Editor Didier Ghez's series *Walt's People,* which showcases interviews with the folks who worked at Disney, has proven quite valuable, although a cautionary note must be sounded: always try to substantiate statements, when possible; memories often blur after half a century.

Particularly useful in the discovery of Disney's lost songs have been the two books by J.B. Kaufman and the Walt Disney Family Museum that detail the creation of two of Walt's greatest films, *Snow White and the Seven Dwarfs* and *Pinocchio.* Kaufman's thorough research helped place many deleted songs within their proper context.

Although the exercise of researching and collating material for a specific subject and the discoveries that ensue can be rewarding in itself, and indeed many subjects benefit from a detached view that allows a balanced, thoughtful perspective, the pleasure is increased many fold when that subject is one for which the researcher has a passion. In that, I have been most fortunate in my chosen area of research.

© 2015 Russell Schroeder

• •

RUSSELL SCHROEDER was employed as an artist for The Walt Disney Company for twenty-nine years. He worked in a variety of creative artistic areas, including the design of figurines, t-shirts, candy tins, meal boxes, and posters both at the Walt Disney Studio in California and at Walt Disney World in Florida where he first started working in 1971. A life-long fan of Disney music, his ten years of research into unused songs created by Disney's celebrated composers resulted in two extraordinary books as well as a series of CDs from Walt Disney Records featuring some of this previously lost music.

His Disney-related books include:

- *Cookie Carnival: The Complete Cartoon Score* (2015)
- *Funny Little Bunnies :The Complete Cartoon Score* (2015)
- *Ye Olden Days: The Complete Cartoon Score* (2014)
- *Songs from Walt Disney's Animated Shorts and Featurettes* (2014)
- *Disney's Lost Chords 2* (2008)

- *Disney's Lost Chords* (2007)
- *Disney: The Ultimate Visual Guide* (2002)
- *Disney's Tarzan: Special Collector's Edition* (1999)
- *Disney's Mulan: Special Collector's Edition* (1998)
- *Mickey Mouse: My Life in Pictures* (1997)
- *The Disney Sing Along Book* (1997) with Jim Fanning
- *Walt Disney: His Life in Pictures* (1996)

For links to Russell Schroeder's books, visit:

themeparkpress.com/historians

Brian Sibley

The Interview: What to Do, What Not to Do, and What Might Be Worth Trying

So you're about to do your first interview as a Disney historian? What do you need to know?

To begin with, I have to come clean and tell you that not everything you are about to read will be relevant to you: I have had the privilege of interviewing many "Disney names", some of whom have worked in front of the camera and (a great many more) behind the scenes. Some of my interviews were for books, but most were made for inclusion in radio or TV programs that I was making where the requirements are often quite different to those of the writer of a book, essay, or article, since they need not just stories and facts, but also a sense of performance.

Some of the best conversations I have ever had about Disney were with a veteran storyman with whom I became good friends; yet whenever I put a microphone in front of him, he totally dried up. Although we had many hours of fascinating conversation over lunch or dinner, he made only rare appearances in my programs. In contrast, I have had interviewees who have talked incessantly without saying anything interesting (or, often, succinct enough) to make the final cut.

So, you have been warned and given license to ignore all that follows.

There's something important you must know before you set off for your interview: the burden of your Disney fandom! I'm sorry to put it so crudely, but the first time you are faced with meeting someone whose work you know about and, possibly, much admire, you may find yourself a tad star struck.

I well remember a long-awaited interview with Julie Andrews (it had been on and off for a month or more) and when the final moment came and we were sitting next to one another on a sofa in her suite at the Dorchester Hotel in London, I wondered whether I would be able to ask even a single intelligible question.

The real danger about such encounters is that the weight your own knowledge (combined with a perfectly understandable anxiety that your interviewee should know that *you know* all there *is* to know about his or her work) can all too easily result in your asking questions that include so much information that the person you are talking to has nothing left to say in reply. So, here's Rule Number One: try and hold your personal excitement safely short of a full-on gush—at least until the interview is over.

And, please, don't try too hard to impress your interviewee with how much you know. I made that mistake once in interviewing Roald Dahl and was very nearly shown the door!

I say this because we are not always aware of the danger that is represented by the extent and weight all that Disney history piled up in our heads: the facts and figures (as well as, probably, the myths and legends) that we've read about in books and articles and heard discussed on DVD bonus extras, TV programs, and convention platforms. Our acquired knowledge (and knowledge is an indispensable requisite for every historian) needs to be mentally stored, ordered, and filed so as be available for effective retrieval, but we really don't want to display it all at every possible opportunity.

Also, and this is very important, try and remember that, however much you think you know, your knowledge should always be open to challenge and review.

The best advice I can give is to begin your preparation as if you were about to go into an exam. So—*do your Disney revision*.

Ask yourself what are you wanting to get from the interview: it might be new facts and details, confirmation of things you have read, an answer to some conflict in more than one version of past events, or, like me, you may be looking for those gems that the broadcaster refers to as the "sound-bite".

Personally, and it may not work for others, I have always written out my rough questions, refined and polished them, and then written them out again (*written*, not typed) in clear handwriting. I then rehearse the questions, like the script of a play but with the exception that I know I may end up leaving the script in favor of some unexpected ad-libbing.

What is curious is that having put it all down on paper and rehearsed it, I find I rarely need look at the questions during the actual interview. As a result, I can focus my attention on the interviewee, silently encouraging them, listening to what they say—and *don't* say.

The single most important thing about question writing is to avoid the trap of what is called "the closed question"—that's a question that is actually nothing more than a statement: "So, then, in 1964, you made *Mary Poppins*."

Closed questions have to be avoided at all costs because—like a closed door—they lead nowhere. Many interviewees will do their best to answer a question even if you haven't actually asked one, but, be warned, closed questions can all too often be answered with a simple "Yes," which will get you no further than confirming what you already knew! Always aim for *open* questions—ones that invariably begin with an "H" or a "W": "How...?" "Who...?" "What...?" "Where...?" "When...?" or "Why...?"

Be prepared for the curious experience of interviewing someone and hearing them answer your questions in exactly the same words as you have heard or read somewhere else. This really isn't too surprising because people who get interviewed will have probably been asked the same questions so many times before that their answers have inevitably settled into a well-rehearsed pattern that provides what they think of as the "best version".

Add in the further consideration that the events about which they are being questioned probably happened a long time ago and which, at the time, may not have seemed as important as later turned out.

Your real job as an interviewer is not to get your interviewee to tell the story you know they can tell, but tell you in a way they haven't told it before—or, better still, tell you a story they *haven't* told before!

So, *how* do you do that?

First, always encourage your interviewee. Depending on who they are and what they do, they may be shy or inexperienced at being interviewed, or they may have done it so many times that it's routine and, possibly, boring. Don't just listen, *show* that you are listening: an occasional nod or a smile can work wonders. Above all, try to look (even if you're not feeling it) relaxed, as if it were perfectly normal to be sitting in Angela Lansbury's house trying *not* to think about the fact that Mrs Potts is pouring you a cup of tea.

Initially, I always let an interviewee answer in the way they want to: what they say may all be terribly familiar, but it is much nicer, when you are later writing it up, to be able use the version told to *you* rather than to someone else—even if it is almost word-for-word the same as many versions you've heard before.

Once you have got that first answer, your aim should then be to see if they can tell you something more: "What specifically appealed to you about working at Disney?"; "How would you describe the atmosphere at the studio?"; "What were your impressions when you walked onto the set on the first day of shooting?"

Questions about "feelings" will often bring out far more from an interviewee than just asking for "facts". I have often asked follow-up questions such as "How did that make you feel?" or "What was your reaction?" Sometimes you don't need anything more than a simple "Why was that?"

Asking such questions is like exploring an unknown territory: you do not know, in advance, how a person will answer and, indeed, they may not *have* an answer! But the unexpected question, that invites them to think and then articulate their thoughts, can give you something unexpected and potentially valuable in return.

Asking questions like these requires two things: first being prepared to leave your pre-thought-out list of questions and go off at a tangent without quite knowing where that might take you, and second, a level of concentration where *listening* takes precedence over *speaking*. If you don't listen—*really* listen—to what someone says, you can easily miss an opportunity to get something new, different—even surprising.

So, if you need a moment to think through a follow-up question, take it. Remember, you are the interviewer; the person you are speaking with will wait for your next question whether it's the next one on your list or the one that's trying to form itself in your head. Of course, a few seconds can feel like an eternity—especially in conversations with strangers; we all tend to rush to fill the awkward vacuum of silence.

This prompts me to share with you another useful interviewing technique. Sometimes, people answer in the way they do because it is more comfortable than saying anything more or something different. If you think that *might be* the case, you can use that silence vacuum to your advantage.

Don't look back down at your questions and don't say anything. Hold their eye-line and if you're even a moderately good amateur actor indicate that you know there's something more that's waiting to be said. I've always found the merest hint of a quizzical look, a slight raising of an eyebrow, a questioning tilt of the head can prompt a longer, fuller answer.

Mention must be made of what can be a testing moment that requires nerves of steel. I refer to the interviewee who gives an answer that you know (or, at least, are pretty sure) is inaccurate: a mistaken name, perhaps, or an incorrect date.

What you do next depends on how you are using the interview and how certain you are that the answer is wrong. If no one else is going to ever hear the actual tape, it's up to you whether you correct the subject and run the risk of causing embarrassment.

If however, you intend to use the recorded answer, then you may not have a choice but to "have another go". Obviously, diplomacy is essential: "I think it was *October* 1982, wasn't it?" But be prepared for a range of responses from "Yes, of course!" to "No, I don't think so!" or, simply, "Was it?"

Of course, some facts can be easily checked, but you might well get an answer that includes detail that appears to contradict what is already known. Your task then is to try and find out whether you have uncovered something previously unknown or whether it is nothing more than a possibly biased or misconceived personal opinion.

So, how do you cope with all these complicated requirements at once? By keeping your questions in mind, mentally crosschecking facts as they surface, and by being alert and focused enough to respond to what is being said.

Two final pieces of advice: if you are using a recording device, ensure you have more than enough tapes or discs and all the cables, extensions, and adaptors that you might need or, if using battery power, enough spare batteries to be able to change them at least four times more than is ever likely to be necessary.

And don't forget to check that the machine is working—and that you know how to use it! I mention this because I once interviewed Disney Archivist Dave Smith for over an hour on an unfamiliar, borrowed machine only to find that I had pressed the PLAY button rather than the one to RECORD! Dave, being a consummate professional and an old friend, spent the next hour recreating all his earlier answers. I doubt I'd have had quite that level of cooperation if it had happened in one of my interviews with Michael Eisner.

Lastly, never forget that we are uniquely privileged whenever we get to meet and talk with the people who helped create Disney magic. As such, we have a dual responsibility of asking questions on behalf of everyone who doesn't have that same privilege while, at the same time, helping to chronicle the history of probably the most prestigious entertainment company in the world.

© 2015 Brian Sibley

- - -

BRIAN SIBLEY [briansibleysblog.blogspot.com] has been a professional writer for thirty years and a freelance broadcaster for the BBC in London for almost as long. His popular radio programs featured a wide variety of topics from the history of magic to the crimes of Jack the Ripper to Disney. He writes extensively about animation and children's literature and has written "making of" books on film series including *Harry Potter*, *The Lord of the Rings*, and *The Hobbit*. As an expert on Disney, he has appeared in bonus extras on eight different Disney Blu-Ray releases of its films.

His Disney-related books include:

- *Mary Poppins: Anything Can Happen If You Let It* (2007) with Michael Lassell
- *The Disney Studio Story* (1988) with Richard Holliss
- *Walt Disney's Snow White and the Seven Dwarfs: The Making of the Classic Film* (1987) with Richard Holliss
- *Mickey Mouse: His Life and Times* (1986) with Richard Holliss
- *Alice's Adventures in Wonderland* (1986)

Other books include *The Land of Narnia: Brian Sibley Explores the World of C.S. Lewis* (1990), *Chicken Run: Hatching the Movie* (2000), *Creating 3-D*

Animation: The Aardman Book of Filmmaking (2004) with Peter Lord, *The Lord of the Rings: The Making of the Movie Trilogy* (2002), *Peter Jackson: A Film-Maker's Journey* (2006), *Harry Potter Film Wizardry* (2012), and *The Hobbit: Official Movie Guides* (2012–14).

For links to Brian Sibley's books, visit:

themeparkpress.com/historians

Paula Sigman Lowery

Tell Me a Story

History has been defined as a chronology of events, an account of what has or might have happened in the past, even a dialogue between past and present. A historian might be considered a chronicler.

But embedded in the word "history" is another, more powerful word: STORY. The more complex role of a historian is to take the facts of the events as we know them, to delve deeply into the lives and passions of the people involved, and to weave them together in such a way that Story emerges.

To be a historian is to be a storyteller, because that's what people remember: we remember stories.

I did not come to Disney history as someone who had majored in historical studies. I was merely a librarian skilled in reference and research. But I was also a children's librarian, helping youngsters find treasure in books and stories. I loved telling stories. And working at the Walt Disney Archives was like being the guardian of Aladdin's Cave of Wonders, with untold stories to be discovered in the artifacts and documents contained within its vaults.

It was our role to guide people to the appropriate materials and help them figure out what they meant, or how they could be used in new projects.

Disney historians do not invent or create "new" history, but examine and often find new stories within the familiar, and make the stories we've heard or read even more meaningful.

How do you become a Disney historian? I suggest starting with what could be called the "Four Rs (plus one)."

Read. This is how I started. Read *everything* you can about the subjects that interest you, especially the things about which you are passionate. BUT—and yes, it's a big one—DON'T always believe everything you read. (Especially on the internet.) Check and double-check the sources that were used in developing what you read. Wherever you can, go back to what educators and historians call "primary" sources. These can be documents, letters, notes, journals, diaries, artwork, and even publications or other materials written at the time of a specific event. If you don't have access to the primary sources, perhaps give more credence to the books and articles that include documentation of those sources.

Read interviews on the subject—and when reading those interviews, also learn as much as you can about the people being interviewed, to put their comments into the context of their own personalities and experiences. What I mean by this is that if you read a quote by a Ward Kimball, for example, remember that Ward liked to present himself as a bit of a bad boy and often delighted in shocking people. Think about the context in which the quote was said, and to whom it was said.

Research. In doing research, be as objective as possible while gathering information. You may have a preconceived notion about where your research will take you, but be open to new information that might change your mind, or lead you in a new direction. Going in with an agenda can cloud your objectivity.

Record and Respect. Document what you do and find. Seek out and interview people who have been involved in past Disney projects, as well as those who are involved in Disney projects today, since they are the creators of tomorrow's history. In conducting interviews, be respectful of the subject and the people who are generous enough to share their time and memories with you.

Once again, read everything you can about what you will be asking, partly so you can prompt your interviewee if he or she seems to falter. If they go off on a tangent, be patient—you may be delightfully surprised by previously unsuspected connections to your key subject.

When I'm being interviewed, I always ask for a general idea of what we'll be talking about, so that I can prepare and think about what I might want to say. In turn, whenever possible I give an interviewee an advance outline of our overall discussion, so they can do the same. It's fine to have specific questions prepared, and you may even want to preview those with your interviewee.

Always ask politely if you may record the interview, and if possible, note how, when, and where you intend to use it. You may want to provide a transcript of your interview so that the interviewee has an opportunity to correct inadvertent errors or mistakes in spelling. Do note the time and place of each interview, and transcribe it promptly while the discussion is fresh in your mind. If you paraphrase something that your interviewee said, be sure you make it clear that these are not his or her actual words.

Reference. It's wise not only to document each specific source, but also note exactly where you found it in case you need to go back and check it again. In a library or archive setting, that should include its collection information, call number, or other identifying data such as box or folder number.

In the "olden" days, we used to do this sort of thing on index cards; these days, sophisticated computer programs can track and organize this information, allowing for easy search and retrieval. Be sure to note full author, title, date, and publisher information of the works that you consult. You may want to create and attach a source ID symbol for every quotation or note.

When you do get around to writing up your findings, having such documentation will allow you to easily credit your sources. The style for footnotes, endnotes, or bibliographies (if used) will depend on where you publish—but you definitely should have everything logged at the time you're creating your notes, rather than having to try to re-create them later. Thoroughly crediting your sources helps establish *your* credibility.

As you write, be clear, concise, and absolutely accurate. Use correct spelling and grammar, and make sure that your work is appropriate for your projected audience. When Frank Thomas and Ollie Johnston were writing their landmark book, *Disney Animation: The Illusion of Life*, they asked us in the Archives to read their manuscript to ensure that a broader audience than the young animators they had mentored could understand it.

By the time you have done your research, you probably will find that your new story is telling itself. You just need to put it together. When you do, you'll be contributing to Disney history, creating an invaluable resource for historians to come.

© 2015 Paula Sigman Lowery

· ·

PAULA SIGMAN LOWERY [howardlowery.com] is an internationally recognized expert on Walt Disney and the history of The Walt Disney Company. A former archivist for the Walt Disney Archives for fifteen years, she was one of the lead creative consultants in the design and development of the critically acclaimed Walt Disney Family Museum. Lowery serves as a lead story and curatorial consultant for a series of Disney exhibits in Japan.

A respected film authority, she has been featured in numerous Disney DVD and Blu-Ray film documentaries. As writer and editor, Lowery has written scripts for storytelling records and books, and articles for *Disney Magazine* and the Walt Disney Family Museum. She was a chapter author for *Marc Davis: Walt Disney's Renaissance Man* and provided the liner notes for the Walt Disney Records Legacy Collection releases of the *Sleeping Beauty* and *Cinderella* soundtracks. Most recently, she wrote the historical text for the Walt Disney Archives presentation of "Disneyland: the Exhibit" at the 2015 D23 Expo.

Her Disney-related books include:

- *Marc Davis: Walt Disney's Renaissance Man* (2014) chapter author
- *The Art of Marc Davis* (1993) introduction author

For links to Paula Sigman Lowery's books, visit:

themeparkpress.com/historians

Werner Weiss

I accidentally became a Disney historian. Working in the computer network industry in 1994, I could not ignore the emerging public Internet. The Next Big Thing would be the combination of widespread online access, graphic web browsers, and websites with images. I would need to become proficient in all things Internet for my career to have a future. What better way to learn than to start my own website? As a lifelong Disney fan, I thought there might be interest in color slides of Disneyland that I had taken 20 years earlier. I launched Yesterland in 1995, focusing on Disneyland features that were gone.

For more than 20 years, Yesterland has grown. My early text relied on my own memories and a few dates and other facts pulled from books and old Disneyland brochures. Over the years, my articles became much longer, with larger images and more of them. The site's scope has broadened to include other Disney parks. But the biggest change is that I now do extensive research for each article.

I've also become 20 years older during that time. It's exciting to see interest in Disney history growing. People who were young children or not yet born when Yesterland launched in 1995 will be the next generation of Disney historians. When Jim Korkis invited me to be part of this book, I welcomed the opportunity to share my thoughts and advice. My advice concentrates on a few areas.

Approaching a Disney history topic

Traditional outlets for Disney history include books, periodicals, academic papers, museum displays, and live presentations. Digital technology has added such outlets as blogs, websites, podcasts, ebooks, Wiki entries, and even location-aware mobile apps. Future technology will bring more options. Within each medium, the content can be an essay, an interview, a photo gallery, a list, or any other format the Disney historian wants to use. Disney history is a broad umbrella that can include the life of Walt Disney, animation, live-action movies, theme parks, merchandising, and even the many non-Disney facets of today's media giant, The Walt Disney Company.

Research, writing, and publishing have never been easier. It's the age of Google, copy and paste, and WordPress.

Unfortunately, some people think that all they have to do is to Google a search term, copy something they find, change a few words to "make it their own," and paste it into a blog or read it aloud on a podcast—not even with an acknowledgment of the source. Starting with someone else's work and then editing it to make it "different" is neither research nor writing. It's lazy. It's plagiarism. Readers and listeners will notice.

Nobody reading this book would do such a thing. Otherwise, you wouldn't be reading it, right?

That doesn't mean you should never copy and paste. Quoting another work, with attribution, can be very good (more on that later). Also, newspaper writers have long relied on company press releases as the basis for articles, harvesting facts and official quotations, and that's fine for bloggers and others, too.

Striving for accuracy

The web is an incredible repository of information and misinformation.

Just because the same fact appears dozens of times does not make it true. It can mean that it has been copied and pasted many times. One clue is when the entire sentence is identical in each search result.

When I was doing online research about the PeopleMover at Disneyland, I kept seeing the "fact" that Goodyear Tire & Rubber Co. sponsored the ride for its entire 28-year run, a remarkably long Disneyland sponsorship. But I noticed that Goodyear's name did not appear on my Disneyland guides and maps from the 1980s and 1990s. With more research, I confirmed that Goodyear's sponsorship only lasted until December 31, 1981—roughly half of the attraction's 28-year life. No sponsor replaced Goodyear.

Figure out which sources you can trust. Wikipedia is a great starting point for research, but not a definitive reference. Double-check anything you get from Wikipedia and blogs. Ideally, consult period sources, such as historical newspaper archives. You might be able to access historical newspapers online with your local library card. Use books from your bookshelf or from the library, even if it's not as easy as using Google.

I've published mistakes and typos on Yesterland. When kind readers let me know about things I should fix, I try to do so very quickly. I assume I still have some mistakes, although my goal is to have none.

Credit where credit is due

Many nonfiction books (not just about Disney subjects) rely heavily on quotations from historical sources—newspapers, speeches, interviews, government documents, and older books. Biographers quote prior biographers. It's a great way not only to present historical details, but also to capture historical wording. For example, how did newspapers describe the opening of Disneyland in 1955? Attribution can involve footnotes, endnotes, or formal inline notes. Or you can simply identify the source within your text. What is best depends on the nature of your work.

What about copyright? The doctrine of Fair Use allows you to cite a reasonable amount of copyrighted material without permission from the copyright holder. There are no hard-and-fast rules about how many words constitute Fair Use, but there are tests that you can apply to the nature of your use. You might want to read up on Fair Use.

Even if you don't cite copyrighted work, there are times when attribution is appropriate. Let's suppose you paraphrase an unusual story from an exclusive interview that a Disney historian had the foresight to pursue. Perhaps the interviewee passed away a decade ago. Instead of simply retelling the story, tell your readers where the story originated. Doing so will add to your credibility because your readers will know you didn't make it up.

Precision vs accuracy

"Werner, you're being too precise!"

That criticism has been leveled against me when I've pointed out factual errors in the work of others. "No," I reply, "it has nothing to do with precision. It's simply that Disney history should be accurate."

Many people use *accurate* and *precise* interchangeably. These words tend to show up in each other's dictionary definitions, which just adds to the confusion.

Accuracy is about being correct—getting the facts, names, and events right. It's always better to be accurate than inaccurate.

Precision relates to the level of detail. The exact day, date, and time that something happened is more precise than simply the year. But it's not necessarily better.

Strive always to be accurate, but only be as precise as your context calls for.

Fact vs opinion

"I'm entitled to my opinion."

That's true in a free country, and it should be true everywhere. However, in the words of the late senator, ambassador, and presidential advisor Daniel Patrick Moynihan, "Everyone is entitled to his own opinion, but not to his own facts."

Know the difference.

Nomenclature

It's Main Street Electrical Parade, not Electric Light Parade. It's Adventure Thru Inner Space, but Mine Train through Nature's Wonderland (with Thru/

through spelled and capitalized differently). And, for some odd reason, it's Astro Orbitor (with *or*) at Disneyland and Astro Orbiter (with *er*) at Walt Disney World.

It's easy to get attraction names, movie titles, and names of individuals wrong. But it's also easy to look them up and get them right. For example, I use Disney's official theme park websites to make sure I use the right nomenclature for current attractions, shops, restaurants, and shows.

With correct nomenclature, your work will come across as more professional and reliable. Also, users will have more success finding your online work with search engines.

Some nomenclature is quite long—for example, The Disneyland Story presenting Great Moments with Mr. Lincoln. If you use the full name once, you can safely write Mr. Lincoln or just Lincoln for subsequent occurrences.

In its early years, Disneyland was less careful with nomenclature than today. For example, the 1961 edition of *Walt Disney's Guide to Disneyland*, the park's souvenir book, called the same attraction Jungle River Boat Safari inside and Jungle Cruise on the back cover. But there's usually a most common, "best" title or name.

When writing about the company, keep in mind that it has had four names since being founded in 1923: Disney Brothers Cartoon Studio (1923–1926), Walt Disney Studio (1926–1929), Walt Disney Productions (1929–1986), and The Walt Disney Company (1986–present). I'm not suggesting that you always have to spell out the entire name, but don't use the wrong name for historical work. The Walt Disney Company did not produce *Steamboat Willie* in 1928.

It's common to write about Walt Disney as Disney. And it's common to write about the company as Disney. Just make sure readers understand whether you mean the man or the company—or possibly both (as in the term "Disney history").

Ever-changing history

Historians still write new books about people and events of decades (or centuries) ago. They make new discoveries about the past, re-discover lost details, make new correlations, and re-examine the past from the perspective of today. They reach new audiences through new media. All that applies to Disney history, too.

Also, Disney history isn't just what happened long ago. It's happening right now. Walt Disney lived from 1901 to 1966, but his creative legacy continues at the company that he and his brother Roy founded.

When you're at the parks, take photos. Things you think will always be there might be gone the next time you visit. Save advertising materials and park guides. Take notes—with your brain and with pencil and paper.

To build your own reference library, buy books about Disney history when they're published. They tend to go out-of-print and usually cost far more on the collector market afterwards.

I don't consider myself an interviewer, but I'm grateful that others have the interest and skill to capture the memories of people with firsthand Disney knowledge. (Thank you!) Maybe you'll be part of the next generation of interviewers. Seek out subjects. Prepare properly. Keep your notes and recordings safe. They're irreplaceable.

Putting it all together

Presumably, you want to be a Disney historian to advance knowledge of some aspect of Disney. You want to uncover long-hidden details, or to offer a contemporary perspective on something from the past, or to jog readers' memories, or to add to Disney history by preserving recent news and events, or to share insights from someone you interviewed, or to tie something to a personal experience, or … whatever. Not everything has to be a never-before-published revelation. Often, you can add value just by telling a story well.

Start by studying multiple sources. Build an outline. Make your own connections and draw your own conclusions. Write in your own voice. Include quotations with proper attribution. Have fun. You're doing this because you love it, right? After all, this is not a way to get rich.

© 2015 Werner Weiss

• •

WERNER WEISS has been the "curator" of Yesterland.com since May 1995. It is one of the most respected Disney-related websites and focuses on discontinued Disney theme park rides, shows, parades, and restaurants, with commentary and historical photos.

Weiss' fascination with Disneyland began as a young child visiting the park in 1958. The favorite television programs of his youth were when Walt Disney would show off the latest plans to enhance Disneyland. His site has expanded to include articles on Walt Disney World, debunking Disney myths, and other topics.

Recommended Resources

"You are only as good as your source."

This time-honored phrase over the decades has been applied to everything from newspaper reporters to intelligence agents and has always proven to be correct.

Information comes from many different types of sources including books, magazines, videos, and even the internet. Each source has its own purpose, but it will be up to you to determine which are reliable for your needs.

Researching is a journey and sometimes you will not immediately be able to determine which sources are best. Over time, you will learn what sources to trust as you begin to use them or see others use them.

Three questions you might ask to help determine a reliable source are:

- Has this source proven reliable in the past? Does it contain facts or opinions? One of the reasons some Disney historians dislike certain biographies of Walt is that the author makes assumptions rather than just relaying the facts. The author tries to psychoanalyze Walt's motives or make guesses why he did something. Even when Walt was alive, no one could guess what he would do or what he might like. He was constantly surprising most people. Someone should understand the process of animation before writing about animation. Someone should have visited Disneyland, maybe even frequently, before writing about the theme park.

- Is this source complete? Does it say all there is to say on the topic? Sometimes a writer will leave gaps, and often those gaps omit important information that may contradict or undermine the author's thesis. Is the information just a quick "snapshot" or does it go into detail?

- Is this source up-to-date? Was it written recently? Some things will never change, like the original release date of *Snow White and the Seven Dwarfs* (1937), but new discoveries in Disney history are being made weekly that may change things that were previously accepted as true.

Usually, it is best to start with a broader general approach and then continue to narrow it down to something more specific. So the first source you consult might be simply to find the basic facts to build a strong foundation and get a general overview. If you know that general information, it might help point you in a more specific direction. A good foundation will support the rest of the article.

It is possible to start with a Wikipedia entry, but you shouldn't depend upon it for accuracy or completeness or even objectivity. Websites and blogs can be valuable as a place to start your research, but anyone can write for these venues so there is no consistency or independent review and the sites often repeat falsities that "everyone knows". However, you have to start somewhere, and it is always wise to know what is already available and what others are using as their primary sources.

The resources in this section are provided to give you a good start. These are not the only resources you should use. This is simply a selection. There are other sources just as good or perhaps even better for your specific purposes.

There are hundreds of websites about Disney. Some of them are quite good, but they often go on hiatus or disappear completely, so it would not be helpful to list all of them here. In addition, listing a website that is focused on Walt Disney World would not be helpful if you are concentrating on Disney animation. Go explore.

If you find something on a website that you like, my advice is to make a copy and put it in your file because that information may be difficult if not impossible to find again.

A good place to start is Didier Ghez's Disney History site at disneybooks. blogspot.com. It has always been the epicenter for all true Disney historians and a place to get up-to-date information about discoveries in Disney history as well as newly released books.

Disney has produced a lot of documentation about things over the decades, from pressbooks for movies to training manuals for the Disney theme parks to internal newsletters to press releases to special promotions, and many more treasures can often be found on eBay or at conventions. The joy of the hunt can sometimes be greater than the actual acquisition.

Often, just by causally browsing eBay, Amazon, websites, or an actual flea market or comic book convention, I have found magazines and books with a Disney connection that I never knew ever existed. As Calvin told his friend Hobbes, "There is Treasure Everywhere!" However, you have to make the time and effort to look.

Books

There is more treasure in books than in all the pirates' loot on Treasure Island and at the bottom of the Spanish Main ... and best of all, you can enjoy these riches every day of your life,.

— Walt Disney for *Wisdom* magazine (Volume 32, 1959).

Though he only had one year of high school education, Walt loved books. The books that he read as well as the books he had in both his home and office libraries waiting to be read helped define who Walt Disney was.

Good books are a valuable resource for research, inspiration, confirming information, and just plain enjoyment. Until the 1980s, there were less than a half dozen books devoted to Walt Disney and his work. Today, there are hundreds with more coming out each week.

It is important not just to have these books in your possession, but to be able to locate the information that is in them. Even books with an index are often inadequate in this regard. In the old days, historians would dog-ear a page and with a yellow highlighter mark the appropriate information on the page.

Today, many historians use post-it notes to mark a page. Some even write notes on the post-it or use the margins of the book to list corrections and additions. One historian used to buy two copies of every book: one to keep in mint condition on his shelves and the other to mark up vigorously with notes. With the flood of expensive books related to Disney, that plan became unfeasible.

A bibliography or end notes section at the back of the book will offer examples of many resources that you may wish to explore or add to your personal library.

My personal library also includes books about animation (especially animation history) and amusement parks because there are often references to Disney and information about Disney's competitors throughout history.

However, other books may contain valuable facts and details as well, such as autobiographies of entertainment people from performers to directors to musicians who worked at Disney, out-of-date annual travel guides, trivia books, or supplemental books that were included with laser discs, CDs, or similar material.

In particular, Jim Fanning has done some outstanding work on such booklets for releases of *Pinocchio* and *Jungle Book*, among others, and Jeff Kurtti's work has enriched similar publications, to name just two experts. A hidden treasure is Kurtti's 48-page booklet *Sleeping Beauty Castle: Building the Most Magical Castle on Earth* (2014) that was only available in the Sterling Innovation hobby kit "Build Sleeping Beauty Castle", a deluxe paper model kit.

For the Disney animated feature films, the many books discussing the art and making of individual films are extremely useful.

I have purposely limited the following list to what I consider some of the "key" books in particular areas of Disney history that would be able provide a broad and accurate perspective. Most historians end up with a personal library many, many times this size.

Some of my personal favorite books (including most of my own) did not make my final cut as well as some favorite obscure books that just contain a chapter or two about Disney like *Bread and Butter Days* (1992) by LaVerne Stevens recounting the life of Clem Flickinger who grew up with Walt Disney in Marceline, Missouri, from 1906–1909.

Just because a book does not appear in this listing does not mean it lacks value. Quite the contrary, several significant books do not appear here simply because of the space restrictions, such as the many books devoted to a single film or character. This listing is meant to give a broad general overview of different Disney aspects and a starting point for further exploration.

Of course, every book written by the contributors to this book should be on your bookshelves, as they are on mine. Many of these contributors have written multiple books and all of them are recommended and will offer accurate insight into the multiple worlds of Disney.

Remember one of the purposes of lists is to spark intelligent discussion about what should and should not be on the list. I certainly debated many times before this version. Once it is published, I am sure I will wonder why I included one book and left off another.

Besides using Amazon.com, good places to look for older books are Bookfinder.com and AbeBooks.com.

One of the top Disney historians in the world, Didier Ghez, started the Ultimate Disney Books Network (DidierGhez.com) in December 1998 to document all of the Disney-related books in print, out of print, forthcoming, and foreign. He has maintained his extensive listing for nearly fifteen years and continues to add to its contents each month. Browsing his site will introduce you to many interesting and valuable books not listed here.

Allan, Robin: *Walt Disney and Europe* (Indiana University Press and John Libbey & Co. Ltd, 1999). An expanded version of his doctoral thesis, with tons of new original research.

Apgar, Garry: *A Mickey Mouse Reader* published by (University Press of Mississippi, 2014). An excellent collection of essays and articles about Mickey Mouse over the decades so you can examine how Disney scholarship has changed and what you might discover when researching old articles.

Ballard, Donald W.: *The Disneyland Hotel: The Early Years 1954–1988* (Ape Pen Publishing, 2005). Covers not only the Disneyland Hotel but also some astonishing information and photos of early Disneyland. Additional information is presented in Ballard's 2011 book *Disneyland Hotel 1954–1959: The Little Motel in the Middle of the Orange Grove.*

Barrier, Mike J.: *Hollywood Cartoons—American Animation in Its Golden Age* (Oxford University Press, 1999). Barrier spent decades working on this book, including conducting hundreds of new interviews. Some new insights and information about Disney animation as well.

Barrier, Michael: *Animated Man—A Life of Walt Disney* (University of California Press, 2007). One of the best biographies of Walt Disney, with information you will not find in other biographies.

Bright, Randy: *Disneyland Inside Story* (Crown, 1987). One of the first histories of Disneyland written by an Imagineer who interviewed and worked with those who were involved with the theme park, although many will find that his great stories have been borrowed elsewhere over the decades.

Broggie, Michael: *Walt Disney's Railroad Story* (Pentrex, 1997). Broggie is the son of legendary Imagineer Roger Broggie. His book is an accurate and complete look at Disney parks railroads.

Burnes, Brian, Dan Viets, and Robert W. Butler: *Walt Disney's Missouri* (Kansas City Star Books, 2002). A well-researched book about Walt Disney's many connections to Missouri, including detailed information about his early years growing up in the state.

Canemaker, John: *The Art and Flair of Mary Blair* (Hyperion, 2003). A widely lauded book about the influential artist.

Canemaker, John: *Before the Animation Begins* (Hyperion, 1996). A look at the great Disney concept artists, once again demonstrating Canemaker's wonderful research and insight.

Canemaker, John: *Walt Disney's Nine Old Men and the Art of Animation* (Hyperion, 2001). The primary reference source for these talented men who are each given their own individual chapter.

Canemaker, John: *Paper Dreams—The Art and Artists of Disney Storyboards*, 1999). Another look at Disney artists enriched by Canemaker's own understanding of art.

Cotter, Bill: *The Wonderful World of Disney Television, A Complete History* (Hyperion, 1997). Comprehensive book (up to its date of publication) of all Disney television shows. Cotter also produced a limited-edition CD with all the additional information he could not cram into the book.

Disney Miller, Diane: *The Story of Walt Disney* (Holt, 1957; paperback version by Dell, 1959). The first biography of Walt Disney. It was written by his eldest daughter and *Saturday Evening Post* writer Pete Martin. Add the 2005 limited edition to your collection because of the end notes by Dave Smith making the appropriate corrections.

Dunlop, Beth: *Building a Dream, The Art of Disney Architecture* (Hyperion, 1996; updated in 2011). A detailed examination of the ideas and stories behind Disney theme park architecture.

Fanning, Jim: *The Disney Book* (DK, 2015). A nice overview of all things Disney with the typical DK book emphasis on amazing visuals with the addition of Fanning's informed text.

Feild, Robert D.: *The Art of Walt Disney* (Macmillan & Co., 1942; English version by Collins, 1944). The first book published about Disney animation. While giving a nice overview of the Disney animation process at the time, it sadly omits all names except Walt's and Roy's, but you can make some good guesses.

Finch, Christopher: *The Art of Walt Disney: From Mickey Mouse to the Magic Kingdoms and Beyond* (Harry N. Abrams, 1973). The book has been updated several times with the most recent edition released in 2011. A nice overview of the Disney company.

Finch, Chistopher: *Walt Disney's America* (Abbeville Press, 1978). This book contains material that Finch was unable to include in his original book.

Genaway, Sam: *Walt Disney and the Promise of Progress City* (Theme Park Press, 2014). Well researched and widely lauded look at Walt's Epcot project.

Gennaway, Sam: *The Disneyland Story: The Unofficial Guide to the Evolution of Walt Disney's Dream* (Unofficial Guides, 2013). Covers the entire history of Disneyland up to the book's publication date.

Gerstein, David: *Mickey and the Gang—Classic Stories in Verse* (Gemstone Publishing, 2005). The complete Disney *Good Housekeeping* magazine pages supplemented by Gerstein's always superior research.

Ghez, Didier, and Alain Litaye : *Disneyland Paris—From Sketch to Reality*

(Nouveau Millenaire Edition, 2002). Covers the art and the making of Disneyland Paris, in English.

Ghez, Didier (editor): *Walt's People*—Volumes 1–17. (Theme Park Press). This critically praised series includes hundreds of interviews done by top researchers. If you are a true Disney historian, you need to have every volume, even if you have no other book in your Disney library, and read each carefully. New volumes come out annually. This is truly the one "must have" set of books on this list.

Gordon, Bruce, and David Mumford: *Disneyland, the Nickel Tour* (Camphor Tree Publishers, 1995; updated version, 2000). The most in-depth and entertaining history of Disneyland to date by two of the most knowledge-able Imagineers on the subject.

Grant, John: *Encyclopedia of Walt Disney's Animated Characters* (Hamlyn, 1987; updated versions by Hyperion 1993 and 1998). Contains much infor-mation on major and minor characters and on the animated features.

Greene, Katherine and Richard: *Inside the Dream : The Personal Story of Walt Disney* (Hyperion, 2001). Sponsored by the Walt Disney Family Foundation, it's a nice overview of the life of Walt Disney.

Green, Howard, and Amy Boothe: *Remembering Walt—Favorite Memories of Walt Disney* (Hyperion, 1999). Outstanding collection of memories from people who actually knew and worked with Walt.

Heide, Robert, and John Gilman: *Cartoon Collectibles* (Doubleday, 1983; updated as *Disneyana* by Hyperion in 1994). A nice overview of early Disney merchandise.

Holliss, Richard, and Brian Sibley: *The Disney Studio Story* (Crown, 1988). A complete history of the Disney Studio during Walt's life and a complete filmography with commentaries.

Hollis, Tim, and Gregory Ehrbar: *Mouse Tracks—The Story of Walt Disney Records* (University Press of Mississippi, 2006). Excellent reference on the history of Disney records as well as personality profiles.

Jackson, Kathy Merlock (editor): *Walt Disney—Conversations* (University Press of Mississippi, 2006). A collection of interviews with Walt Disney over the years.

Kaufman, J.B.: *South of the Border with Disney: Walt Disney and the Good Neighbor Program 1941–1948* (Disney Editions, 2009). The best book to cover this aspect of Disney history.

Korkis, Jim: *The Vault of Walt* Volumes 1–4 (Theme Park Press, 2012–2015). A look at the many nooks and crannies and generally unreported stories of Disney history are divided into four sections: Walt, Theme Parks, Films, and Miscellaneous. Even though they are authored by me, others have found these volumes to be informative so I have included them.

Kurtti, Jeff: *Since the World Began* (Hyperion, 1996). Still considered one of the best resources on the history of Walt Disney World.

Kurtti, Jeff: *Walt Disney's Legends of Imagineering and the Genesis of the Disney Theme Parks* (Disney Press, 2008). Terrific well-researched look at individual Imagineers.

Lesjak, David: *Service With Character: The Disney Studio and World War II* (Theme Park Press, 2014). The digital edition contains artwork. Written by an acknowledged specialist in this area.

Maltin, Leonard: *Of Mice and Magic* (Plume, 1980). One of the best overviews of early American animation ever published, with valuable filmographies.

Maltin, Leonard: *The Disney Films* (Crown, 1973; updated in 1984, 1995, and 2000). It has been described as the ultimate reference for pre-1966 Disney movies history.

Marling, Karal Ann (editor): *Designing Disney's Theme Parks: The Architecture of Reassurance* (Flammarion and Centre Canadien d'Architecture, 1998). Written as a catalog to supplement the exhibit of the same name, it is a mixture of illustrations and academic examination.

Merritt, Russell, and J.B. Kaufman: *Walt in Wonderland: The Silent Films of Walt Disney* (John Hopkins University Press, 1994). Outstanding examination of the films of Walt Disney before the birth of Mickey Mouse.

Munsey, Cecil: *Disneyana* (Hawthorn Books, 1974). The first book ever on collecting Disney memorabilia.

Peri, Don: *Working with Walt: Interviews with Disney Artists* (University of Mississippi Press, 2008) and *Working with Disney: Interviews with Animators, Producers, and Artists* (University Press of Mississippi, 2011). Similar in format to the *Walt's People* series.

Rafferty, Kevin, and Bruce Gordon: *Walt Disney Imagineering: A Behind the Dreams Look At Making the Magic Real* (Hyperion, 1996; updated in 2010). The official Disney-approved story of Imagineering.

Schroeder, Russell: *Disney's Lost Chords* Volumes 1 and 2 (Voigt Publications, 2006 and 2008). A fascinating glimpse into the Disney that never was with rare artwork and informative text as well as the actual songs.

Shale, Richard: *Donald Duck Joins Up, The Walt Disney Studio during WWII* (UMI Research Press, 1976). The first book to cover in depth the Disney Studio during World War II.

Smith, Dave (editor): *Quotable Walt Disney* (Disney Editions Deluxe, 2001). A good selection of quotations credited to Walt Disney.

Smith, Dave: *Disney A to Z, The Official Encyclopedia* (Hyperion, 1996). There have been three updates, the latest in a limited edition released in 2014 through Sam's Club exclusively.

Smith, Dave, and Steven Clark: *Disney—The First 100 Years* (Hyperion, 1999). A good general overview of the history of the Disney company.

Smith, Dave: *Disney Trivia from the Vault: Secrets Revealed and Questions Answered* (Disney Editions, 2012). A compilation of questions and answers from Smith's popular "Ask Dave" column.

Solomon, Charles: *The Disney that Never Was* (Hyperion, 1995). Well-illustrated look at Disney animated films that never developed. Solomon wrote a sequel for Disney Editions in 2008 entitled *Disney Lost and Found: Exploring the Hidden Artwork from Never-Produced Animation.*

Surrell, Jason: *Haunted Mansion: Imagineering a Disney Classic* (2015), *Pirates of the Caribbean: From the Magic Kingdom to the Movies* (Disney Editions, 2006), and *The Disney Mountains—Imagineering at its Peak* (Disney Editions, 2007) An Imagineer's perspective into these Disney theme park attractions.

Susanin, Timothy: *Walt before Mickey: Disney's Early Years, 1919-1928* (University Press of Mississippi, 2011). Outstanding example of original, well-cited research into Walt Disney's early life. Sadly, the movie of the same name did not use anything from this book other than the title.

Thomas, Bob: *Building a Company: Roy O. Disney and the Creation of an Entertainment Empire* (Hyperion, 1998). Though not as strong as his biography of Walt, Thomas still produces a fine book on a man deserving of much more attention.

Thomas, Bob: *Walt Disney, An American Original* (Simon and Shuster, 1976; revised, 1994). This is the official biography of Walt and one of the absolute best. It has remained in print for decades because it is a fair and complete look at Walt, mentioning his flaws but never dwelling on them and never making a pseudo-psychoanalysis of the man or jumping to assumptions.

Thomas, Frank, and Ollie Johnston: *Disney Animation: The Illusion of Life* (Abbeville, 1981). Considered the "bible" of Disney animation, it offers insights not only into the process of animation but the people, ideas, and behind-the-scenes stories from two top animators who were actually there.

Tieman, Robert: *The Disney Treasures* (Disney Editions, 2003). A former Disney archivist, Tieman is sadly unknown or underappreciated but has contributed significantly to Disney scholarship. This is an entertaining and informative book.

Tieman, Robert: *The Disney Keepsakes* (Disney Editions, 2005). This is also an entertaining and informative book that is the sequel to Tieman's previous book.

Tietyen, David: *The Musical World of Walt Disney* (Harry N. Abrams, 1990). Great overview of the history of Disney music.

Tumbusch, Tom: *Tomart's Merchadise History of Disneyana—Disney Merchandise of the 1930s* (Tomart Publications, 2014). This listing is here to remind you to look at all of the Tumbusch books on Disney merchandise.

Watts, Steven: *The Magic Kingdom, Walt Disney and the American Way of Life* (Houghton-Miflin, 1998). A scholarly look at the life of Walt Disney.

West, John G.: *The Disney Live-Action Productions* (Hawthorne and Peabody, 1994). A good example of original research to reveal more about some of the Disney live-action films.

Williams, Pat, Art Linkletter, and Jim Denney: *How to Be Like Walt—Capturing the Disney Magic in your Every Day Life* (Health Communications, 2004). A surprising book filled with original interview material and an interesting perspective on the life and impact of Walt Disney.

Magazines

Today, most people who would have produced magazines now have websites or on-line "magazines" connected to a website or blog.

Some of the older, out-of-print magazines can be found on eBay, usually at premium prices. Remember they are just paper and need to be protected and organized. The covers may not necessarily reflect all the contents, so you may need to find some way of identifying what is inside each issue.

Here are some suggestions of "key" magazines to have in your collection:

E-Ticket was the universally lauded magazine about Disneyland produced from 1986–2009 by Leon and Jack Janzen. The Walt Disney Family Museum acquired all the assets of the magazine, including back issues and CD ROMs (which had the early out-of-print issues as well as additional material) and sells them at their museum store.

Perisistence of Vision, produced from 1992–1998 by Paul F. Anderson for ten issues, was considered the gold standard of Disney history research. Today, Anderson and Todd James Pierce supply intriguing glimpses into previously undiscussed Disney history at the online Disney History Institute.

Tomart's Disneyana Update began in 1994 and is produced by Tom Tumbusch. Besides the prices on Disneyana merchandise, there are many fine Disney history articles and it is a fine looking, slick magazine.

The Disney News/Disney Magazine was published by the Disney company from 1965–2005. It was reasonably priced, packed with informative Disney material for the entire family, and contained many treasures still waiting to be uncovered. The earlier issues are sometimes difficult and expensive to acquire. With the Spring 1994 issue it became a newsstand periodical, and that is a good place to start a collection since it featured an expanded page count, full color interior, and many interesting Disney history bits and news.

D23 Magazine is the current quarterly magazine of the Official Disney Fan Club operated by the Disney company. *Disney Magazine* was replaced by this expensive, overly large (11" by 12") and cumbersome magazine in Spring 2009. It has received criticism, as has the organization that produces it, but it contains many fine articles and illustrations. There was a short-lived attempt to sell it at newsstands, but now it is only available through D23.

DVD/BluRay

There are a plethora of videos, some professional and some homemade, available covering many aspects of Disney, from animation to the theme parks.

Here are a few that would make a good start to a collection, in addition to copies of the Disney films, especially releases that include extras. Remember that earlier releases of these films (and especially the LaserDisc versions) often had different extras that are not included in recent releases but contain valuable information.

Walt Disney: The Man Behind the Myth (2001), produced in cooperation with Diane Disney Miller to commemorate the 100th birthday of Walt Disney, is a balanced overview of his life. At the same time, a companion book, *Inside the Dream: The Personal Story of Walt Disney* (Disney Editions Deluxe, 2001), was released.

Disney Parks: The Secrets, Stories and Magic Behind the Scenes (Walt Disney World Resort: Behind the Scenes / Disneyland Resort: Behind the Scenes / Ultimate Walt Disney World / Disney s Animal Kingdom / Disney Cruise Line / Undiscovered Disney Parks (2010) is a six-disc set produced by Lightship Productions (with the supervision and approval of the Disney Company). The individual segments are often shown on the History and Travel channels.

Disneyland Resort: Imagineering the Magic (2008) is a two-disc set covering the history of Disneyland with interviews from Imagineers.

Magic Kingdom: Imagineering the Magic (2009) is a two-disc set covering the early history of Walt Disney World with interviews from Imagineers.

Walt Disney Treasures was a series that began in 2001 and ended in 2009 of limited-edition special DVD releases with multiple extras. This series was the inspiration of Leonard Maltin who hosted all the sets and realized there was a lot of great Disney material not easily available on video. The DVDs include animation, episodes of the weekly anthology series with glimpses of Disneyland, and live-action gems including *Zorro* and *The Scarecrow of Romney Marsh*.

Walt Disney World: 100 Years of Magic (2001) was released by Walt Disney Parks and Resorts as the souvenir DVD sold at the park. Some clever person included on this DVD a copy of "The Walt Disney Story", the twenty-eight minute finale film shown in the attraction of the same name that was at both Disneyland and Walt Disney World starting in 1973.

Frank and Ollie (1995) is a loving documentary of two of Disney's top animators, Frank Thomas and Ollie Johnston, whose work graces many of the classic Disney animated features and whose personal friendship was legendary. A nice glimpse into how animation was done during the time of Walt Disney.

Waking Sleeping Beauty (2010) is an eye-opening documentary on how Disney Feature animation was revitalized in the late 1980s. It does not shy away from studio turmoil, management mistakes, and how the creative process works. For younger historians, this is an insight into the era in which they were growing up.

Walt Disney Records: The Legacy Collection is a series of CDs featuring previously unreleased music, concept art, and detailed liner notes. These editions as well as many others were prepared by Randy Thornton who has been a vital and often unrecognized hero in the preservation of Disney music and its heritage.

The *Mary Poppins* collection features over 2½ hours of content, including the original soundtrack, "The Lost Chords" (previously released demos and newly recorded versions), cast and filmmaker interviews, and a collectible 20-page booklet. Also included are audio excerpts from the historic *Mary Poppins* story meetings in 1961 with author P.L. Travers.

The four-hour documentary *Walt Disney* on the *American Experience* on PBS was a highly flawed film that depended on highly questionable authorities and emphasized Walt's one-day testimony to the House on UnAmerican Activities Committee while omitting all mention of Disney's participation in the 1964–65 New York World's Fair that evolved audio-animatronics and was the springboard for Walt to create Walt Disney World on the East Coast. As Imagineer Marty Sklar who worked with Walt starting in 1955 wrote, "So did PBS' the *American Experience* truly capture the Walt Disney that I knew? Not even close." Floyd Norman who worked as an animator and storyman for Walt wrote, "*The American Experience* gave us 'warts and all' but they did not give us Walt Disney."

The recent independent biographical films about Walt Disney (*Walt Before Mickey* and *As Dreamers Do*) should also be avoided as not only factually inaccurate but not even in keeping with the spirit of the events. Most biographical films are inaccurate and these films are in that same tradition

The Story of Theme Park Press

Theme Park Press debuted in November 2012 as an independent publisher concentrating on releasing Disney-related books. In just over three years, it has become the leading independent publisher of Disney-related books, producing many highly acclaimed titles written by well-known authors.

The Theme Park Press catalog of over 100 titles includes guidebooks, memoirs, fiction, popular history, scholarly works, books about animation, theme parks, Walt himself, the original Mouseketeers, and Disney Legends, with new books being released each month.

I interviewed publisher Bob McLain, who has earned a reputation for integrity and the admiration of many authors, about this company that was truly "one man's dream".

> I wasn't a Disney fan growing up. I was more interested in Marvel comics. When I stopped reading Marvel comics, around the age of 14 or so, my parents took me to Walt Disney World. I have pleasant memories of that trip, and of staying at the Contemporary. Billy Eckstine was playing in the lounge. The magic shop was still on Main Street.
>
> There was a trip to Disneyland the next year, of which I have no recollection whatsoever, and then another trip to Disney World. Other than a drive to Niagara Falls, those were the only vacations I had as a child, and so they stuck with me.
>
> Then I started taking my own kids to Disney World. I became interested in the history of the place, the people who built the attractions, and then Walt himself, as a historical figure.
>
> Over the years, I earned my living in a lot of different ways. I've had other start-ups, in and out of publishing. My first venture, when I was still in high school, was a gaming magazine that I edited and published in the days before affordable personal computers, and the days before email and the internet.
>
> In the intervening three decades, the obstacles to print production had become much less daunting, which led me to resuscitate and combine two lost joys of my youth - publishing and Disney - into Theme Park Press.

My initial goal was to find enough authors to use up the ten ISBNs I bought when I set up the company. At the time there were so few unofficial Disney books on the market that I expected to put out ten books, give or take, and then move on to something else.

Once word got around that I was accepting authors to write books about Disney, however, I reset my goal to 50 books. Then 100. Now it looks as if I'll have well over 150 books on the market by Christmas 2016, with 200 sometime in 2017.

Just as Walt said it all started with a mouse, I have to say it all started with a Korkis. Had I not brought Jim aboard as my first author, many doors that opened would have remained closed. Without Jim, Theme Park Press would have had a much tougher road in its first year.

In November 2012, I released his books *The Revised Vault of Walt* and *Who's Afraid of the Song of the South?* and they remain strong sellers today. Jim has produced several books for me with more on the way.

I think one of the keys to the success of Theme Park Press is its diversity. I don't turn my nose up at anything, as long as it's well-written and the author has a story to tell.

Sometimes the author is a Disney Legend, a retired Disney executive, Imagineer, or a Disney historian. Other times the author is just an eager fan who has a vision from a trivia book to a memory of working for the WDW college program to something more scholarly. Despite all the Disney books I've published, and all the Disney books that Disney itself has published, there are so many more stories left to tell.

I use professional tools, like Adobe InDesign, and I've written (or had written for me) scripts to automate much of the grunt work, while still giving me hands-on control over the layout, the typography, and everything else that sets a professional book apart from one that's self-published or the product of a vanity press.

Even though Theme Park Press has been around for a bit over three years, I still get excited whenever I receive a new query from a prospective author (several of these arrive every week). It's like Christmas; you never know what you're opening up and are always surprised.

That, in part, is what keeps me forging ahead with the company. And the books aren't just commodities to me, parcels of ink and paper and gloss, they're the realization of someone's dream, someone who'll hold his fresh-off-the-press book in his hands and remember that feeling until the day he dies. It's important work to make that happen.

Maybe it's not Disney magic, strictly speaking, but you can't tell me that there isn't a speck or two of pixie dust in there, somewhere."

To keep up to date with the latest titles to add to your personal Disney history collection, go to ThemeParkPress.com.

Final Thoughts of a Cheshire Cat

"But I don't want to go among mad people," Alice remarked.
"Oh, you can't help that," said the Cat. "We're all mad here. I'm mad. You're mad."
"How do you know I'm mad?" said Alice.
"You must be," said the Cat, "or you wouldn't have come here."

> — Lewis Carroll, *Alice in Wonderland*

If you want to be a Disney historian, it may be because you have no other choice. The thrill of discovery accompanied by the satisfaction of sharing the information can be addictive for some people.

According to the *Psychology Today* website:

> Addiction is a condition that results when a person ingests a physical substance (e.g., alcohol, cocaine, nicotine) or engages in a psychologically influenced activity (e.g., gambling, sex, shopping) that can be pleasurable but the continued use/act of which becomes compulsive and often interferes with ordinary life responsibilities, such as work, relationships, or health.

Emotional trauma or a feeling of social isolation can fuel an addictive personality. Disney magic can and has offered comfort and a sense of community. That is a good thing in this troubled world, but find balance in your life.

There is more to life than Disney. Pay your bills before buying that Disney treasure. Get out of the house and walk around and enjoy the life that is happening now. Engage people in frequent conversations that have nothing to do with Disney. Develop some other unrelated interests. Focusing solely on Disney robs the subject of some of its magic and changes a happy fan into an obsessed fanatic.

Ironically, doing some of these other things on a consistent basis will bring fresh perspective and renewed energy and increased joy when you return to your responsiblities as a Disney historian.

Welcome to the Disney history community. Enjoy your time here. Play well with others. Please try to leave it all better than you found it.

"Would you tell me, please, which way I ought to go from here?"
"That depends a good deal on where you want to get to," said the Cat.
"I don't much care where," said Alice.
"Then it doesn't matter which way you go," said the Cat.
"... so long as I get SOMEWHERE," Alice added as an explanation.
"Oh, you're sure to do that," said the Cat, "if you only walk long enough."

— Lewis Carroll, *Alice in Wonderland*

Acknowledgments

As always, I would like to acknowledge not only the people who directly helped me with this specific book, but those who have inspired or supported me over the years. There are indeed angels in this world, and I have been blessed to know so many of them.

I would like to thank all the people who have bought my Disney history books, because their support has allowed this book to be published.

This book would not have been possible without the skills and encouragement of publisher Bob McLain and his Theme Park Press.

Thanks to my brothers, Michael and Chris, and their families, including their children—Amber, Keith, Autumn, and Story. Also, my grand-nieces Skylar, Shea, and Sidnee. None of them have ever read any of my books and one day will hopefully be pleasantly surprised to find their names listed in all of them. During the course of writing this book, my grand-nephew Alexander Thomas Johansen was born. He hasn't read any of my books either.

Michael Barrier, Alberto Becattini, Jerry Beck, Greg Ehrbar, Jim Fanning, Sam Gennawey, Didier Ghez, J.B. Kaufman, Jeff Kurtti, David Lesjak, Leonard Maltin, Todd James Pierce, Russell Schroeder, Brian Sibley, Paula Sigman Lowery, Dave R. Smith, and Werner Weiss gave generously of their time and expertise so that all of us would be better Disney historians. Ignore their wisdom at your own peril.

Robin Allan, Paul F. Anderson, Garry Apgar, Jeff Baham, Donald Ballard, Randy Bright, Michael Broggie, John Canemaker, Dave DeCaro, John Cawley, John Culhane, Jerry Edwards, John Gilman, Becky Cline, Bill Cotter, Matt Crandall, Christopher Finch, David Gerstein, Bruce Gordon, George Grant, John Grant, Howard Green, Katherine and Richard Greene, Robert Heide, Jim Hill, Brian Holliss, Kevin Kidney, Pierre Lambert, Michael Lyons, Howard Lowery, Stacia Martin, Russell Merritt, David Mumford, Cecil Munsey, Tim O'Day, Don Peri, Wade Sampson, Jason Schultz, Shawn Slater, Charles Solomon, Jason Surrell, Tim Susanin, Randy Thornton, Robert Tieman, Tom Tumbusch, John G. West Jr., Scott Wolf, Alex Wright and fortunately many others whose efforts have enriched the understanding of Disney history.

To all those other Disney historians who continue to produce outstanding work and inspire me to do better work, thank you all so much.

And sadly some people that I have foolishly forgotten for the moment. Their kindness and generosity, like those names listed here, have lightened my journey through life and made this book possible. I hope all of you, both acknowledged and temporarily missing, live happily ever after and enjoy this book.

About the Author

Jim Korkis is an internationally respected Disney historian who has written hundreds of articles about all things Disney for over three decades. He is also an award-winning teacher, professional actor, and magician, and author of many books and articles.

Jim grew up in Glendale, California. He enjoyed several concurrent careers, including performing on stage and television, being a public school teacher, co-writing four books on animation history with his friend and business partner John Cawley, being co-owner of Korkis and Cawley's Cartoon and Comic Company, as well as writing, directing and performing at Six Flags Magic Mountain where he was responsible for the park's longest running show, Lucky Louie's Roaring 20s Revue.

In 1995, he relocated to Orlando, Florida, to take care of his ailing parents. He got a job doing magic and making balloon animals for guests at Pleasure Island. Within a month, he was moved over to the Magic Kingdom, where he "assisted in the portrayal of" Prospector Pat in Frontierland as well as Merlin the Magician in Fantasyland for the Sword in the Stone ceremony.

In 1996, he became a full-time salaried animation instructor at the Disney Institute where he taught every animation class, including several that only he taught. He also instructed classes on animation history and improvisational acting techniques for the interns at Disney Feature Animation Florida. As the Disney Institute re-organized, Jim joined Disney Adult Discoveries, the group that researched, wrote, and facilitated backstage tours and programs for Disney guests and Disneyana conventions.

Eventually, Jim moved to Epcot where he was a coordinator with College and International Programs and then a coordinator for the Epcot Disney Learning Center. During his time at Epcot, Jim researched, wrote, and facilitated over two hundred different presentations on Disney history for Disney cast members and Disney's corporate clients including Feld Entertainment, Kodak, Blue Cross, Toys "R" Us, and Military Sales.

Jim was the off-camera announcer for the syndicated television series *Secrets of the Animal Kingdom*; wrote articles for Disney publications like *Disney Adventures*, *Disney Files* (DVC), *Sketches*, and *Disney Insider*. He worked on special projects like writing text for WDW trading cards, as the on-camera host for the *100 Years of Magic Vacation* planning video, as facilitator with the Disney Crew puppet show, and countless other credits, such as assisting Disney Cruise Line, WDW Travel Company, Imagineering, and Disney Design Group with Disney historical material. As a result, Jim was the recipient of the prestigious Disney award, Partners in Excellence, in 2004.

Jim is not currently an employee of the Disney company.

Several websites feature Jim's essays about Disney history:

- MousePlanet.com
- AllEars.net
- Yesterland.com
- CartoonResearch.com
- WDWRadio.com
- YourFirstVisit.net

More Books from Theme Park Press

Theme Park Press publishes dozens of books each year for Disney fans and for general and academic audiences. Here are just a few of our titles. For the complete catalog, including book descriptions and excerpts, please visit:

ThemeParkPress.com

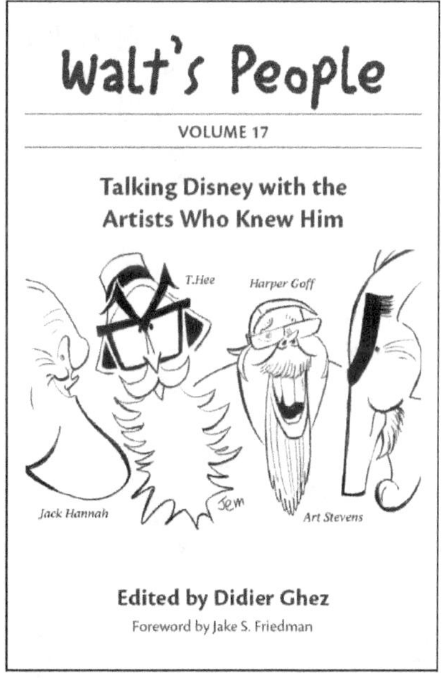

50 YEARS IN THE MOUSE HOUSE
The Lost Memoir of One of Disney's Nine Old Men
ERIC LARSON
Edited by Didier Ghez and Joe Campana

From Disneyland's
Tom Sawyer
to Disney Legend
The Adventures of Tom Nabbe
TOM NABBE

The
BOOK of MOUSE
A Celebration of Walt Disney's Mickey Mouse
Jim Korkis
Foreword by Senior Disney Character Artist
Don "Ducky" Williams

HORATIU
DISNEY'S GRAND TOUR
WALT AND ROY'S EUROPEAN VACATION
SUMMER 1935
DIDIER GHEZ

From
Jungle Cruise Skipper
to Disney Legend
40 Years of Magical Memories at Disney
William "Sully" Sullivan

EVERYTHING
I KNOW
I LEARNED FROM
DISNEY ANIMATED
FEATURE FILMS
Advice for Living Happily Ever After
JIM KORKIS
Author of
The Vault of Walt
A Disney Historian FUN FACT Book

Great Big
Beautiful
Tomorrow
Walt Disney
and Technology
Christian Moran
with Rolly Crump,
Bob Gurr, Jim Korkis,
Sam Gennawey, and Dr.
Maureen Furniss, Ph.D

Walt Disney
AND THE PROMISE OF
Progress City
SAM GENNAWEY
Foreword by Werner Weiss

Who's the Leader
of the Club?
Walt Disney's Leadership Lessons
JIM KORKIS
Foreword by Henry Hardt
Professor of Business Law and Professor of Finance
Buena Vista University

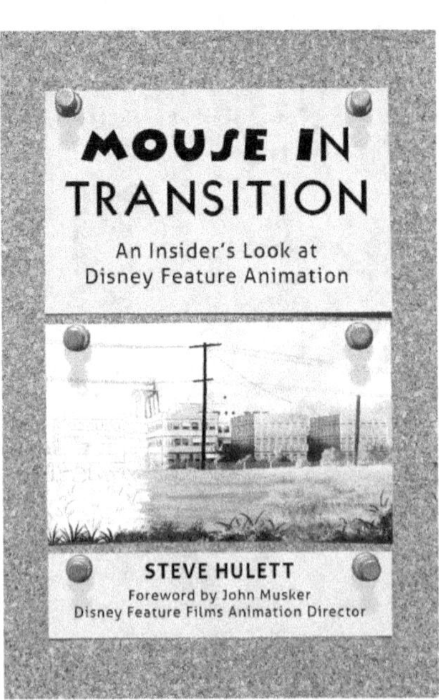

MOUSE IN
TRANSITION
An Insider's Look at
Disney Feature Animation
STEVE HULETT
Foreword by John Musker
Disney Feature Films Animation Director

SERVICE
With
CHARACTER
The Disney Studio & World War II
by David Lesjak

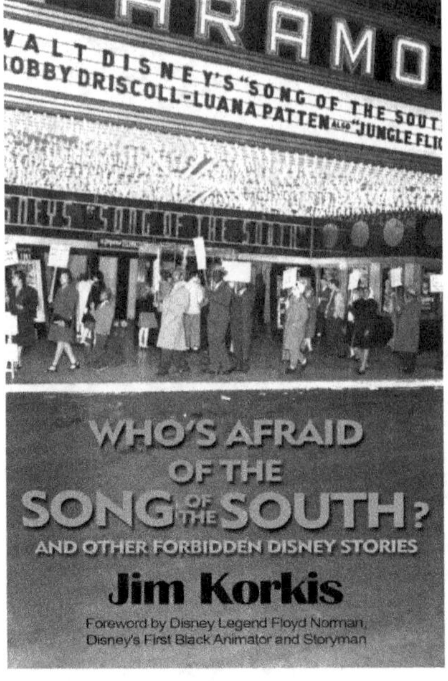

RAMO
WALT DISNEY'S "SONG OF THE SOUT
BOBBY DRISCOLL-LUANA PATTEN ALSO "JUNGLE FLIC
WHO'S AFRAID
OF THE
SONG OF THE SOUTH?
AND OTHER FORBIDDEN DISNEY STORIES
Jim Korkis
Foreword by Disney Legend Floyd Norman,
Disney's First Black Animator and Storyman